Transforming the Countryside

It is now almost impossible to conceive of life in western Europe, either in the towns or the countryside, without a reliable mains electricity supply. By 1938, two-thirds of rural dwellings had been connected to a centrally generated supply, but the majority of farms in Britain were not linked to the mains until sometime between 1950 and 1970. Given the significance of electricity for modern life, the difficulties of supplying it to isolated communities, and the parallels with current discussions over the provision of high-speed broadband connections, it is surprising that until now there has been little academic discussion of this vast and protracted undertaking. This book fills that gap. It is divided into three parts. The first, on the progress of electrification, explores the timing and extent of electrification in rural England, Wales and Scotland; the second examines the effects of electrification on rural life and the rural landscape; and the third makes comparisons over space and time, looking at electrification in Canada and Sweden and comparing electrification with the current problems of rural broadband.

Paul Brassley is Visiting Research Fellow in the Land, Environment, Economics and Policy Institute, University of Exeter.

Jeremy Burchardt is Associate Professor in the Department of History, University of Reading.

Karen Sayer is Professor of Social and Cultural History, Leeds Trinity University.

Rural Worlds: Economic, Social and Cultural Histories of Agricultures and Rural Societies
Series Editor: Richard W. Hoyle, University of Reading, UK

We like to forget that agriculture is one of the core human activities. In historic societies most people lived in the countryside: a high, if falling proportion of the population were engaged in the production and processing of foodstuffs. The possession of land was a key form of wealth: it brought not only income from tenants but prestige, access to a rural lifestyle and often political power. Nor could government ever be disinterested in the countryside, whether to maintain urban food supply, as a source of taxation, or to maintain social peace. Increasingly it managed every aspect of the countryside. Agriculture itself and the social relations within the countryside were in constant flux as farmers reacted to new or changing opportunities, and landlords sought to maintain or increase their incomes. Moreover, urban attitudes to the landscape and its inhabitants were constantly shifting.

These questions of competition and change, production, power and perception are the primary themes of the series. It looks at change and competition in the countryside: social relations within it and between urban and rural societies. The series offers a forum for the publication of the best work on all of these issues, straddling the economic, social and cultural, concentrating on the rural history of Britain and Ireland, Europe and its colonial empires, and North America over the past millennium.

Series Advisory Board:

Paul Brassley, University of Exeter, UK
R. Douglas Hurt, Purdue University, USA
Leen Van Molle, KU Leuven, Belgium
Mats Morell, Stockholm University, Sweden
Phillipp Schofield, Aberystwyth University, UK
Nicola Verdon, Sheffield Hallam University, UK
Paul Warde, University of Cambridge, UK

https://www.routledge.com/history/series/RW

Transforming the Countryside
The Electrification of Rural Britain

Edited by Paul Brassley, Jeremy Burchardt and Karen Sayer

LONDON AND NEW YORK

First published 2017
by Routledge
2 Park Square, Milton Park, Abingdon, Oxon OX14 4RN

and by Routledge
711 Third Avenue, New York, NY 10017

Routledge is an imprint of the Taylor & Francis Group, an informa business

© 2017 selection and editorial matter, Paul Brassley, Jeremy Burchardt and Karen Sayer; individual chapters, the contributors

The right of Paul Brassley, Jeremy Burchardt and Karen Sayer to be identified as the authors of the editorial material, and of the authors for their individual chapters, has been asserted in accordance with sections 77 and 78 of the Copyright, Designs and Patents Act 1988.

All rights reserved. No part of this book may be reprinted or reproduced or utilised in any form or by any electronic, mechanical, or other means, now known or hereafter invented, including photocopying and recording, or in any information storage or retrieval system, without permission in writing from the publishers.

Trademark notice: Product or corporate names may be trademarks or registered trademarks, and are used only for identification and explanation without intent to infringe.

British Library Cataloguing in Publication Data
A catalogue record for this book is available from the British Library

Library of Congress Cataloging in Publication Data
A catalog record for this book has been requested

ISBN: 978-1-4724-4127-0 (hbk)
ISBN: 978-1-315-55006-0 (ebk)

Typeset in Sabon
by Apex CoVantage, LLC

Printed in the United Kingdom
by Henry Ling Limited

Contents

List of figures	vii
List of tables	viii
Acknowledgements	x
Contributors	xi

1	**Introduction** PAUL BRASSLEY, JEREMY BURCHARDT AND KAREN SAYER	1

PART I
The progress of electrification 13

2	**The electrification of the countryside: the interests of electrical enterprises and the rural population in England, 1888–1939** KARL DITT	15
3	**Power to the people: power stations and the national grid** JOHN SHEAIL	38
4	**Lighting the landscape: rural electrification in Wales** RICHARD MOORE-COLYER	51
5	**The electrification of Highland Scotland** DAVID FLEETWOOD	69
6	**Electrifying farms in England** PAUL BRASSLEY	83

vi *Contents*

PART II
The effects of electrification

115

7 Electrification and its alternatives in the farmer's and
   labourer's home   117
   KAREN SAYER

8 Pylons and frozen peas: the Women's Institute
   goes electric   135
   ROSEMARY SHIRLEY

PART III
Comparisons over space and time

155

9 Rural electrification in Sweden: a comparison   157
   CARIN MARTIIN

10 People, place and power: rural electrification in Canada,
    1890–1950   178
    RUTH W. SANDWELL

11 Rural broadband: a twenty-first-century comparison with
    electrification   205
    MARTYN WARREN

12 Conclusion: electricity, rurality and modernity   221
    PAUL BRASSLEY, JEREMY BURCHARDT AND KAREN SAYER

   Index   246

Figures

Cover: Pylons and power lines over the harvest at Doune, Perthshire, September 1961. Photograph P FW PH2 S30/21, Museum of English Rural Life, University of Reading

6.1 Proportion of agricultural holdings with a public or private supply of electricity in each county of England and Wales in 1942. 90

6.2 Development of high-voltage mains in the West Devon district, 1950 and 1967. 102

8.1 *A Collage to Suggest Binsted*: front cover of the Binsted scrapbook. 137

8.2 Detail from the Binsted WI scrapbook, 1965. 145

9.1 Degree of electrification of the Swedish countryside in 1945 and 1950. 165

9.2 Degree of rural electrification in the two main regions of Götaland and Svealand, shown at parish level. 166

9.3 Electrified, at last. Electric pole in a village on the island of Gotland by 1950. 166

9.4 Farmyard, buildings and the electric line into the farm, where internal electrification took over. 168

9.5 The electric stove was no immediate success. 174

10.1 Electrical generation by prime mover, Canada, 1919–1976 (millions of kWh). 182

10.2 Percentage of households with central station electricity, Canada and the provinces, 1921–1951. 183

10.3 Percentage of Canadian farm dwellings and all Canadian households with central station electrical service, 1921–1951. 186

10.4 Percentage of farm, rural non-farm and urban households with specified conveniences, Canada, 1941. 188

10.5 Average monthly consumption of electricity (kWh) by province, Canada, 1931, 1941, 1951. 189

11.1 Individual use of the internet anywhere, United Kingdom, 2013. 208

Tables

4.1	Electricity supply to farmsteads, 1955 (number of farms).	60
4.2	Analysis of work in mid-Wales on approved schemes under the Hill Farming Act and the Livestock Rearing Act (as at 30 June 1955).	61
4.3	Percentage of farms connected to public electricity supplies between nationalisation in 1948 and 31 March 1961.	62
4.4	Mean numbers of Welsh farms (thousands) connected to public electricity supplies and annual electricity consumption (millions of units), 1949–1980.	63
6.1	Mains electrification 1920–1940.	87
6.2	Stationary power on farms in Great Britain, 1908–1939.	88
6.3	Percentage of holdings with an electricity supply (of which % with private supply %P).	89
6.4	Mains electrification 1940–1970.	92
6.5	Farms as a % of all rural consumers.	97
6.6	Date of electrification of a sample of 125 farms in Devon, Cornwall and Dorset.	103
6.7	Number of farms connected to mains supplies in England and Wales.	110
9.1	Number of farm holdings in each of the three major regions of Sweden and per cent with electric light by the middle of the 1940s.	163
9.2	Use of electricity for various kinds of farm work, based on the investigation of 419 farm holdings of different size and located all around the country (in per cent).	170
9.3	Access to electricity at Swedish farm holdings in 1944, categorised according to arable area (per cent of all Swedish farm holdings).	171
9.4	Electric equipment in farmers' households by the mid-1940s (per cent of the households surveyed).	172
11.1	Household internet take-up, UK, 2001–2013 (% adults).	214

11.2	Average download speeds (in Mbps) for fixed broadband connections in urban, suburban and rural areas: May 2011 to November 2013.	215
11.3	Average download speeds (in Mbps) experienced by panellists in rural areas: May 2010 to November 2013.	215

Acknowledgements

This book is a collective intellectual product. Its origins can be traced back to discussions in 2007–2008 funded by a network grant of the Arts and Humanities Research Council of the UK under the title of *The Landscape and Environment of Rural England, 1918–1939*, organised by a working group chaired by Professor Alun Howkins. From these talks it became clear that the changing service provision in the interwar countryside was an under-researched area, and one of the results was a conference on rural electrification organised by Professor Karen Sayer at Leeds Trinity University in March 2013. Most of the chapters of this book had their first exposure at this conference, and we are grateful to Leeds Trinity University, the Social History Society, the British Association for Victorian Studies, the Leeds Centre for Victorian Studies, and the Interwar Rural History Research Group for their financial assistance. We also thank the participants at the conference, especially Clare Griffiths, for their interest in the topic and their valuable comments. Finally we would like to thank those who have been concerned with the commissioning and production of the book, especially Richard Hoyle and Emily Yates.

Contributors

Paul Brassley is Visiting Research Fellow in the Land, Environment, Economics and Policy Institute, University of Exeter

Jeremy Burchardt is Associate Professor in the Department of History, University of Reading

Karl Ditt is a retired historian at the Landschaftsverband Westfalen-Lippe: Institut für westfälische Regionalgeschichte in Münster

David Fleetwood is Head of Sponsorship and Policy Co-ordination in the Historic Environment Policy Unit of the Scottish Government in Edinburgh

Carin Martiin is Associate Professor of Agricultural History, Swedish University of Agricultural Sciences, Uppsala

Richard Moore-Colyer is Emeritus Professor of Agrarian History, University of Wales, Aberystwyth

Ruth W. Sandwell is Associate Professor in the Ontario Institute for Studies in Education, University of Toronto

Karen Sayer is Professor of Social and Cultural History, Leeds Trinity University

John Sheail is a research fellow at the Centre for Ecology and Hydrology (Natural Environment Research Council)

Rosemary Shirley is a lecturer in Art and Design History at Manchester Metropolitan University

Martyn Warren is Visiting Research Fellow in the Land, Environment, Economics and Policy Institute, University of Exeter

1 Introduction

Paul Brassley, Jeremy Burchardt and Karen Sayer

Electricity is ubiquitous in the modern world. Almost all the key technologies of twenty-first-century life depend on it. Communications and media, often regarded as the most fundamental and distinctive elements of modernity, have become almost wholly electronic: the internet, social media, phones, television and radio are all entirely dependent on electricity. The knowledge economy of the developed world is inconceivable without it. Transport is perhaps a little less reliant on electricity, although most trains, trams and urban transport systems are electrically powered, and even cars, aeroplanes and other vehicles that generate their own power now invariably incorporate subsidiary electronic systems. Industry makes very heavy use of electricity, to the point where some large industrial plants (steel and aluminium works, for example) possess their own power stations. Domestically, electricity is equally universal, at least in the developed world. Most homes run numerous electric devices including vacuum cleaners, radios, televisions, phones, refrigerators, freezers, washing machines, kettles, cookers, musical equipment, computers, printers, hairdryers, and countless other gadgets and devices.

The ubiquity of electricity is a reflection of its remarkable properties as a source of power. Many economists and historians of technology argue that power availability per head is one of the fundamental determinants of economic performance. The superior productivity of English agriculture in the eighteenth century is, for example, often attributed to the prevalence of horses as a power source at a time when oxen or even human muscle were still the predominant forms of agricultural draught power across much of continental Europe. In the same way that the use of horse rather than human muscle power represented a technological step change, so in many contexts did the adoption of electricity. An obvious example is the replacement of hand tools such as drills, saws and hammers by power tools. However, it was not only, and possibly not even principally, because electricity increased power availability that it proved such a transformative technology in so many different fields. At least as important were a number of other distinctive advantages. Electricity is almost uniquely flexible and versatile as a power source. It can be converted into kinetic energy in many forms,

2   Paul Brassley et al.

into light or other forms of electromagnetic radiation, into sound or into heat. At the point of use, electricity is also an exceptionally clean form of power, leaving no waste by-product behind. Coal, one of its chief competitors, by contrast leaves smoke, soot and ash behind, which can be expensive to remove and inappropriate or disfiguring in some settings. Electricity is silent, and although its applications, particularly those involving dynamos, are not necessarily so, they are usually quieter than comparable applications powered by alternative means. In many respects electricity is also an unusually safe form of power. While high currents and voltages pose a danger of electric shock, so long as the wires are properly insulated and earthed, this should not occur. Unlike combustion fuels, electricity rarely causes fires and does not explode. While it cannot easily be stored, it can be transported over long distances by means of wires, although as several of the chapters of this book describe, the dependence of electricity transmission on a fixed physical infrastructure did prove a significant limitation in some historical contexts. This notwithstanding, electricity was perhaps the closest thing there was to an ideal modern source of power.

The close association of electricity with modernity also implies a nexus between electricity and that other icon of modernity, the city. Unsurprisingly, therefore, most histories of electricity and electrification have had an urban focus. Examples can be found in both national surveys and local studies, such as those of Leeds and Lyme Regis, and across the Atlantic, as in David Nye's celebration of the 'Electric Cityscape' of New York, or his account of its impact on the homes and factories of 'Middletown'.[1] The conflation of electrification with modernity, urbanity and 'progress' tends to produce, in both writers and readers, a search for a linear thread to its history, leading from the unelectrified origin to the networked, centrally supplied present. This has had a number of questionable consequences, among them four that are especially pertinent to the themes addressed in this book. First, the countryside, with its very different geography, settlement pattern and socio-economic structure, has been recurrently marginalised by, or even written out of, most histories of electrification. It is the principal aim of this volume to redress this imbalance. Second, there is a widespread assumption that the delay in rural, and especially farm, electrification with a mains supply hindered rural and farm life from joining in with the rest of the rational modern economy, society and culture, and that this affected the relationship between the country and the city. Third, it is often assumed that a central or mains supply was the only realistic option for the provision of electricity in villages and farms, an assumption that can certainly be questioned for the first half of the twentieth century, and perhaps increasingly for the twenty-first century. And the final consequence is that many historians have neglected any examination of the demand for electricity while concentrating upon its supply.

Existing histories of electrification in the United Kingdom are remarkable for their concentration on the political, administrative and industrial aspects of the story, as opposed to any examination of the effects of electrification on the lives of consumers. Byatt's account of the years before the First World War is specifically about the British electrical *industry*, and when he discusses consumers they are industrial consumers, in the form of trams, railways and lighting manufacturers.[2] Sir Henry Self, a leading figure in the post–World War II nationalised electricity industry, wrote a book (with Elizabeth Watson) on the history of electricity supply, in which the only account of consumers or demand was a four-page chapter on the statutory representation of the consumer.[3] Similarly, Hannah's two magisterial accounts of the electrification of Britain were commissioned by the Electricity Council on behalf of the Central Electricity Generating Board and the area distribution boards, and based upon their records, and not surprisingly they also see the story from the perspective of the supplier.[4] More recently, John Baker approached the subject in an equally top-down, supply centred manner in his PhD thesis on debates about the reorganisation of the electricity supply industry between 1935 and 1948.[5]

In outline, the story these studies tell is one of gradual adjustment to the changing technologies and economics of electricity generation and distribution. In the 1820s and '30s Michael Faraday identified the principles of dynamos and electric motors, and in 1878 Joseph Swan first demonstrated an electrically powered incandescent carbon filament lamp. From these discoveries emerged, quite rapidly, the idea of a public supply of electricity and the means to produce it. The first public generator was installed at Godalming in Surrey in 1881, and in the following year an Electric Light Act had been brought into being which recognised the existence of public electricity suppliers, and in fact restricted their expansion by giving local authorities the power to purchase them after a period of time. Nevertheless, by 1900 there were sixty-five private supply companies and 164 municipal undertakings in being.[6] As with many other technologies, war accelerated change. In 1918 the Coal Conservation Committee of the Ministry of Reconstruction advocated the establishment of large power stations near coalfields, and an Act of 1919 established the Electricity Commission, which in turn led to the Electricity (Supply) Act of 1926 setting up the Central Electricity Board. The Board's functions were to generate electricity efficiently and construct a national transmission grid system.[7] The national grid was completed in 1933, but, in the words of the McGowan Committee in 1936, 'the problems arising in connection with distribution are entirely different in character from, and far more complex than, those arising in connection with generation.'[8] They were later described as 'almost chaotic', and arose from the large number of electricity undertakings, of very different sizes, and the associated variability in tariffs and charging systems, which was one of the main reasons, it was generally felt, holding back growth in demand, especially for the use of electricity for heating and power.[9] The Second World War led to further rationalisation and concentration. A national voltage was established in 1945, and a report produced (probably for internal use)

4   *Paul Brassley et al.*

within the Ministry of Agriculture in September of that year discussed 'the belief that electricity is a social service which should be provided by right to every citizen', although it noted that 'there may be some justification for this opinion but the satisfaction of such a demand will depend on the readiness of the urban population to bear part of the cost of distributing electricity to rural areas.'[10] The same report noted that while the private undertakings had distributed 54 per cent of their surpluses on interest and dividend payments in 1937, the public companies had only needed to use 27 per cent of their surpluses for interest payments and were therefore in a much better position to expand services.[11] Given these statements in official documents it was hardly surprising that the industry was nationalised in 1948. From then on, until privatisation in 1990, the Central Electricity Generating Board was responsible for generating and transmitting electricity and selling it to the fifteen area electricity boards that handled retail sales.[12]

A supply of electricity could be taken to within reach of potential consumers, but they still had to make the decision to use it. Alternative sources of light and power were already in existence, and the firms that supplied them were unlikely simply to surrender their markets to the electricity companies. Indeed, the present position of mains gas as a fuel for cooking and heating in towns, and of oil for heating in rural areas, demonstrates their survival powers. As Graeme Gooday argues, the idea of an inevitable and steady uptake of electricity by consumers underestimates both the problems of early electricity and the innovative abilities of alternative energy suppliers.[13] Nevertheless, the use of electricity did expand. For most families in Britain, domestic electricity first became available in the interwar period, when most new houses first incorporated electric wiring, and many older houses were wired for the first time. The number of consumers increased tenfold, and electricity consumption increased dramatically, albeit from a low base. Whereas in 1920 the UK generated 154 kWh (kilowatt-hours) per head of population, by 1938 the figure was 712 kWh. However, in comparison with some other countries, the British performance was less impressive. By 1938 the German figure was 843 kWh; the USA was generating over 1,000 kWh per head of population; Sweden even more; and Canada and Norway at least twice as much as the USA, although UK consumption did exceed that of Denmark, France, Italy and Spain.[14] A post-war report suggested that although the experience of the Tennessee Valley Authority in the USA demonstrated that lower prices could have a significant effect on increasing demand, it was not the only factor involved. In New Zealand, where prices were similar to those in the UK, electricity use was greater, and nearly all urban households, and 90 per cent of rural households, used it. The explanation lay in the much higher price of alternative fuels such as coal. By the outbreak of the Second World War it was estimated that about 8.5 million of the 12.75 million domestic premises in the Great Britain had been connected to a mains supply. Of these, 1.2 million out of a total of 2.25 million were located in rural (but not necessarily agricultural) areas. Even after the

Introduction 5

war it was estimated that about 20 per cent of urban households remained unconnected, mainly in poorer working class areas.[15]

Before proceeding to consider the historiography of rural electrification, it may be as well to clarify some of the conceptual issues involved. In the first place, then, it is important to be clear that electricity generation requiring a centralised operating system was only one of several possible 'sociotechnical translations'.[16] There were two basic options. One was to generate electricity centrally, as close to the source of energy as possible. In most of England and Wales this was initially coal, although later coastal and estuarial oil- and gas-fired power stations became important.[17] The other was to generate it locally. The first was likely to incur lower energy or generation costs but higher transmission costs, while locally generated electricity might cost more to produce but less to transmit. Generation costs could also be divided into capital and running costs (or fixed and variable costs). The main variable or running cost was for fuel, so for hydroelectricity (and, in more recent contexts, wind, wave and solar power), running costs would be more or less limited to control and maintenance costs, with the capital required to install the generating and transmission equipment forming the major cost item. The proportion of running costs in the total would clearly be much higher when other energy sources, such as coal or oil, were used. The problem faced by all would-be providers of electricity in the late nineteenth and twentieth centuries (and still to some degree today) was to work out which of these alternatives offered the best option, taking convenience, reliability and safety into account. The answer was by no means obvious, as the following chapters demonstrate.

While calculating the long-term costs of local versus central generation was often complex, the cheapest and most straightforward approach in terms of the initial capital outlay required was almost always local generation at the level of the individual consuming unit – in a rural context, typically the farm or estate. Unsurprisingly, therefore, this kind of very small-scale self-supply preceded central generation. To a large extent, its history remains to be written, mainly because by its nature the sources are scattered and incomplete. While the present book is mainly concerned with larger-scale provision, especially although not solely mains electrification, it is important to provide a brief overview of self-supply here, as it is impossible to understand the timing, trajectory and implications of mains electrification in rural areas without an awareness of the significant role played by self-supply in the countryside. While individual households, urban or rural, could rarely be self-sufficient in electricity – at least with twentieth-century technology – farms and estates were potentially much heavier users and the economies of scale were such as to justify a range of oil, petrol and diesel generators and even small hydroelectric plants. Among the earliest adopters, in Britain at least, were the great country houses, several of which had built their own generating stations (hydroelectric and steam) and (glass tank) accumulator storage systems to form private lighting plants before the First

6 Paul Brassley et al.

World War.[18] Many estates still had private installations and some farms tapped into these. However, even after the Second World War many farmers simply used DC generators, and batteries charged at a local hardware store or garage, to generate electric power for lighting, radios and other domestic uses. Generators of all sorts powered other equipment on the farm more directly. If static, these generators would run in a shed/lean-to near to where the power was wanted, as DC current drops rapidly the further it has to travel. Later, AC generators (alternators) were more widely used.

It is difficult to estimate how widely used generators were in British agriculture. According to Collins, there were about 2,000 electric motors in operation on British farms in 1910, mainly used for barn work and machine milking. These must almost all have been powered by generators but the figure is almost negligible in comparison to the more than 800,000 agricultural horses at the same date. The number of electric motors on British farms had increased to 11,000 by 1939, providing a total brake horsepower of 47,300. What proportion of these were powered by generators is unclear, but the overall figure is still rather small in relation to the total draw-bar horsepower of over 1 million supplied by tractors and farm horses at this date. Farmers were not, then, wholly dependent on mains electricity to take advantage of major electricity-powered innovations such as the milking machine (a point made in several of the chapters that follow), but on the other hand the rate of uptake in the absence of mains electricity was not necessarily all that high. Collins concludes starkly that 'the electric motor was far less popular in Britain than in other European countries due to the lack of electrical power. As late as 1938, only 7 per cent of farms were connected to the mains supply.'[19]

The timing and impact of central generation and transmission on rural areas has received a little more attention from historians but remains a very under-researched subject. One approach is to focus on the political implications of electricity as a network, and consequently in the way in which different political circumstances produced different electrification histories.[20] This can help to explain why rural electrification took longer to be brought about in many contexts. In the case of the United States, Nye outlines the reasons why farmers were increasingly interested in buying electric power, whereas private utility companies 'saw little profit' in supplying them.[21] The State Commission for the Electrification of Russia, formed in 1920, faced opposition for a variety of conflicting reasons from agricultural specialists and bureaucrats, electrification enthusiasts, electrical engineers and peasants, according to Coopersmith.[22] On the other hand, Nye argues that government policy in Germany, France, the Netherlands and Scandinavia promoted rural electrification so that two-thirds of farmers had access to it by the end of the 1920s, Austria had large numbers of electricity supply cooperatives, and in Czechoslovakia by 1930 over 8,000 communities were electrified, some through the work of cooperatives, although about 7,000, especially in the less-industrialised east of the country, remained without a

Introduction   7

supply. In Finland the presence of an Agrarian League party in government also promoted rural electrification after the Second World War.[23] The impact of electrification on the lives of rural people is also a recurrent theme, with Nye, for example, arguing that it eased the work of women on the farm, whereas Katherine Jellison suggests that it raised some problematic gender and farming family issues, with women often resisting it.[24] Her argument is that women's history often focuses on the urban experience, so that if some urban consumers at a particular time had, for example, electrically powered washing machines, then there is a dubious tendency to assume that all women at the same time had bought into the same equipment. Moreover, she points out, it is an assumption that electric water heating and power, for example, actually help women; they may just increase the perceived obligation to do the laundry more frequently.

Historical studies of rural electrification in Britain are few and far between. Apart from the late Leslie Newman's unpublished MPhil thesis and Moore-Colyer's pioneering study of the subject in Wales (reprinted in this volume), there has hitherto been little further academic investigation of this vast, protracted, and sometimes contested undertaking.[25] We know little about the timing or geography of rural electrification, about the providers, beneficiaries or indeed losers. The decision-making process that led to electrification remains unclear: how much local input was there? When, and to what extent, did local authorities become important players? How did the rise of planning impact electrification projects? Did remote areas, at the end of the queue for mains electricity, lose population more rapidly than those parts of the countryside that were electrified earlier, and were their farms less prosperous? To what extent were relevant Whitehall departments such as the Ministry of Agriculture able to influence decisions, or did policy statements such as the Scott Report of 1942 remain largely aspirational?

If the process by which electrification occurred remains unclear, the consequences are even more so. Plainly, questions of the available technical alternatives and issues of regional geography are equally critical here, but also remain largely unexplored. The following chapters in this book will demonstrate that the history of rural electrification does not simply end in the early 1970s, when a mains connection became nearly universal, because the story involves not only connection and supply, but also use. And while most villages, houses and farms might have been connected by the early 1970s, that did not necessarily mean that all the machines and appliances that could and would eventually use electricity immediately came on-stream. What, therefore, was the impact on farming methods? Equally, was the effect on domestic life, through changing lighting and heating options, and making consumer durables such as television, washing machines, refrigerators and hi-fi systems available during the 1950s and 1960s, perhaps more significant in the long run, paving as it may have done the way to counter-urbanisation? Just as intriguing is the cultural response to rural electrification. The early years of rural electrification coincided with the rise of a

8   Paul Brassley et al.

powerful preservationist discourse that valued tradition, local distinctiveness and small-scale features. Yet surprisingly, many preservationists enthused about the 'right kind' of pylons. To engage in counterfactual history, what would have happened if the mains network had not been expanded? Would there have been more noisy diesel or petrol-powered generators in the countryside? Would that have had a more damaging impact on the rural landscape and soundscape than pylons and power lines did? How, then, should electrification be situated in relation to discourses of preservation, modernity and national identity? To what extent should we see electrification as a form of urban conquest of the rural, the imposition of an alien technology on a reluctant but ultimately subordinate rural world? Certainly this is how it was sometimes imagined, for example in Lenin's dictum that 'Communism is Soviet power plus the electrification of the whole country.'[26] Or is the implication that the countryside was somehow 'less modern' than the city, and therefore less receptive to electrification, a naïve myth? These are some of the principal questions informing this book.

In the present volume we have to some extent followed the previous pattern of examining the structural changes involved, the development and spread of the infrastructure of generation and distribution. But we also address what we might think of as the cultural/human aspects of adoption – the ways in which mains electricity was presented to consumers by its enthusiasts, politicians and so forth, and the negotiations involved in its adoption, what this intangible thing meant and how electrical devices came to be absorbed in the village, on the farm and into the farmer's home, despite or perhaps because of its competitors.[27] The geographical focus is primarily on Great Britain, that is to say England, Wales and Scotland, but not Ireland. While electricity supply in rural Ireland is an interesting historiographical issue, it is in many respects a different story. The national grid, which became the cornerstone of electricity supply in Great Britain, did not, for obvious reasons, extend to Ireland, and electrification in Ireland (both North and South) had different administrative and technical characteristics (for example with respect to voltage). Issues of national identity and citizenship loom large in the history of Irish rural electrification, not questions that on the whole are central to the English, Welsh and Scottish experiences. On the whole, and bearing in mind that the topic has already been addressed by Michael Shiel's well-received book, it seemed better to limit the present book to Great Britain, but with some comparative chapters.[28] It is therefore divided into three parts, the first on the spread of rural electrification, the second on its effects, and the third comparing electrification in Britain with Canada and Sweden, and with the more recent story of the spread of rural broadband.

In the first part Karl Ditt puts some detail into the story of the slow progress of rural electrification before the Second World War, explaining how high infrastructure costs, low rural demand, dubious local authority decisions and continuing arguments over central control restricted any

Introduction 9

expansion in England. John Sheail then takes over the story with an account of the development of the national grid from the legislative problems of its establishment in the interwar period to the post-war impact of nationalisation. He also examines its environmental implications, as power lines and pylons crossed the countryside and the cooling demands of new power stations affected river water temperatures. Richard Moore-Colyer's chapter on Wales charts not only the spread of electrification but also its economic, social and cultural impact in different parts of the principality.[29] David Fleetwood charts the development of hydroelectricity in the Highlands of Scotland. Paul Brassley concentrates on farm electrification, explaining why, in general, it came later than the electrification of the villages, and exploring its impact on farming and the lives of farmers, especially in the south-west of England.

The second part of the book concentrates on the effects of electrification on the lives of country people. Karen Sayer uses the memoirs of two families in particular to show how it changed home life. Rosemary Shirley analyses a scrapbook compiled by the Binsted Women's Institute as part of the WI Golden Jubilee celebrations in 1965 to show how village women perceived the impact of electrification on both the landscape outside their homes and their cookery practices inside them.

The third part of the book is concerned with comparisons over space and time. Ruth Sandwell shows how, in the very different environment of rural Canada, some of the same problems of providing mains supplies to communities and farms that had other established energy sources delayed widespread electrification in the first half of the twentieth century, just as they did in Britain. Sweden, in contrast, saw an earlier spread of at least some form of electric power, but, as Carin Martiin's chapter reveals, there were still significant differences between different parts of the country, and also between different uses of electricity in the home and the farmstead. Martyn Warren examines a much more recent issue: the spread of broadband connections in rural areas of the UK, a process that has exhibited some interesting, if not complete, parallels with the process of rural electrification. Finally the editors draw some of the main issues that emerge from all of these chapters together and attempt to identify the questions that remain unanswered.

Notes

1 G. Weightman, *Children of light: How electricity changed Britain forever.* London: Atlantic Books, 2011; J.D. Poulter, *An early history of electricity supply: The story of electric light in Victorian Leeds.* London: Peter Peregrinus, on behalf of the Institution of Electrical Engineers, 1986; M.R. Green, *Electric Lyme: The coming of electricity to an English seaside town.* Crewkerne: M.R. Green, 2006; D. Nye, *American technological sublime.* Cambridge, MA: MIT Press, 1994, pp. 173–198; D. Nye, *Electrifying America: Social meanings of a new technology, 1880–1940.* Cambridge, MA: MIT Press, 1990.

2 I.C.R. Byatt, *The British electrical industry 1875–1914: The economic returns to a new technology.* Oxford: Clarendon Press, 1979.

10   *Paul Brassley et al.*

3 H. Self and E.M. Watson, *Electricity supply in Great Britain: Its development and organisation.* London: George Allen and Unwin, 1952, pp. 146–149.

4 Leslie Hannah, *Electricity before nationalisation: A study of the development of the electricity supply industry in Britain to 1948.* London: Macmillan, 1979; Hannah, *Engineers, managers and politicians: The first fifteen years of nationalised electricity supply in Britain.* London: Macmillan, 1982. See also Bill Luckin, *Questions of power: Electricity and environment in interwar Britain.* Manchester: Manchester University Press, 1990.

5 John Leon Baker, *Planning the future of the electricity supply industry, 1935–48.* PhD thesis, University of Birmingham, 1991.

6 R. Millward, 'Business and government in electricity network integration in western Europe, c.1900–1950', *Business History*, vol. 48 (4), 2006, p. 486; R.J. Moore-Colyer, 'Lighting the landscape: Rural electrification in Wales', *Welsh History Review*, vol. 23 (4), 2007, p. 73. A revised version of this paper is included in this book as chapter 4.

7 Hannah, *Electricity before nationalisation*, p. 116; C. Chant (ed.), *Science, technology and everyday life 1870–1950.* London: Routledge/Open University, 1989, p. 92; Millward, 'Business and government in electricity network integration', p. 486; Moore-Colyer, 'Lighting the landscape', p. 75.

8 Ministry of Transport, *Report of the Committee on Electricity Distribution* (the McGowan Committee), London: HMSO, 1936, p. 4.

9 The National Archives of the UK, Kew (henceforth TNA), MAF 38/695, Ministry of Agriculture and Fisheries, Economics and Statistics division, *Reports on the Economic Position of Agriculture No. 23: Farm Water and Electricity Supplies*, September 1945, pp. 28 and 42–3. The editors are grateful to Professor Richard Hoyle for bringing this report to their attention.

10 MAF, *Farm Water and Electricity Supplies*, p. 43.

11 MAF, *Farm Water and Electricity Supplies*, p. 54.

12 Chant, *Science, technology and everyday life*, p. 110; Millward, 'Business and government in electricity network integration', p. 486.

13 Gooday, *Domesticating electricity: Technology, uncertainty and gender, 1880–1914.* London: Pickering & Chatto, 2008, pp. 15–16.

14 Millward, 'Business and government in electricity network integration', p. 482; Chant, *Science, technology and everyday life*, p. 110. See also Baker, *Planning the future of the electricity supply industry*, p. 97.

15 MAF, *Farm Water and Electricity Supplies*, pp. 27, 50–51.

16 S. Hinchliffe, 'Technology, power and space: The means and ends of geographies of technology', *Environment and Planning D: Society and Space*, vol. 14, 1996, p. 665.

17 Nuclear power was rather different, since the principal determinant of the location of nuclear power stations was neither minimising generation nor transmission costs but obtaining copious supplies of water for cooling, and avoiding large population centres. Nuclear energy only began to make a significant contribution to electricity generation in the UK in the late 1960s, although the UK's first nuclear power station was Calder Hall in Cumberland, opened in 1956. See C.N. Hill, *An atomic empire: A technical history of the rise and fall of the UK atomic energy programme.* London: Imperial College Press, 2013.

18 F.C. Allsop, *Practical electric-light fitting: A treatise on the wiring and fitting-up of buildings deriving current from central station mains, and the laying down of private installations*, 7th edn. London and New York: Whittaker, c. 1915; e.g. see plate facing p. 268 – originally a series of articles in the *English Mechanic*, first edn. 1892.

19 E.J.T. Collins, 'Power availability and agricultural productivity in England and Wales', in Bas J.P. van Bavel and Erik Thoen (eds), *Land productivity and*

agro-systems in the North Sea Area (Middle Ages–20th century). Elements for comparison. Turnhout: Brepols, 1999, pp. 209–225, esp. pp. 215, 221.

20 Jonathan Coopersmith, *The electrification of Russia, 1880-–1926.* Ithaca, NY: Cornell University Press, 1992, p. 5; T.P. Hughes, *Networks of power: Electrification in western society, 1880–1930.* Baltimore, MD: Johns Hopkins Press, 1983.

21 Nye, *Electrifying America*, pp. 287–314.

22 Coopersmith, *The electrification of Russia*, p. 164.

23 Nye, *Electrifying America*, p. 287; O.S. Morgan (ed.), *Agricultural systems of middle Europe: A symposium.* New York, 1933, pp. 27 and 129; T. Myllyntaus, *Electrifying Finland: The transfer of a new technology into a late-industrialising economy.* Basingstoke: Macmillan, 1991, p. 249. The first and last of these authors give figures for the extent of rural or farm electrification, but Nye gives no source for his data and Myllyntaus (p. 364) simply states that it is unreliable.

24 Nye, *Electrifying America,* pp. 303–304; K. Jellison, *Entitled to power: Farm women and technology.* Chapel Hill: University of North Carolina Press, 1993.

25 Leslie T. Newman, *The electrification of Rural England and Wales.* Unpublished MPhil thesis, Institute of Agricultural History & Museum of English Rural Life, March 1991; Moore-Colyer, 'Lighting the landscape'; and on a specific technology, see, K. Sayer, 'Battery birds, 'stimulighting' and 'twilighting': The ecology of standardised poultry technology', *History of Technology*, special issue, 'By whose standards? Standardization, stability and uniformity in the history of information and electrical technologies', vol. 28, 2008, pp. 149–168.

26 Vladimir Lenin, *Our foreign and domestic position and party tasks.* Moscow, 1920.

27 This is the approach taken by historians of technology and science, e.g. Gooday, *Domesticating electricity*, p. 3: 'an innovation will only gain a permanent footing in the home if its role is made meaningful and unthreatening.'

28 Michael Shiel, *The quiet revolution: The electrification of rural Ireland 1946–1976.* Dublin: O'Brien Press, 2003. The original edition was published in 1984.

29 A previous version of this chapter was first published in 2007. See note 6.

Part I

The progress of electrification

2 The electrification of the countryside

The interests of electrical enterprises and the rural population in England, 1888–1939

Karl Ditt[1]

The question of rural power supply

England not only pioneered industrialisation, but also set up an effective energy supply system at a relatively early period. By the mid-nineteenth century almost all local authorities with a population of over 2,500 had access to gas supplies.[2] The construction of electricity supply also began relatively early. After it became clear at both the International and the World Exhibitions in Paris in 1878 and 1881[3] that electricity had more advantages than gas – it was easier to handle and transport, it was safer and could be used in many more ways – this new form of energy began to be used in 1878 in London for lighting a theatre, a promenade along the Thames and a fish market, as well as in an ironworks in nearby Shoreditch. The first public electricity power stations went into operation in 1881 in small towns in Derbyshire and Surrey.[4] The subsequent, rapid growth of electricity consumption in factories, theatres, cafés, department stores and public buildings demonstrated that its advantages were reckoned to far outweigh the fact that it was more expensive.

Nonetheless the process of electrification in England began to slow down as early as the 1880s. One reason was the 1882 Electric Lighting Act which stipulated that business companies that wanted to supply an area with electricity had to have the consent of the respective local authority before the Board of Trade could give them a concession. The consent was valid for a period of twenty-one years – the original proposal was only fifteen years – and after that the local authority would be able to buy up a company's installations at the current market value.[5] This restrictive law can be traced back to the influence of the towns which, because of their poor experience with privately owned gas and water monopolies, wanted to be able to take over electricity companies as early as possible.

The consequences of the Act were considerable. Privately owned companies regarded the concession period as too short for them to commit themselves to the necessarily high investment costs and risks. As a result, from

16   *Karl Ditt*

1882 onwards, there were next to no applications for concessions and the spread of electricity supply also slowed down considerably.[6] However, representatives from local authorities played down the consequences of legal restriction. Thus, when George W. Morrison, the mayor of Leeds, was questioned by a committee of the House of Lords, he replied that he had no doubt that the lack of applications for concessions could be attributed to the Act of 1882. Like other mayors, however, he thought that the main reason was because the price of electricity could not compete with gas.[7] But when Parliament doubled the concession period to forty-two years in 1888 and gave the Board of Trade the right to overrule local authorities' objections to applications for concessions by private electricity companies, the number of applications rose dramatically.[8]

After its early beginnings, the delay in electrification hit the town and countryside alike. In England, however, the subsequent electrification of rural areas developed relatively slowly, not only in comparison to urban areas but also at an international level. What was responsible for this? In order to answer this question it is necessary to examine the interests of the electricity companies and those of rural populations in closer detail.

Electricity companies and rural areas until 1918

The private companies that were initially prepared to risk investing the necessary capital to set up electricity supplies concentrated primarily on towns and cities. Here there was a high population density of private households and business companies – their two main potential consumers – and this meant that investment costs would be considerably smaller and the ensuing revenue larger than in comparatively thinly populated rural areas.[9] Furthermore the use of direct current, which could not be 'transported' as easily as alternating current, limited the range of electricity supply.[10] Thus there were both technical and financial problems to extending the grid beyond the towns into rural areas.

At a technical level the transport of electricity clearly became easier in the course of time thanks to the switch from direct to alternating current. But because investment costs in rural areas remained high in comparison to towns and cities, electricity companies were still reluctant to supply thinly populated areas. At most they were interested in supplying industrial companies, quarries or complete villages, but not scattered farmhouses whose electricity consumption in the 1920s was often only the equivalent of that of an urban middle class household.[11]

True, individuals interested in being supplied with electricity could demand a connection in areas already owned by approved electricity suppliers, but they had to pay a price for it. If a building belonging to a prospective consumer lay within a radius of 50 yards from a supply line, the 1899 Electric Lighting (Clauses) Act gave electricity companies the right, either to pass on the capital costs of connecting the consumer or to raise the cost of the electricity to such a level as to ensure they retrieved their investment costs, and to demand a consumption guarantee for a minimum of three years. That said, they were not permitted to raise the surcharge on investment costs higher than 20% per year. At least six potential consumers were necessary for connecting buildings beyond the 50-yard radius. But as a rule they also had to enable electricity companies to make a gross profit of 20% on the price of their electricity.[12] All in all, the price of supplying electricity to rural areas was higher than that in towns because distribution costs, which as a rule made up more than half the cost of electricity supplies, were higher.[13] This deterred potential rural customers more than their urban counterparts, all the more so because average incomes in the countryside were lower.

The readiness of electricity companies to bear the disproportionately high costs of any such infrastructure was thus dependent on the readiness of consumers to pay high prices, on the number of consumers and the amount of electricity they consumed. It was above all necessary to ensure a high level of consumption of power electricity, for as a rule the demand for lighting electricity alone was insufficient to retrieve investment costs. Furthermore electricity for lighting was generally only necessary at night-time; hence this only led to temporary peak loads, that is to a temporary utilisation of the requisite capacities. It is worth noting that in order to reduce the lopsided usage rate electricity companies invested very little in advertising electric light after the turn of the century, even in towns. Instead they concentrated much more on promoting the use of domestic electric gadgets and electrically driven motors, which were principally used during the daytime and consumed more electricity.

Before the First World War the public required next to no electric power because the use of domestic electric household equipment like washing machines, cookers and vacuum cleaners, not to speak of hot water devices which ran on electric power, was still in its infancy. At the most electric irons had begun to spread in towns and cities. Until well into the 1920s such equipment, especially electric cookers, was also likely to break down and need repairs. People living in the countryside were probably even more reluctant to purchase domestic electrical equipment. Alongside electric light they had to drive electrical machines by day to make investment attractive for the electricity companies and to set in motion (via the economies of scale) the spiral of growing demand and consumption with a concomitant reduction in the price of electricity. To achieve this, it was necessary to ensure that electric motors were in continual use in workshops, factories and on farms. Here equipment like threshing machines, chaff and beet cutters, cream separators, milking machines and transport engines, water and sewage pumps, circular saws and so forth all came into question.[14] In villages cooperative cooking and washing facilities held open the promise of high power consumption.

Nonetheless there was no great demand for electricity to drive agricultural machines until well into the 1920s. British scholars are unanimous in their

18 *Karl Ditt*

findings[15] that during this time agriculture was dominated by simple equipment like mechanical reaper-binders and horse power. As a rule only dairy and poultry farms had machines which required a large amount of electricity. Furthermore there was a huge amount of seasonal agricultural work which made it scarcely worthwhile for many farmers to invest in electrical equipment. Mobile agrarian service providers and farming cooperatives which might have made the most of such machines scarcely existed. Apart from tractors, in the mid-1920s there were only around 80,000 machines on farms in Great Britain. Of these more than 80% ran on oil and petrol, 8% were hydraulically driven, 5% used steam and only 1% electricity.[16]

It was only around this time that people began to promote the electrification of agriculture. The Institution of Electrical Engineers and the British Electrical Development Association began to publicise the advantages of electro-farming and organise corresponding exhibitions.[17] In addition electric companies like General Electric began to manufacture machines for sterilisation, butter production, heating greenhouses and henhouse incubators and so forth.[18] Many farmers used hydraulic power to drive their own power and lighting generators. The problem was that this form of self-help and consumption reduced the need for third-party electricity supplies and slowed down any attempt by the electricity companies to construct a centralised nationwide grid.

All in all, there appears to have been a deadlock in rural electricity supply until well into the 1920s. The electricity companies concentrated on supplying towns and were reluctant to spread their grids to the countryside because it was simply not worth their while. For their part rural inhabitants regarded electricity as too expensive and therefore used traditional methods to cover their lighting and power requirements. Electricity companies often discovered that, even when farmers were prepared to connect a supply line, they often used it simply for lighting purposes, at the most for an electric fire and much less for power needs.[19] It was clearly sufficient for them to use electricity for lighting purposes because they thought it involved lower fire risk, enabled them to prolong working hours into dusk, and was more comfortable than gas lighting, above all when compared to oil lamps and candles.

Given the problems and difficulties involved in electrifying the countryside, there were four possible solutions. The first involved electricity companies using their own capital to invest in the construction of a suitable infrastructure for a specific area – lines, pylons, substations and so forth – on a step-by-step basis.[20] As a rule this solution was not practiced by local authority electricity suppliers whose tariffs and profit levels were often held down because their primary aim was to supply companies and individuals with electricity as cheaply as possible. Hence it was only the financially powerful private Power Companies for whom this was possible. Such companies, of which there were about thirty in 1918, were mostly set up and financed by urban entrepreneurs from the turn of the century onwards.[21]

They wanted to supply authorised undertakers, moreover companies and individuals in areas without concessions.[22]

However, the Power Companies suffered from the selfish policies of the local authorities who possessed around two-thirds of all the authorised electricity companies in England at the turn of the century.[23] What this meant can be illustrated by the story of an industrial group in Chesterfield which planned to exploit the potentials inherent in alternating current in 1898 by setting up a Power Company to provide electricity to rural areas. To do so, however, the group would have competed with some of the local authority urban power suppliers within the concession area. Thus the local authorities in question objected to the application for a concession on the grounds that the area was protected by their monopoly. Their objection was supported by the Association of Municipal Corporations, and the responsible Board of Trade also took their side. The upshot was that the group's application for a concession was rejected and it was unable to put its plans into action.[24] Subsequently in the same year the government set up a joint committee of the House of Lords and the House of Commons under the leadership of Lord Cross in order to examine the pros and cons of regional electricity supplies. The committee came to the conclusion that private and public companies should be given the right to produce electricity in bulk and to supply rural areas where local electricity companies already existed, that is to allow competition in cases 'where sufficient public advantage is shown'.[25]

However, the towns appealed against this recommendation because their potential expansion targets would have been restricted. The upshot was that Parliament rejected the idea. Following this, the MP Sir James Kitson proposed a compromise solution that would allow private Power Companies to supply electricity to power suppliers with a concession. In areas not occupied by concessioned companies they should have the right to supply electricity of power. On the other hand, in areas already covered by an electricity distribution concession Power Companies would only be able to deliver power electricity with the consent of the concession holder. This consent could only be withheld if there was a good reason, for example when the concession holder itself was in a position to deliver the desired electricity at the same time and price. The Power Companies had to give up their supply rights if local authorities in their delivery area produced and wanted to supply their own electricity, or when towns which had incorporated rural areas wanted to extend their delivery area accordingly.[26] Following the spirit of the so-called Kitson clause the Board of Trade began to issues concessions to the power companies. Thus local private and local authority electricity suppliers were given powers of veto which enabled them to put a brake on the establishment and expansion of large regional and national electric companies.[27]

Nonetheless the municipalities were unable to prevent the creation of larger electricity companies. Shortly after the turn of the twentieth century

Parliament issued concessions to the likes of the Lancashire Power Company, the Cleveland and Durham County Power Company, the Nottinghamshire Power Company and the Yorkshire Electric Power Company, all of which primarily delivered electricity to rural areas – but only where it appeared profitable. Thanks to their huge power stations these financially powerful companies were able to supply electricity at comparatively cheap rates. But for a long time they were unable to do business with the municipalities because the latter wanted to retain their autonomy in supplying electricity at all costs.[28] Thus Power Companies were deprived of a clear growth in demand for electricity, which meant that they were unable to enjoy the advantages provided by economies of scale, and rural consumers were unable to enjoy the corresponding advantages of cheaper prices.

The 1909 Electric Lighting Act then gave the Board of Trade powers to give consent to companies to construct power lines and supply electricity in areas outside their own concessions. However the expansion of Power Companies into rural areas largely depended on negotiations with the local authorities that had powers of veto, with the result that rural electrification only progressed slowly.[29] Given the power of local authorities to block the companies' plans, their best way for them to be given – and to retain – a large-scale concession was to announce the construction of large power stations and concomitantly cheaper tariffs. Local authorities would also be able to profit from this when they at least took part of their electricity requirements from the large power station. Otherwise power companies were restricted to supplying electricity to free, non-concessioned rural areas, that is to less profitable areas.

A second possible potential for electricity companies to raise capital for investment in rural areas was to charge urban customers disproportionately high prices and use the profits to invest in rural electrification, so to speak to redistribute costs to the detriment of urban consumers. That said, townsfolk tended as a rule to oppose the extension of the grid beyond their own municipal borders, for they feared that the electricity companies would shift a part of the high costs of power lines and administration onto their own bills, thereby delaying any possible price reductions. As long as the potential for winning new customers within municipal borders was not exhausted, urban electricity companies and their customers were hardly interested in extending power supplies to the countryside.

Furthermore until 1909 the 1899 Electric Lighting (Clauses) Act forbade any fusion between adjacent local authority electricity companies or cooperation between local authorities which might have eased the supply of power to areas between two neighbouring towns. But even after the Act became invalid in 1909, towns neither cooperated with each other nor with private Power Companies, in contrast with Germany where there were mixed economy enterprises. In England the towns mainly wanted to avoid becoming dependent on private companies in order to be able to determine price levels alone. Their background motive was not only to maintain their own autonomy but to respond to the interests of local industrialists and inhabitants. Hence many urban authorities often kept their prices relatively low out of regard for private and business interests, that is they mostly decided to desist from making high profits and not to milk their customers to help them balance their books. Whatever the case, as censuses in 1910 and 1911 showed, local authority electricity works in England often delivered power at cheaper prices than their private counterparts, with little or no profits as a result.[30] Such parochial policies slowed down regional and national solutions which might not only have improved supplies to the countryside but also, in the final analysis, might have led to a general reduction in prices because of the economies of scale.

A third possible way of financing rural electrification was for the electricity companies to receive public grants, either from rural authorities or from the state, to extend the grid to the countryside. But this was seldom the case. On occasions during the 1920s state support could be gained for simple earthworks (to erect pylons, for example) as part of job creation programmes.

The fourth and most obvious possibility for electrifying the countryside occurred when the rural population itself wished to be connected to the grid and/or could be persuaded to do so by the electricity companies. These would then have been able to charge a relatively high price for connections and power to those sections of the rural population that were prepared to take large supplies of electricity on a long-term basis. Furthermore by demonstrating the uses of electricity the companies hoped that they would rapidly be able to persuade other consumers to ask for connections, thereby setting in motion a spiral of profit making and price reductions. In other words they had to use the same strategies for the countryside as they had used in setting up power supplies in the towns.

The German solution often used for preparing rural electrification seems scarcely to have applied in England. Before 1914 in some regions of the German Reich, like Westphalia, Württemberg or Saxony, people or companies (as a rule farmers or independent businesses) joined forces to set up cooperative electricity works. Some of them began to produce electricity themselves, while others tried to take electricity from electricity companies and then distribute it themselves. To do this they offered guaranteed purchase commitments and a partial share in meeting the costs of constructing a low-tension grid, whereas the electricity companies should take over the construction of high-tension power lines.[31] It is possible that the lack of cooperative electricity companies in England can be attributed to business companies blocking areas which failed to make the most of their concessions or from the fact that cooperative companies in England were traditionally set up by the working class rather than the middle class.

The imbalance in the electrification between town and country before the First World War was clear. The large number of local electricity works also led to a large number of technical solutions. This meant that the electricity

22   Karl Ditt

economy was technically and geographically very fragmented and therefore worked inefficiently. For this reason in 1910 the well-known engineer Ferranti was one of the first to demand the creation of a systematic national power grid.[32] At the start of the First World War similar ideas were once more being put forward in trade journals, mainly when it became clear that the armaments industry would require an enormous amount of electricity and when there were difficulties in linking existing electricity works in order to balance supplies in the different regions. In 1916 the Prime Minister Herbert Asquith tackled the problem by setting up a Coal Conservation Committee (the Haldane Committee) to come up with recommendations for economising on coal consumption. After the report was submitted, the Board of Trade – which was responsible for electricity supply – created the Electric Power Supply Committee (the Williamson Committee) to specify more closely the results in the report and implement them in a legislation proposal.[33] The recommendations of this and other committees were basically the same. After the end of the First World War they therefore formed the basis for restructuring electricity supplies in Great Britain.

The electrification of the countryside from the 1920s

The committees had come to the conclusion that the central problem of English electricity supply was the fact there were too many (ca. 600) power stations and many companies were too small to be able to work efficiently on both a technical and financial level. Furthermore because of the high number of companies production fragmentation would mean a waste of coal. In order to solve these problems the electricity system should be reorganised. It was first necessary to set up a Board of Electricity Commissioners. This should be broadly independent of government and Parliament and work strictly according to practical requirements. It should divide England into sixteen electricity supply areas each of which would have a District Electricity Board. The Boards were to organise the construction of regional electricity supplies by purchasing electricity from the individual power stations and distributing it according to requirements, that is balance out disparities within the district. Thus instead of nationalising electricity producers, as had been proposed by the Williamson Committee, the state should initiate, set up and control self-governing boards consisting of private and public electricity companies at a regional level. In this way power supply in a district would no longer be concentrated on urban areas but also benefit rural consumers.

However the proposed legislation was rejected not only by the private and local authority companies but also by industrial concerns.[34] The Conservatives deprived it of its teeth in Parliament by turning the District Electricity Boards, which the Electricity Commissioners could insist on, into so-called joint electricity authorities, that is voluntary units with no powers to enforce businesses to cooperate. The Electricity (Supply) Act passed on

The electrification of the countryside 23

23 December 1919 and remained fundamentally unchanged in the following years despite many attempts to reform it.[35] It failed to fulfil the hopes either of concentrating and rationalising electricity supplies or speeding up the electrification of rural areas. Only in very few regions did local authority and private electricity companies work together. There continued to be a complete lack of mixed economy companies which enjoyed the advantages of great creditworthiness on the one hand and a freer management hand on the other.[36]

A further problem was that there was no real improvement in the material conditions of the rural population between the two wars. Agriculture in England suffered particularly from global market imports and falling prices in the 1920s.[37] Consequently many rural people suffered from a lack of capital to make their businesses more efficient with the help of electricity.

The inefficient fragmentation of electricity production, high electricity prices, the low level of cooperation between producers at a district level – only three Joint Electricity authorities had been set up by the mid-1920s – and the lack of interest on behalf of the electricity companies meant that they did not put as much effort into winning new rural customers by offering two-part tariffs and hire purchase schemes, as they did in the towns.[38] All these developments were followed with increasing displeasure by trade journals, the Electricity Commissioners and the government.[39] They attributed the low level of success in setting up joint authorities to the irresponsibility and self-interest of the towns and cities. 'The chief offenders are undoubtedly some of the municipal authorities.'[40] Even the president of the Incorporated Municipal Electrical Association, S. E. Britton, put down the slow spread of electricity in Great Britain to the fragmentation of local interests. In this he was supported by the trade journal, *The Electrician*, which wrote: 'The essential fact remains that we cannot go on as we are. In this country electricity supply has been hampered through being considered as a parochial affair.'[41]

There were two main grounds for an increased national commitment to improving electricity supply in England. On an international level progress in improving electricity supply lagged behind that in the USA and the German Empire and it was felt that attempts should be made to remedy this state of affairs. Second, in the cities the companies had to contend increasingly with a lack of space, the high price of land and to some extent with a lack of workers, and were therefore beginning to move to the countryside. Hence the electrification of rural areas in particular needed to be accelerated in order to keep pace with this trend. In addition, it was argued that electrification of the countryside would give rural inhabitants the chance of enjoying a standard of living similar to that of the urban population. This was not merely a democratic attitude but was also linked with the hope of being able to put a brake on emigration from the countryside.

In 1925 Prime Minister Stanley Baldwin set up a commission under Lord Weir to come up with proposals for improving national electricity supplies.[42] The subsequent report recommended the creation of networks not only within but also between districts, in other words a unified technical national grid. The planning and implementation of this grid should be the responsibility of a new, non-government, but nationally acting and self-financing Central Electricity Board (CEB) under the supervision of the Ministry of Transport. With the advice of the Electricity Commissioners it was to select the most efficient and economical electricity works in England and/or allow private companies to set them up, and ensure that they were networked via high-tension power lines. Thus the powers of the CEB recommendations were to be strengthened by giving the Ministry of Transport (after parliamentary approval) the right to buy up selected electricity works where necessary. In the final analysis the Weir Committee did not think it reasonable to nationalise the electricity industry because central administration would not be flexible enough. Furthermore the committee expected high purchase prices and a time lag before they could be transferred to the state because existing power stations were protected by a forty-two-year concession period.

The Weir Committee hoped to rationalise electricity production and clean up the market by making the stations selected by the CEB duty-bound to sell their complete electricity production to the Board. The Board was to standardise electricity frequencies and in turn sell back electricity to all existing electricity works at a somewhat higher price, which these could then deliver to consumers. All in all this system would reduce the average price of electricity. The surcharge on the buying price would help the CEB to finance the costs of networking 'selected stations', thereby creating a part of the infrastructure with whose help other electricity producers and distributors would be able to electrify rural areas. In this way a unified national electricity grid could be created which would ensure electricity supply to town and country alike, and charges could be gradually reduced.

More rational and cheaper electricity production was expected to follow from the fact that the larger, more economical high performance works privileged by the CEB would be able to raise their capacity levels, thereby enabling them to lower their prices to such an extent as to make the prices charged by other works who were not on the national grid uncompetitive. Hence the idea was to give the CEB the role of a nationwide wholesale dealer and distributor, with a dominant position on the electricity market thanks to its potential for wholesale purchases and ability to deliver large amounts of electricity via the national grid. In comparison with the existing, mostly voluntary, organisation of power production and distribution on a limited regional level, the implementation of the Weir proposals meant a sharpening of state regulations and control. The fact was, however, that because the CEB (and its experts, who had close links to industry) was an independent body with its own budget, this measure was far from being a nationalisation. For 1940 the Weir Committee forecast only fifty-eight electricity works, an increase in electricity consumption from 110 to 500 kWh per capita, a rise in installed electricity capacity from 3.1 to 10 million KW, and of sales from 4 to 21 million kWh with a simultaneous fall in average prices from around 2d. to 1d. per kWh.[43]

In opposition to the proposals put forward by the Weir Report, whose basic thinking was to concentrate electricity production in a few major works – which corresponded to the experts' advice – the representatives of urban and privately owned electricity works, the Institution of Electrical Engineers and the chambers of commerce, not to speak of a number of individual MPs, pointed out that such a solution would hamper the free development of market forces which would automatically lead to the creation of large power stations and more rationalisation. Above all the large, efficient electricity companies would have to submit to unnecessary regulations. The Weir proposals would lead to top-heavy bureaucratisation and unnecessary expenses – for example for standardisation – whereas a continuation of the status quo would mean savings on the cost of constructing overhead lines and expensive intermediary distribution by the CEB. The lord mayor of Leeds, Sir Charles Wilson, vehemently rejected the bill put forward in the House of Commons when he declared that it was 'nationalisation of a very bad kind' that would be greeted with loathing in the North of England. For if, for example a local authority opposed the plans of the CEB its management could be taken over and the power station bought up at an unfair price if necessary. Furthermore Leeds, which produced electricity at a particularly cheap price, would be forced to sell it to the Board, which would in turn then sell it back to the city at a surcharge. All this meant that urban consumers would be paying higher prices than they would if the city was alone responsible for electricity production.[44] The opponents from the circle of major cities therefore pleaded in favour of retaining and/or creating regional supply areas, a solution which also would avoid the danger of a widespread breakdown in supplies caused by individual disruptions. All in all they regarded the creation of a CEB as a 'thinly veiled nationalisation'.[45]

Notwithstanding the protests, the solutions put forward by the Weir Committee 'to establish public control without public ownership' prevailed.[46] Prime Minister Baldwin, who had publicly admitted in early 1926 that electricity consumption in Great Britain lagged behind other nations,[47] accepted its most important proposals and these were included in the Electricity (Supply) Act which passed through Parliament on 15 December 1926. Lord Weir himself cautiously described the new Act to improve national electricity supply as 'like a man's second marriage, as it represented the triumph of hope over experience'.[48]

The CEB was set up in the same year, 1926, with eight members under the leadership of Andrew R. Duncan.[49] The CEB's legal position and identity was not so much that of a regulatory authority but more of a private company. For credit it could fall back on a state guarantee of up to £33.5 million, but basically it financed itself by issuing its own shares, which meant that in one essential point it could only be indirectly controlled by the Ministry

26   Karl Ditt

of Transport. The Board organised power supply on the basis of the plans worked out by the Electricity Commissioners (who were still active), that is it conducted negotiations with the electricity producers with regard to the upgrading of their works to 'selected stations', ordered the construction of 132-volt high-tension lines, took electricity from the 'selected stations' and distributed it to other electricity stations with a surcharge of 10% to cover its own costs and to build up capital.

For their part the Electricity Commissioners attempted to push forward the electrification of the countryside, appealed for the cooperation of the electricity companies, parishes and landowners, organised a conference to this end in 1927, and attempted to demonstrate the advantages of electricity consumption in the rural areas around Bedford and Norwich. Furthermore they encouraged power stations to advertise in rural areas and offer attractive tariffs and hire purchase schemes. Finally they ensured that rural areas were increasingly integrated into the electricity companies' supply areas.[50]

Thus between 1927 and 1938 the CEB was able to build up a national grid and reduce the number of public electricity producers from 491 in 1926 to 171 by 1938, all of whom were linked into the national grid. In this way electricity prices could be substantially reduced. Within the space of a few years it was clear that the construction of the national grid had proved to be a powerful and profitable programme of rationalisation of electricity production. Although it was mainly rural areas which profited from the construction of high-tension lines because they could be led off to villages and their surrounding areas, thereby tending to reduce connection costs, towns and cities remained unconvinced.

When, for example, after the Electricity Commissioners had set up the Central Eastern England area they urged the city of York to go ahead with electrifying its rural neighbourhoods – the more so because the parishes themselves wanted to receive electricity – the city dragged its feet because of the expense involved and only cooperated in areas which paid off.[51] When the rural inhabitants petitioned their MP R.H. Turton to stand up for their interests, upon which he requested the Electricity Commissioners to push through supplies to these parishes, the city of York first countered this strategy with the results of a census showing that only a minority of the rural population wanted electricity. When Turton disputed this, the city once again refused to act on the grounds that financial aid from the Ministry's fund to help the unemployed was inadequate or had already been exhausted.[52]

Despite the effects of rationalisation the government considered that the construction of the national grid had not sufficiently reduced the cost of electricity. As early as 1930 the Ministry of Transport therefore demanded that the Electricity Commissioners look for further rationalisation measures to reduce costs. The upshot was that in March 1931 the leader of the Electricity Commissioners, John Snell, put forward the following alternative in a report: either the CEB should take over the responsibility for power

The electrification of the countryside   27

production at its own expense or it should speed up the merging of electricity producers: that is, he was hinting in the direction of nationalisation or at least stronger state interference. But since there was no political majority in favour of nationalising the electricity industry, rationalisation by concentration was the only other alternative. This meant waiting for market powers, judicious insights and voluntary action or a government initiative: on this point representatives from the electricity industry and the Electricity Commissioners were unanimous at a meeting held in June 1933. Proposals put forward by the Ministry of Transport at the end of 1933 to close stations which only produced a small amount of electricity were not implemented, because such measures would have hit public power stations which were often prestige objects.[53] One year later, however, a law gave the CEB the right to reduce electricity production from stations outside the 135 selected major companies, or even to close them down.[54]

At the start of the 1930s new attempts at rationalising the electricity industry were no longer aimed at production but at distribution. In this field, too, mergers had to be pushed through since the cost of electricity production only made up the lesser proportion of the selling price.[55] This varied considerably both locally and regionally depending on the different costs and policies of the distributors, although the CEB provided electricity to the distributors at a standard price. Even after the discussions in 1933 finally led to a legislative proposal, delays continued because of the growing difficulties in implementing it at a political level. Finally in July 1935 the Ministry of Transport set up a three-man committee under the chairman of Imperial Chemical Industries (ICI), Sir Harry McGowan, to deal with questions of standardisation and optimising organisation, which also implied extending electricity supplies to rural areas.[56] It confirmed that at the start of 1934 there was a total of 643 electricity companies in England delivering different forms of power and current strengths. Thus pre-war levels had to all intents and purposes not changed because, despite the rationalisation efforts of the Electricity Commissioners and the electricity industry, the number of new stations was roughly equal to the number of closures. That said, this development could not have been prevented because this would have otherwise meant excluding certain areas of the population from power supplies. The output of the companies differed greatly. Whereas average per capita consumption was 253 kWh, more than two-thirds of electricity distributors provided less than this amount. The McGowan Committee therefore argued in favour of a substantial reduction of the number of companies to a few major stations and standardising the distribution of electricity.

Since a voluntary concentration of distribution seemed to be out of the question, the Committee considered two alternative ideas for the compulsory reduction of the number of distributors. First, regional administrations could be set up under state supervision or merged by combining them. Thus the number of existing electricity companies could be reduced by purchasing them and closing them down. Second, large-scale power producers should

28   Karl Ditt

be allowed to purchase and close down smaller businesses producing less than 20 million kWh per year.[57] The first variation meant nothing more than the nationalisation of electricity supplies. In the 1930s it was mainly supported by the Labour Party, which had been a proponent of electricity nationalisation since 1924 in order to supply the population in the whole of England with cheap electricity – 'the handmaiden of our working women'[58] – at standard prices. But this idea came up against considerable opposition. Electricity experts and entrepreneurs rejected the creation of a further controlling authority and regarded the organisation of electricity sales as a pure business duty.[59] The Conservative Party pointed out that after the nationalisation of the telephone system call prices had risen from 2d. to 4d. between 1913 and 1936 and this had held back growth in the industry, whereas the cost of electricity from privately owned companies had fallen and consumption had risen rapidly.[60] The Ministry of Trade rejected the idea of a National Electricity Board because excessive bureaucracy would make it almost impossible to control. In 1936 the Electricity Commissioners estimated the costs of nationalisation as follows: the value of current power stations in private hands would amount to £168.7 million and that of local authority stations £256.6 million, a total of £425.3 million. In addition compensation for profits from private companies over a period of twenty-five years would amount to a further £98 million. Thus total compensation for nationalising electricity production would cost the government more than half a billion pounds.[61]

Given these misgivings and the sums involved, the McGowan Committee voted for the non-state takeover of the smaller companies by the large electricity suppliers, and here they received the support of an independent group of experts in 1936.[62] The number of 635 electricity distributors should be reduced to around 200, and the boundaries of business viability should not be less than 10 million kWh. In April 1937 the Ministry of Transport and consumers' organisations agreed to these recommendations which were then published in the form of a White Paper.[63]

But this solution also had its critics. Once again they came from the towns and cities whose own power stations were threatened with closure or takeover. They enjoyed a powerful position within the electricity industry because, at the end of the 1920s in terms of investment, capacity and production, about two-thirds of the English electricity system relied on local authority power stations.[64] The towns and cities emphasised that the decisive criterion for selecting power distributors should not be their size but rather their efficiency. A small station could very well work more economically than a large one. Furthermore in disputed cases they demanded there should in any case be a public hearing and a parliamentary vote before the matter was decided by the Electricity Commissioners, thereby hoping that this procedure would at least make the takeover process as slow as possible. Finally they pointed out that selecting power distributors by size would lead to a reduction in local authority control. With the exception of the last argument their point of view was widely shared by a huge number of private companies and chambers of commerce. They pointed to the concession period and argued that the system would be cleaned up by market forces. In addition the towns and cities continued to remain extremely cautious with regard to the tasks expected of them in extending their grid to rural areas. They preferred to connect the last remaining houses in their area and insisted on retaining a 20% profit margin on their investment when they connected buildings in the countryside.[65] As early as 1944 the electricity supply industry was also issuing warnings about the unlimited extension of the urban grid to rural areas, for in reality this would be nothing other than urban inhabitants subsidising rural consumers.[66] Given these controversial positions and the reluctance of the urban authorities – and despite the general consensus that power supplies and distribution had to be improved – the British government postponed making a decision for quite some time before giving up plans to introduce legislation for the time being in 1938. In the end protests from the urban authorities seem to have been decisive in influencing the government.[67]

Summary

When surveying the process of electrification in England, the first thing which becomes clear is its relatively slow development in the period leading up to the First World War. Not surprisingly the main emphasis was on connecting businesses and households in urban areas: by contrast very few rural areas were connected to the grid. Here electrification only began in the 1920s. If we assume for the 1920s and '30s that total rural areas covered 81,000 square miles with a population of 9.4 million, statistics were as follows:

In 1920, there were supplies to 7% of rural areas and 21% of the population.
In 1928, there were supplies to 42% of rural areas and 67% of the population.
In 1930, there were supplies to 59% of rural areas and 82% of the population.
In 1936, there were supplies to 90% of rural areas and 85% of the population.

By contrast, 89% of urban areas and 97% of the urban population had been connected to the grid by 1928.[68] The fact is that the electrification of rural areas lagged about a decade behind that of urban areas in the period before 1945.

The electrification of the countryside seems even more underdeveloped when we consider the number of farms which were connected to the grid. By 1930 this amounted to a mere 4,000. This had risen to 25,000 by 1936

30   Karl Ditt

when the total number of farms was almost 400,000.[69] Although connections continued to increase, the National Farm Survey of England and Wales taken in 1941 and 1943 showed that only 78,000 or 27% of holdings of five acres or more had access to electricity (England 30%, Wales 11%). A great deal of these were in Central England and remarkably few in South West England, East Anglia and Wales. The farms which had access to electricity took 89% of their requirements from a public grid and produced 11% themselves, above all with petrol engines.[70] By contrast, as noted at the 1936 World Power Conference in Washington, 80% of all farms in Germany, 65% in France and 50% in Sweden were connected to the grid.[71]

How do we explain the delay in the electrification of the countryside, particularly of farms? The primary cause of this lack of development was the size of investment required and the price of electricity. Up until 1914 electricity was to all intents and purposes a luxury because its price could not compete with traditional lighting sources like candles, oil lamps and gas, or power from wood, coal and water. Furthermore the average citizen was unable to meet the costs of a power line which in country areas outside villages and hamlets could be as high as several hundred pounds. The census conducted by the National Farm Survey clearly shows that a comparatively high number of rural areas in the direct vicinity of towns were connected to the grid and by contrast non-urban areas had a comparatively low access to electricity supplies.[72] The question of who was to take responsibility for financing rural areas was therefore decisive. So long as consumption potentials remained in urban areas the companies which held concessions there had very little interest in the high cost of investing in connections in the countryside, let alone in waiting for a long time for the amortisation of their investments before they could begin to make a profit. Hence the first power companies to supply electricity to rural areas primarily concentrated on business requirements and villages rather than those of scattered inhabitants.

Rural consumers considered the price of electricity and the costs of connection too high and the electricity companies thought that the complete electrification of the countryside was not worth the effort. This situation resulted in a deadlock which continued right into the First World War and the early 1920s, and was only broken when the state decided to take a hand in the matter. However, it refused to nationalise electricity production and distribution but, rather on the grounds of rationalisation and democratisation, began take direct responsibility for organising the electricity industry. After an initial attempt to regionalise electricity supplies on a voluntary basis which failed because of the reluctance of the electricity suppliers and the lack of powers given to the Electricity Commissioners, a second attempt following the 1926 Electricity (Supply) Act by means of constructing a national grid, proved a success. In the 1920s and '30s there was a clear reduction in production and supply prices and this made electricity affordable for the great majority of the population.[73]

The electrification of the countryside 31

It seems that investment in the electricity infrastructure, whose costs were reckoned to be about £250 million by the 1920s, was mainly provided by those electricity companies who were urged by the CEB to construct power lines, and partly by the CEB itself.[74] In the final analysis the extension of the electricity system to rural areas seems to have benefited to a high degree from rationalisation. For the resulting spiral of economy of scale – considerably higher levels of consumption in town and country, the greater use of capacity, reduction of production costs and lower electricity prices – was by far the most important reason for consumers to switch to electricity from traditional sources of power like gas, oil and coal because there were fewer and fewer differences in prices. The profit maximisation strategies of companies producing and distributing electricity – and therefore their reluctance to reduce prices – were also hampered by the intervention powers of the CEB. In addition the advantages of comfort, safety and cleanliness, not to speak of the extension of the possibilities of electric consumption due to the invention of a huge number of household gadgets and other power-driven machines, were important factors in motivating people's desire to be connected to the grid. However, the National Farm Survey makes it quite clear that even those farmers who were potentially the first members of the rural population to have access to electric power supplies were primarily interested in using it for lighting purposes.[75] It was after the nationalisation of the electricity industry in 1948 that the state abandoned its objections to providing financial support to electrify the countryside, and agreed to take over a part of the costs of constructing power lines and providing connections in order to enable the remainder of the rural population to have access to the grid.[76]

Notes

1 Translated from the original German by Roy Kift.
2 Cf. M.E. Falkus, 'The British gas industry before 1850', *Economic History Review*, vol. 20, 1967, pp. 494–508; Francis Goodall, *Burning to serve. Selling gas in competitive markets*. Ashbourne: Landmark, 1999, pp. 23–24.
3 Cf. Francois Caron and Christine Berthet, 'Electrical innovation: State initiative or private initiative? Observations on the 1881 Paris exhibition', *History and Technology*, vol. 1, 1983–1984, pp. 307–318.
4 Cf. Patrick Strange, 'Early electricity supply in Britain: Chesterfield and Godalming', *Proceedings of the Institution of Electrical Engineers*, vol. 126, 1979, pp. 863–868. Cf. generally PEP (Political and Economic Planning), *Report on the supply of electricity in Great Britain. A survey of present-day problems of the industry with proposals for reorganisation of electricity distribution*. London: PEP, 1936; R.H. Parsons, *The early days of the power station industry*. Cambridge: Cambridge University Press, 1939; I.C.R. Byatt, *The British electrical industry 1875–1914. The economic returns to a new technology*. Oxford: Oxford University Press, 1979; Leslie Hannah, *Electricity before nationalisation. A study of the development of the electricity supply industry in Britain to 1948*. London: Macmillan, 1979; Brian Bowers, *A history of light & power*. Stevenage: Peregrinus in association with the Science Museum, 1982.

32   *Karl Ditt*

5 Cf. The Public General Statutes passed in the Forty-Fifth and Forty-Sixth Years of the Reign of Her Majesty Queen Victoria, 1882 (London 1882), pp. 335–349. Cf. also Parsons, *The early days*, pp. 184–200; Bowers, *A history*, pp. 152–165.

6 Cf. H. H. Ballin, *The organisation of electricity supply in Great Britain*. London: Electrical Press, 1946, pp. 6–12; John F. Wilson, *Ferranti and the British electrical industry, 1864–1930*. Manchester: Manchester University Press, 1988, pp. 19, 39. For a critical argument on this thesis see Hannah, *Electricity before nationalisation*, pp. 5–6; Thomas Parke Hughes, 'British electrical industry lag: 1882–1888', *Technology and Culture*, vol. 3, 1962, pp. 27–44.

7 Cf. *Yorkshire Post* 13.8.1886, in: Sir George Morrison, *Newspaper cuttings. Leeds municipal affairs 1885–86*, in: Leeds Local History Library.

8 Cf. Ballin, *The organisation*, pp. 12–15.

9 Cf. for example PEP, *Report on the supply of electricity*, p. 87.

10 People thought that alternating current was less efficient than direct current. In addition it was impossible to load accumulators with alternating current. On the other hand 'simple' and three-phase alternating current made it possible to attain higher voltage levels, reduce the cross-section of copper lines, and enabled electricity to be transported over greater distances. Cf. Parsons, *The early days*, pp. 136–150; Paul A. David, 'Heroes, herds and hysteresis in technological history: Thomas Edison and "the battle of the systems" reconsidered', *Industrial and Corporate Change*, vol. 1, 1992, pp. 129–179.

11 Cf. PEP, *Report on the supply of electricity*, p. 87. Cf. an exemplary case concerning the difficulties of an urban electricity supplier in delivering superfluous electricity to a rural area in D. G. Tucker, 'Rural electrification and the pioneering scheme of the Hereford Corporation (1918–1928)', *Transactions of the Newcomen Society for the Study of the History of Engineering*, vol. 51, 1981, pp. 111–128.

12   In cases where a consumer is unlikely to use an amount of electricity sufficient to provide a gross return of 20 per cent allowed by law . . ., the consumer is generally asked to pay the difference between the capital upon which he can guarantee a return of 20 per cent . . . and the capital necessary to connect him to the mains. For example, if a country house nearly a mile from the nearest distributing main, costs say £350 . . . to connect, and the rates charged an annual revenue of £40 is guaranteed, the guarantee would represent 20 per cent on £200 and the balance of capital expenditure, namely £150, would be payable by the consumer.

PEP, *Report on the Supply of Electricity*, p. 46; Report of the Committee on Electricity Distribution [Chairman: Harry McGowan], May 1936, in Public Record Office [PRO], CAB 27, 617, pp. 69–70.

13 E. W. Golding, *The electrification of agriculture and rural districts*. London: English Universities Press, 1937, p. 6.

14 Cf. Bill Luckin, *Questions of power. Electricity and environment in inter-war Britain*. Manchester: Manchester University Press, 1990, pp. 81–87.

15 Cf. for example S. A. Caunce, 'Mechanisation and society in English agriculture: The experience of the North-East, 1850–1914', *Rural History*, vol. 17, 2006, pp. 23–45.

16 Cf. Electricity Commission, *Report of proceedings of conference on electricity supply in rural areas*. London: HMSO, 1928, pp. 26, 42.

17 Cf. 'Electricity in agriculture. Report of the electricity in agriculture committee to the council', *Journal of the Institution of Electrical Engineers*, vol. 63, 1925, pp. 838–842; R. Borlase Matthews, *Electro-farming: Or the application of electricity to agriculture*. London: Ernest Benn, 1928, pp. 4–6.

18 Cf. Andrew Fenton Cooper, *British agricultural policy, 1912–36. A study in conservative politics*. Manchester: Manchester University Press, 1989, pp. 82–83.

The electrification of the countryside 33

19 Cf. R.J. Moore-Colyer, 'Lighting the landscape: Rural electrification in Wales', *Welsh History Review*, vol. 23, 2007, pp. 72–92, 78. Consumption levels per farm were comparatively low: 1,150 units per year. Cf. Electricity Commission, *Report of Proceedings*, pp. 7, 19. Cf. also specified and with higher consumption figures *Electricity in Agriculture*, p. 839. Cf. for Ireland Michael J. Shiel, *The Quiet Revolution: The Electrification of Rural Ireland 1946–1976*. Dublin: O'Brien Press, 1984, pp. 152–153.

20 Cf. PEP, *Report on the supply of electricity*, p. 87.

21 Cf. PEP, *Report on the supply of electricity*, p. 12.

22 Cf. PEP, *Report on the supply of electricity*, p. 13; Parsons, *The early days*, pp. 196–197; Leslie Hannah, 'Public policy and the advent of large-scale technology: The Case of electricity supply in the U.S.A., Germany and Britain', in Norbert Horn and Jürgen Kocka (eds), *Recht und Entwicklung der Großunternehmen im 19. und frühen 20. Jahrhundert. Wirtschafts-, sozial- und rechtshistorische Untersuchungen zur Industrialisierung in Deutschland, Frankreich, England und den USA*. Göttingen: Vandenhoeck & Ruprecht, 1979, pp. 577–589, 583–584.

23 Cf. Report of the Committee on Electricity Distribution (McGowan Committee), p. 6; Hannah, *Electricity before nationalisation*, p. 22.

24 Cf. also R.H. Morgan, 'The development of the electricity supply industry in Wales to 1919', *Welsh History Review*, vol. 11, 1983, pp. 317–337.

25 Cf. *Report from the Joint Select Committee of the House of Lords and the House of Commons on Electrical Energy (Generating Stations and Supply)* [Chairman Lord Cross], London: HMSO, 1898, quote p. vii; Adam Gowans Whyte, *The electrical industry: Lighting, traction, and power*. London: Methuen, 1904, pp. 145–169; Richard Roberts, 'Business, politics, and municipal socialism', in John Turner (ed.), *Businessmen and politics. Studies of business activity in British politics, 1900–1945*. London: Heinemann, 1984, pp. 20–32; Bowers, *A history of light & power*, pp. 159–161.

26 Cf. Ministry of Reconstruction, Reconstruction Committee. Coal Conservation Sub-Committee, *Interim report on electric power supply in Great Britain* [Chairman Lord Haldane] [Cd. 8880]. London: HMSO, 1917, pp. 23–25; Report of the Committee on Electricity Distribution (McGowan Committee), pp. 7–8; Henry Self and Elizabeth M. Watson, *Electricity supply in Great Britain. Its development and organisation*. London: Allen & Unwin, 1952, p. 27.

27 Cf. also as an example, Morgan, 'The development of the electricity supply industry in Wales'.

28 Cf. Hannah, 'Public policy', p. 584.

29 Cf. Ballin, *The organisation*, pp. 42–57; Wilson, *Ferranti*, p. 123; Hannah, *Electricity before nationalisation*, pp. 24–53.

30 Cf. C. Ashmore Baker, *Public versus private electricity supply*. London: Fabian Society, 1913; Hannah, *Electricity before nationalisation*, pp. 50–51. Cf. the emphasis on the difference between English and German electricity works in the discussion on J.W. Beauchamp and R. Kauffmann, 'State regulation of electricity supply tariffs. Recent German legislation compared with British tendencies', *Journal of the Institution of Electrical Engineers*, vol. 85, 1939, pp. 569–589, 582. Cf. also the discussion on the article by L.J. Lepine and A.R. Stelling, 'Notes on methods and practice in the German electrical industry', *Journal of the Institution of Electrical Engineers*, vol. 44, 1910, pp. 281–300, 309.

31 Cf. e.g. Erich Nagel, *Die Elektrizitätsversorgung der Landwirtschaft im Gebiet des Elektrizitätswerks Westfalen*, in *Die Elektrotechnik im Rhein.-Westf. Industriebezirk. Festschrift aus Anlass der 27. Jahresversammlung des Verbandes Deutscher Elektrotechniker im Mai 1921 in Essen*. Essen: Girardet, 1921, pp. 91–93; Burghard Flieger, 'Elektrizitätsgenossenschaften im ländlichen Raum, dargestellt am Beispiel Teutoburger Energie Netzwerk eG (Ten eG)',

34 *Karl Ditt*

in Heinrich-Kaufmann Stiftung (ed.), *Ländliche Genossenschaften: Contributions to the 5th congress on the history of cooperatives on 5th and 6th November 2010 in the Warburg-Haus in Hamburg*. Norderstedt: Books on Demand, 2012, pp. 106–117.

32 Cf. Wilson, *Ferranti*, p. 108; Hannah, *Electricity before nationalisation*, pp. 34–35.

33 Cf. the forerunner discussion in Ernest T. Williams, 'The electricity supply of great Britain', *Journal of the Institution of Electrical Engineers*, vol. 54, 1916, pp. 581–587, and the discussion on pp. 588–607. Cf. further: Reconstruction Committee, Coal Conservation Sub-Committee, *Interim report on electric power supply in Great Britain*; Ministry of Reconstruction, Coal Conservation Committee, *Final Report* [Chairman Lord Haldane] [Cd. 9084]. London: HMSO, 1918; Electric Power Supply Committee, *Report of the Committee appointed by the Board of Trade to consider the question of electric power supply* [Chairman Sir Archibald Williamson] [Cd. 9062]. London: HMSO, 1918; UK National Archives, Kew (TNA), Reco 1, Nr. 257, 884; Ballin, *The organisation*, pp. 95–112. Cf. generally Hannah, *Electricity before nationalisation*, pp. 53–67; Paul Barton Johnson, *Land fit for heroes: The planning of British Reconstruction 1916–1919*. Chicago: University of Chicago Press, 1968, pp. 426 ff.

34 Cf. Anne Clendinning, *Demons of domesticity. Women and the English gas industry, 1889–1939*. Aldershot: Ashgate, 2004, p. 220.

35 Cf. TNA, Powe 13, Nr. 11; *Electrical Review* 6.10.1922, pp. 472–474; 13.10.1922, pp. 531–532.

36 Cf. Hannah, 'Public policy', pp. 584–585. Cf. on the immediate post-war history of electricity legislation *First Annual Report of the Electricity Commissioners 31st January 1920, to 31st March, 1921*, London 1921, and the review of the activities of the Commissioners in: *Seventh Annual Report of the Electricity Commissioners 1st April, 1926, to 31st March, 1927*, London 1927, pp. 5ff., in: West Yorkshire Archive Service [WYAS] Wakefield, C 550; Ballin, *The organisation*, pp. 113–153; Hannah, *Electricity before nationalisation*, pp. 67–88; Wilson, *Ferranti*, pp. 124–126.

37 Cf. Jonathan Brown, *Agriculture in England. A survey of farming, 1870–1947*. Manchester: Manchester University Press, 1987, pp. 76–124; Paul Brassley, 'British farming between the wars', in P. Brassley, J. Burchardt and L. Thompson (eds), *The English countryside between the wars: Regeneration or decline?* Woodbridge: Boydell Press, 2006, pp. 187–199.

38 Cf. PEP, *Report on the supply of electricity*, pp. 88–89.

39 Cf. e.g. The Conclusions of the Unemployment Policy Committee of 7.7.1924, in: TNA, T 160, Nr. 285. It attributed this to the lack of hydraulic power resources and the widespread supply of gas but also to the lack of demand from industry and 'possibly most important of all' the local fragmentation of electricity production. Cf. also *Electrical Review* 24.4.1925, pp. 644–645; 1.5.1925, pp. 686–688; 8.5.1925, pp. 749–750; Hannah, *Electricity before nationalisation*, pp. 88–89.

40 *Electrical Review* 18.7.1924, p. 85. Cf. also John Snell at the World Power Conference 1924, in ibid., p. 86.

41 Cf. *The Electrician* 20.6.1924, pp. 747–750.

42 Cf. Ministry of Transport, *Report of the committee appointed to review the national problem of the supply of electrical energy* [*Weir Committee*]. London: HMSO, 1926; Self and Watson, *Electricity Supply*, pp. 51–56; Hannah, *Electricity before nationalisation*, pp. 89–100. On Weir and his role in electricity supply cf. William J. Reader, *Architect of air power. The life of the first Viscount Weir of Eastwood 1877–1959*. London: Collins, 1968, pp. 130–136.

The electrification of the countryside 35

43 Cf. on the procedure of the Central Electricity Board, *Fourth annual report 1st January to 31st December, 1931*. London, 1932, in WYAS Wakefield, C 550; Electricity Commission, *Electricity (Supply) Act, 1926. Memorandum on the provisions of the act, prepared by the electricity commissioners*. London 1927, in: York City Archive [YCA], YDD IV, Nr. 1299; Hannah, *Electricity before nationalisation*, pp. 92–100; Ministry of Transport, *Report supply of electrical energy* [*Weir Committee*], p. 9. Cf. generally on the reorganisation of the electricity system since 1925 Ballin, *The organisation*, pp. 184–223.

44 Cf. Parliamentary Debates [Hansard], *Official report*, Fifth Series, 193, 1926, London 1926, c. 1732–1740. Cf. also Leeds Chamber of Commerce Journal, 3, 1926–1927, pp. 51–52. The 1926 Electricity (Supply) Act removed this disadvantage. The selected electricity plant would be able to buy up power from the CEB, at its own original price plus an extra charge for the CEB or at a theoretical price equivalent to the costs which would been incurred if it had not been taken over by the Board as a 'selected station'. Cf. PEP, *Report on the supply of electricity*, p. 29; *Report of the committee of inquiry into the electricity supply industry*. Presented by the Minister of Fuel and Power to Parliament by Command of Her Majesty, January 1956 [Cmd 9672]. London: HMSO, 1956, p. 12.

45 Cf. e.g. for the position of the director of the Yorkshire Electric Power Company, Woodhouse, *Yorkshire Post* 16.1., 26.1. and 25.3.1926, in: WYAS Wakefield, C 550, Box: Press Cuttings, also in: *The Electrician* 9. 4. 1926, p. 405. For critical remarks of the British chambers of commerce cf. *Leeds Chamber of Commerce Journal*, 3, 1926–1927, pp. 22–23, 70–75, 89–90, 94–96, 124, 126–127. Cf. also *Electrical Review* 29.1.1926, pp. 171–173; 2.4.1926, p. 562; 30.4.1926, pp. 719–720; 11.6.1926, pp. 857–858; *The Electrician* 19.3.1926, p. 333; 2.4.1926, pp. 377–378, 380–381; 30. 4.1926, pp. 490, 492, 499; Hannah, *Electricity before Nationalisation*, pp. 96–97.

46 According to the Labour MP William Graham, in: Yorkshire Post, in: WYAS Wakefield, C 550, Box: Press Cuttings.

47 Electricity consumption in Great Britain amounted to 200 kWh per head and year, in the USA 500 and in Canada 900. Cf. *Yorkshire Post* 16. 1. 1926, in: WYAS Wakefield, C 550, Box: Press Cuttings.

48 *The Electrician* 25.11.1927, p. 665.

49 Cf. the ideas of the members of the CEB in: *Electrical Review* 18.2.1927, pp. 244–245; Hannah, *Electricity before Nationalisation*, pp. 100–104.

50 Cf. *Twenty-third and Final Report of the Electricity Commissioners*. 1st April 1947 to 31st July 1948, London: HMSO, 1950, pp. 10, 13–14; PEP, *Report on the Supply of Electricity*, pp. 91–92; Ballin, *The organisation*, pp. 231–238; Luckin, *Questions of Power*, pp. 80–81.

51 Cf. York Minutes 1927–1928, p. 320; Report 15.4.1930, in: Report Book Electricity Engineer Jan. 1928–Dec. 1930, in: Documents of the Northern Electric Company, in the possession of John Ormerod, York; YCA, BC 36–6; Sitting of 5.9.1928, in: PRO, Powe 11, Nr. 13; sitting of 12.10.1932, in: TNA, Powe 11, Nr. 17.

52 Cf. YCA, YCB, York Electricity Extension Order 1929, Misc.; *Electrical Times* 21.5.1931, p. 941; 16.7.1931, p. 106; 17.9.1931, p. 448; York Minutes 1931–1932, p. 370.

53 Cf. TNA, Powe 13, Nr. 62.

54 Cf. TNA, Powe 13, Nr. 67.

55 Cf. J.M. Kennedy and Dorothy M. Noakes, 'An analysis of the costs of electricity supply in great Britain, with some suggestions as to the causes of and remedies for the slow rate of development', *Journal of the Institution of Electrical Engineers*, vol. 73, 1933, pp. 97–168; vol. 75, 1934, pp. 124–130 incl.

36 *Karl Ditt*

discussion; J. A. Sumner, 'Modern factors affecting electricity costs and charges', *Journal of the Institution of Electrical Engineers*, vol. 81, 1937, pp. 429–496; Hannah, *Electricity before nationalisation*, pp. 248–256; Martin Chick, 'The political economy of nationalisation: The electricity industry', in Robert Millward and John Singleton (eds), *The political economy of nationalisation in Britain 1920–1950*. Cambridge: Cambridge University Press, 1995, pp. 257–274.

56 Cf. Report of the Committee on Electricity Distribution (McGowan Committee), pp. 3, 24, 63–72; Ballin, *The organisation*, pp. 250–266; Hannah, *Electricity before nationalisation*, pp. 248–253.

57 Cf. TNA, Powe 13, Nr. 77.

58 Cf. TNA, Powe 13, Nr. 98, Part 2, p. 448 (sitting of the House of Commons).

59 Cf. *The Electrician* 3.2.1933, p. 154; 10.2.1933, pp. 179–180; 17.2.1933, pp. 211–212, 219; 20.10.1933, p. 469; 22.11.1935, p. 627; 29.11.1935, p. 657.

60 Cf. TNA, Powe 13, Nr. 98, Part 2, p. 460 (sitting of the House of Commons). Cf. also the comments in Nr. 99.

61 Cf. TNA, Powe 13, Nr. 86, 93.

62 Cf. sitting of the Cabinet Committee 28. 7. 1936, in: TNA, CAB 27, Nr. 617; PEP, *Report on the supply of electricity*, pp. 98–118; Hannah, *Electricity before nationalisation*, pp. 250–251.

63 Cf. Ministry of Transport, *Electricity distribution: Outline of proposals*, London: HMSO, 1937, in: TNA, Powe 13, Nr. 78, 101 and 120, Part 1; Hannah, *Electricity before nationalisation*, pp. 253–254; PEP, *The British fuel and power industries. A report by PEP*, London: PEP, 1947, pp. 311–314; Ballin, *The organisation*, p. 252.

64 Cf. Memorandum by Sir Harry Howard on the Organisation and Structure of the Electricity Supply Industry, 1929, in: TNA, Powe 13, Nr. 48. Cf. also similarly for 1933–1934 the Report of the Committee on Electricity Distribution, p. 95.

65 Cf. TNA, Powe 13, Nr. 78, 83, 84, 95, 99, 100, 109, 115, 116, 117, 119, 121; *The Electrician* 25.6.1937, p. 853; 16.7.1937, pp. 89–90; 23.7.1937, p. 105; 13.8.1937, pp. 182–183; *Electrical Review* 23.7.1937, pp. 114–115; 15.10.1937, p. 529; 24.6.1938, p. 922; 4.11.1938, pp. 637–638; *Electricity Distribution*. Report of a Conference of Representatives of the Association of Municipal Corporations, the Urban District Councils and the Incorporated Municipal Electrical Association, printed manuscript 5.12.1935; Association of Municipal Corporations, *Electricity Distribution*. Report of the Joint Committee of the General Purposes and Law Committees, printed manuscript 16. October 1936; ibid., *Electricity Distribution*. Report of Law and General Purposes Committees, printed manuscript 20.5.1937; Incorporated Municipal Electrical Association, *Revised Report of Council on the Representations proposed to be made to the Minister of Transport upon the outline of the Government's proposals for re-organisation of Electricity Distribution to be submitted to an Extraordinary General Meeting to be held at Caxton Hall, Caxton Street, Westminster, S. W. 1, on Friday, the 9th July, 1937*, printed manuscript 18th June 1937, all in: YCA, TC 1, Nr. 1578/1; Leeds Chamber of Commerce Journal, 14, 1937–1938, pp. 17–23. Cf. generally Norman Chester, *The nationalisation of British industry, 1945–1951*. London: HMSO, 1975, pp. 17–18; Hannah, *Electricity before nationalisation*, p. 252.

66 Cf. also the similar position of electricity companies in: The Electricity Supply Industry, *Memorandum on electricity distribution with recommendations relating to future policy and practice*. London, 1944, p. 9.

67 Cf. TNA, Powe 13, Nr. 109; CAB 124, Nr. 427; Hannah, *Electricity before nationalisation*, pp. 254–255; Chick, *The political economy of nationalization*.

The electrification of the countryside　37

Cf. on this matter the negotiations and the report of a planning commission dated 28.2.1944, in: TNA, CAB 124, Nr. 427; Chester, *Nationalisation*, pp. 17–18. Cf. generally R. Kelf-Cohen, *Twenty years of nationalisation. The British experience*, London: Macmillan, 1969; Leslie Hannah, *Engineers, managers and politicians. The first fifteen years of nationalised electricity supply in Britain*. London: Macmillan, 1982.

68　Cf. PEP, *Report on the supply of electricity*, p. 86. In 1936 less than 3% of the English population still lived in areas which had no access to electricity supplies. Ibid., p. 35.

69　PEP, *Report on the supply of electricity*, p. 35; Ministry of Works and Planning, *Report of the committee on land utilisation in rural areas* [Scott Committee]. London: HMSO, 1942 [Cmd. 6378], p. 19; Golding, *The electrification*, p. 4, 21, 57.

70　Ministry of Agriculture and Fisheries, *National farm survey of England and Wales. A summary report*, London: HMSO, 1946, pp. 65–69, 107; John Sheail, *Rural conservation in inter-war Britain*. Oxford: Clarendon Press, 1981, pp. 24–26; R. J. Moore-Colyer, 'Lighting the landscape: Rural electrification in Wales', p. 77. Cf. for the post-war era A. W. Gray, *Electricity supply in the rural areas*. Portsmouth: Grosvenor Press, 1968, p. 3.

71　Cf. Klaus Herrmann, 'Die Entwicklung der Elektrotechnik in der Landwirtschaft und in bäuerlichen Haushalten', in Horst A. Wessel (ed.), *Elektrotechnik – Signale, Aufbruch, Perspektiven. Fünftes VDE-Kolloquium am 5. Oktober 1988 in Mannheim*. Berlin: VDE-Verlag, 1988, pp. 11–29, 19.

72　Ministry of Agriculture and Fisheries, *National Farm Survey*. p. 65.

73　Cf. PEP, *Report on the Supply of Electricity*, p. 63. The maximum price for electricity which would be tolerated by the rural population was set at 2d. per unit in 1927 and in 1936 at 1d. Cf. Electricity Commission, *Report of Proceedings*, p. 43; PEP, *Report on the Supply of Electricity*, pp. 44–47.

74　Cf. Ministry of Transport, *Supply of electrical energy (Weir Report)*, p. 18.

75　Ministry of Agriculture and Fisheries, *National farm survey*, pp. 67–69. Cf. also Golding, *The Electrification*, p. 30.

76　*Report of the Committee of Inquiry into the Electricity Supply Industry*, pp. 95–97; G. F. Peirson, 'The development of rural electrification. A review of progress', *Proceedings of the Institution of Electrical Engineers*, vol. 108, 1961, pp. 112–126. Cf. for Ireland Maurice Manning and Moore McDowell, *Electricity supply in Ireland. The history of the ESB*. Dublin: Gill and MacMillan, 1984, pp. 123–142; Shiel, *The quiet revolution*.

3 Power to the people
Power stations and the national grid

John Sheail

Introduction

This chapter outlines the legislative history of the national grid, as it came to assume those iconic expressions of modernity, the 2,000 MW power station and 275 kV super grid, commencing with the nationalisation of the industry following the Second World War. Illustration is drawn from the Uskmouth power station as to the physical impacts upon the rural environment. An outline is provided of the statutory means by which they were generally allayed, if not altogether accommodated.

Rob Cochrane published his illustrated booklet *Power to the People* in 1985, when Britain was probably at the height of its global pre-eminence in the electric power-generating industry. Commissioned by the Central Electricity Generating Board, the booklet marked the fiftieth anniversary of the British electricity transmission network, namely 'a system of major arteries enabling electricity to be fed from wherever it could be generated most cheaply to all parts of the country'. The transmission lines might carry the equivalent to four 1,000 ton trainloads of coal every hour. They enabled the balance of generation to be changed both between power stations, and between the use of different types of fuel, by the minute, hour, day and season, according to the aggregate domestic, commercial and industrial demand in the different parts of the country at any particular moment.[1]

Electricity and the war

There is a huge literature upon the readiness of the armed forces for war in 1939. Comparatively little has been written about the part played by the utilities – electricity, gas, water and telephone – and indeed the roads and railways – in supporting the military effort, affecting both town and countryside alike. Although the grid constructed by the Central Electricity Board had covered the whole country, it was necessarily sectionalised into seven separate geographical divisions, with another in Scotland, each with a sufficient generating plant to meet the area demand and provide the necessary stand-by equipment. Despite being interlinked, there was neither the intention nor the capacity to transfer large quantities of power between the divisions. There had however been some strengthening of the 'tie-lines', and the Board's engineers, entirely without authorisation, undertook an experiment on Friday, 19 October 1937, when the nightly demand was at its lowest. The control engineer, on shift at the south-eastern control room in London, issued switching instructions coupling each of the seven areas in turn until every power station operating that night became part of a completely integrated system for the first time. Whilst senior engineers were censured the next day, the experience proved invaluable in meeting the predicted shortage of generating plant in the 1938–1939 winter. Despite the continued misgivings as to the robustness of the system, a winter contingency plan was devised whereby the south-eastern control room could act as a national control point. The facility proved so successful that it was never withdrawn, thereby establishing the largest integrated network in the world.[2]

The grid, and the fact that half of the total supply to the grid came from the almost continual running of the fourteen most efficient and economical power stations, proved crucial to the war effort. When for example the Fulham power station was bombed, and the Battersea station heavily damaged, London drew heavily upon the power imported from South Wales and Scotland.[3] By the end of the war, a situation had evolved where one-quarter of the generating capacity accounted for 90 per cent of output, distributed by 540 undertakings. Fewer than forty of those stations together accounted for more than half the total number of units of electricity sold to the public. As many as 200 produced just 2 per cent of the aggregate.[4] Max Nicholson recalls, in his unpublished autobiography, how it was assumed that the post-war power cuts would continue for many years, owing to shortages of materials and the plant required to manufacture what were in effect the one-off requirements of the power stations for generating equipment. Prime Minister Clement Attlee (deputising for Herbert Morrison who was ill) summoned engineering leaders to 10 Downing Street, where he indicated that priority would be given to the manufacture of plant of the largest size. Nicholson recalls how quickly the nightmare of recurrent power cuts receded.[5]

Post-war nationalisation

Leslie Hannah wrote, in his study *Electricity before Nationalisation*, of how a Victorian municipal and company enterprise developed organisationally from the Conservative experiments with public ownership in the 1920s, to what became an integral part of the Labour government's nationalisation programme after the Second World War.[6] No politician had been more closely connected with the integration of town and country, as represented by the electricity supply grid, than Herbert Morrison – the Hackney Borough and London County Councillor, the Minister of Transport in the Labour Government of 1929 to 1931, and now the Lord President of the

40 John Sheail

Council in the post-war Labour government – the minister most responsible for the nationalisation of the basic utilities of coal, electricity and gas.

One of Morrison's biographers has described him as the 'supremo on the home front'. He was chairman of the Cabinet's Socialisation of Industry Committee, to which non-Cabinet ministers, such as the Minister of Fuel and Power, submitted their respective draft Bills. Where approved and further drafted, the Bills were resubmitted to the Committee and to the Future Legislation Committee (of which Morrison was also Chairman). They might then be submitted to the Cabinet. It was also Morrison, as leader of the House of Commons, who facilitated their introduction and passage through parliament.[7]

In a speech of June 1947, Morrison spoke of how the previously long and bitterly cold winter had shown how domestic comfort and industrial efficiency depended upon an adequate provision of coal, gas and electricity. With the coal industry nationalised, it became the turn of electricity, thereby making sure, in Morrison's words,

> that development is not guided by profits, but the needs of our homes and factories; to take power and light to the countryside and the farms which private enterprise has so often neglected – neglected quite logically because on the whole their interest is primarily in making good profits, and only indirectly in relating the supply to national purpose.[8]

As he phrased it, in a speech of February 1948, an essential purpose of 'a thorough-going policy for cheaper and plentiful electricity supplies' must be to bring

> cheap electricity to rural areas which have been largely starved of electricity in the past because most supply companies, with one or two honourable exceptions, look to quick profits and were unwilling to undertake long-term development work.[9]

The Central Electricity Generating Board

The Electricity Act of 1947 established a British Electricity Authority with the twofold responsibility for co-ordinating the entire industry (namely the fourteen Area Electricity Boards), except for the North of Scotland (where the North of Scotland Hydro-Electricity Board would remain a separate industry), and second for the construction and operation of the power stations and grid. All were required 'to promote the use of all economical methods of generating, transmitting and distributing electricity', and to 'secure, so far as practicable, the development, extension to rural areas and cheapening of supplies'. The Minister of Fuel and Power would appoint the Boards, and give such general directions as appeared requisite in the national interest. The Minister would similarly appoint Consultative Councils, representative of public and consumer interests, in each area.[10]

As well as embarking upon the construction of a comparatively few power stations of considerably larger size, a technical decision was required as to whether to enlarge the existing 132 kV network or superimpose a new network of fewer but higher-voltage lines, namely a supergrid. As well as further 'pooling' and, therefore, minimising spare generating capacity, it was cheaper to convey electric power by supergrid than to transport the coal-equivalent across Britain. Large power stations were accordingly built upon the East Midlands coalfields, which the National Coal Board had scheduled for particular development. Construction of a 275 kV supergrid began in 1950, the transmission lines being so designed that they could be modified for operation at the even higher voltage of 400 kV in the future.[11]

The British Electricity Authority emphasised, in its first report, the greater general prosperity in agriculture, and the purchasing power of agricultural workers, since the war, and how electricity had begun to provide 'modern amenities to village communities', thereby 'checking the movement of population to the towns, accelerating the mechanisation of agriculture, and bringing power to rural industries'. Operating conditions were however so varied, encompassing 'the plains of Lincolnshire, the dales of Yorkshire, and the high lands of Kirkcudbright'. The basic problem remained whether there would be sufficient return on capital to warrant the extension of rural supply lines 'farther and farther into the less economic districts of the countryside'.[12]

The South West and South East Scotland Electricity Boards were replaced, under the Electricity Reorganisation (Scotland) Act of 1954, by a South of Scotland Board, which became separately responsible for both generation and distribution within those areas. The British Electricity Authority was accordingly renamed the Central Electricity Authority, and its activities made the subject of an enquiry under Sir Edwin Herbert, in July 1954. Where the Committee recommended that the central authority should become purely advisory, the Electricity Act of 1957 established two new bodies, namely an advisory Electricity Council and a Central Electricity Generating Board (CEGB), with such powers of direction, as previously possessed by the Central Electricity Authority, now vested in the Minister of Power.[13]

There was by now some thirty years of achievement. The CEGB might be challenged to increase total power resources by 44 per cent before 1963, most obviously by the construction of between twelve and fifteen base-load nuclear stations, but power supply had already doubled in the previous eight years. The industry was the largest spender (outside Whitehall) in the British economy, operating 238 power stations, with an aggregate output capacity of 25,100 MW and 433 main electricity distribution centres (grid switching stations). The grid itself now comprised over 6,000 miles of high-voltage transmission lines, of which 1,120 miles comprised the supergrid of 5,400 steel towers. The Area Boards would be adjudged on their maintenance of voltages, reinforcement of distribution networks, meeting the demands of both industry and rural supply, and upon their retail tariffs closely matching economical costs. Those same Boards had, over the previous nine years,

42   John Sheail

increased electricity sales by 107 per cent, as compared with an increase in consumers of 35 per cent. The average price per unit had increased by only 28.4 per cent, only 38 per cent above the pre-war figure.[14]

The Uskmouth power station

Power stations represent one of the most intensive forms of land use and, both for their physical bulk and associated transmission lines, they constitute one of the most challenging forms of land use to integrate into what were predominantly rural and coastal parts of the country. Both the construction of the stations and transmission lines required the statutory consent of the Minister of Fuel and Power, as advised by such departments as those of Agriculture and Fisheries, and Housing and Local Government, following public inquiry.

Account had to be taken of both land-use planning and pollution control. Power stations were brought under the scrutiny of the Alkali, &c. Works Regulation Inspectorate in 1958. The Electricity Commissioners had set a standard of particulate matter not exceeding 0.4 grain per cubic foot (920 mg/m³). The Alkali Inspectorate, taking account of what had been achieved for other scheduled industrial emissions and 'the need for a better social environment', raised the target to 0.2 grain per cubic foot (460 mg/m³). The CEGB became 'the country's biggest spender on air pollution control', investing £11 million in upgrading existing plants during its first seven years. New plants had to meet even higher arrestment efficiencies of not less than 99.3 per cent, with greater attention paid to the dispersion of the cleaned gases. The capital cost of the equipment for the giant 2,000 MW stations of the 1960s was nearly £4 million, and that for the largest in Europe at the time, the Drax 4,000 MW station, about £5 million.[15]

The controversies surrounding the development of the Uskmouth power station may be cited for the range of issues which had to be tackled. Although some might be resolved, it was rarely possible to achieve a clear-cut solution, short of closing down the station altogether. The post-war story of station development in South Wales was hardly happy. So many of the valleys were industrialised, and their watercourses polluted, that an even greater premium was placed upon preserving those tracts of unspoilt river and countryside which remained. Having failed in 1946 to secure support for a station at Llanover, in the Usk valley in Monmouthshire, the obvious step in the late 1940s was to double the capacity of the station already being planned further downstream, on the east bank of the river Usk as it flowed into the Severn estuary. The Usk was, however, an outstandingly good salmon river, with a capital value of over £100,000. The Usk Board of Conservators strongly objected to the building of a station on the grounds that it would endanger salmon entering the river to spawn, and the migration of the salmon and sea trout smolts to the sea. The discharge of heated

Power stations and the national grid 43

waters at times of minimum flow would affect the fish directly, and cause an even greater reduction of oxygen in the already badly polluted estuary waters.[16]

After prolonged discussions with the Board of Conservators, the Electricity Commissioners decided, in March 1948, that the need for a new station at Uskmouth, of 360 MW capacity, was so pressing that consent should be given, despite the operation of the circulating water arrangements still being unresolved. A special condition was accordingly included in the consent, whereby the requirements of the Conservators were to be met to the fullest possible extent. To that end, the Electricity Commissioners were empowered to impose any regulations deemed necessary on the cooling arrangements. In a letter to the Board of Conservators, the Commissioners wrote of how it should not be difficult to reach agreement over the quantities to be abstracted, and the temperature of that discharged. The optimism was misplaced.[17]

A survey carried out by the civil engineers, Sir William Halcrow and Partners, indicated that the minimum flow of the river for the short period of dead low water was over 60 million gallons per hour, compared with a requirement of 60 million gallons per hour for a station of an aggregate capacity of 360 MW. Although the findings were confirmed by independent experts, the consulting engineers to the Usk Board arrived at a minimum flow that was only half the Halcrow figure, although admitting the measurements had been taken in difficult circumstances.

Whatever the figures, the British Electricity Authority contended that too much importance was being attached to the minimum flow conditions, which only occurred for very short periods and at widely separated intervals. In 1949, the Authority asked the Minister of Fuel and Power to decide on the limits to be imposed on the amounts of water to be extracted and the temperature of that returned to the river. Ministry officials were at first strongly opposed to laying down any limits. As one remarked, they were 'far too much in the hands of nature'. There was, however, no sign of the negotiations coming to any conclusion, and, after 'unofficial' discussions with the British Electricity Authority, it was decided that the amount of cooling water to be extracted should not exceed 15 million gallons per hour at any time. When the temperature of the water in the river at the inlet point exceeded 50 degrees F, the rise in temperature of the water between the inlet and outlet should not exceed 15 degrees F. When the temperature was 50 degrees F or less, the temperature of the water at the outlet point should not exceed 65 degrees F.[18]

The station commenced operation in December 1952, and was working at about two-thirds capacity two years later. The Usk River Board (as it had become) soon claimed that excessive heating of the river was causing damage to fish. Surveys carried out by the Fisheries Department of the Ministry of Agriculture and Fisheries did not, however, support the contention. Insofar as there was any effect, it was both local and intermittent.

44   *John Sheail*

As anticipated, the Central Electricity Authority applied for a second power station of similar size, Uskmouth 'B', in October 1955. The Usk River Board insisted on the use of cooling towers. The Central Electricity Authority accepted that the conditions laid down by the consent for the first station had been breached a number of times, but contended that there was no cause for concern, except during the migratory period. Surveys had shown that this period might be as short as three days, and seldom more than a fortnight, in May. It would accordingly be grossly wasteful to construct cooling towers at a cost of £750,000, or to impose undue restrictions on the operation of the station for so short a period, particularly as river temperatures were not high at that time of the year.

The Ministry of Fuel and Power once again suggested that consent should be granted in principle, but that the position on the cooling water arrangements should be reserved until further technical discussions had taken place. This time the Central Electricity Authority objected, arguing that the design of the circulating-water works was so integral with the station that any variation that might be required later was likely to have a fundamental effect on the design, and even orientation, of the station. To add to the uncertainty, another issue had come to the fore. Although large numbers of smolts were thought to have been swept by powerful intake currents into the circulating-water system, no one had any idea of the proportion of the total smolt run these losses represented. Whilst devices might be developed to keep the smolts out of the intake, time would be needed to install and test their effectiveness.[19]

In January 1957, representatives from three ministries, namely of Fuel and Power, Agriculture and Fisheries, and Housing and Local Government, decided against cooling towers and the imposition of a maximum temperature at the point of discharge. A condition was however imposed, requiring the Central Electricity Authority to record river temperatures (which it had previously done voluntarily) and that it should take 'such steps as are reasonably practicable to prevent smolts being damaged by the intake of water into the Station, and install such reasonable amount and type of apparatus as investigations may prove to be effective and desirable for this purpose'. The River Board neither accepted nor opposed the new condition, reserving its position in the event of serious damage being inflicted on the fisheries. Formal consent for Uskmouth 'B' was granted in April 1957.[20]

The Authority's scope for satisfying the River Board had always been constrained by an earlier decision taken to meet the fears of the Harbour Commissioners that too little water might be left in the river at low tide. The point of discharge of the cooling water was located upstream of the inlet. The Harbour Commissioners insisted that the same condition should apply to the new station. At low water, and particularly when the freshwater flow was small, the recirculation of discharge water from the upstream outflow to the intake had the effect of creating a narrow band of water reaching temperatures of 100 degrees F adjacent to the east bank. In order to prevent this band becoming hotter and of longer duration when the 'B' station was commissioned, consents were obtained for building a tunnel under the river so as to create a point of discharge in the middle of the river. So as to prove there was no threat to navigation, representatives of the Harbour Commissioners were invited to see for themselves the minimal effect of the mid-river outfall of the Bankside power station on the river Thames in London. A Tate and Lyle sugar molasses tanker was commissioned for the purpose. Such was the stench that it required only a few passes to dispel any doubts. Formal consents, first for the 'B' station, and then for a combined outlet, were granted in August 1959 and December 1960 respectively.[21]

Meanwhile little progress had been made in the search for effective ways of diverting smolts from the circulating water system. The most feasible appeared to be a bubble-screen barrier formed by compressed air escaping from a perforated pipe laid on the river bed. The intensive programme of netting to help assess the effectiveness of the screen soon developed into a rescue operation, returning most fish to the river unharmed. At a very long and tedious meeting at the offices of the Ministry of Power in Cardiff, in October 1962, River Board representatives again pressed for cooling towers. As the Ministry's regional officer minuted, the Central Electricity Generating Board bent over backwards to be helpful, but could not hold out any promise of the problem being solved by the following spring. Representatives of the Ministry of Agriculture and Fisheries were singularly quiet. They appeared embarrassed at the bleak prospect of any solution. Despite rescue operations and further plant modifications, some damage to smolts seemed certain to continue. The Fisheries Adviser to the North of Scotland Hydro-Electric Board confirmed there was no alternative to building a hatchery and smolt-rearing station, their costs being set against the potential loss of availability of 180 MW of the plant during the migration season. The hatchery was completed in 1967 at a final cost of £20,790.[22]

Pylons across the Downs

The decision of the Central Electricity Board to erect overhead transmission lines passing over the South Downs has become something of a cause célèbre, as perpetuated by such historians as Bill Luckin.[23] Herbert Morrison cited the 'first-class row with a substantial body of public opinion and with the newspapers'; in a lecture to the Royal Institute of Public Administration some quarter century later, he wrote:

> I think it is salutary that there should be a row about such matters because it shows that public opinion is alive and is watching public amenity: this puts the Government and local authorities on their guard.[24]

But as he further remarked, 'we had our own way over the pylons in the end and they are now generally accepted.'

46   John Sheail

The previous Minister of Transport, Colonel Wilfred Ashley, had spoken, in an Electricity Supply debate of December 1929, of the need for a sense of proportion in providing both cheap electricity in rural areas and mitigating 'any destruction of the beauty of the scenery'. Herbert Morrison (as the new Minister) had agreed, but remarked 'the nation must live, and the people must have their electrical power.'[25] Prime Minister Ramsay MacDonald asked for his personal intervention on amenity issues. Morrison, anticipating an outcry over a proposal to erect pylons across the South Downs, took the precaution of submitting a Memorandum to the Cabinet on 11 October 1929, indicating that, following the statutory public inquiry and a personal visit, he had given his consent. Even if it had been technically possible to place a 132 kV cable underground, it would have cost nine times as much, and would still have impaired amenity, in that a series of 50-foot high oil towers would have been required to service the cable. Not only was the electricity supply required for the electrification of the main railway line to Brighton, and its coastal extensions, but both Brighton and Eastbourne, and the coastal towns between, would have been excluded from the grid, upon which the whole of the Board's secondary development for Sussex and Kent depended. By so gravely imperilling the finances of the entire South East England Scheme, any 'return to uncoordinated and individualistic development' would mean the denial of 'the cheaper electricity based on the National Scheme'. Rural development of the grid would be retarded. The Cabinet, with the Chancellor of the Exchequer (deputising for MacDonald) in the chair, took note and approved Morrison's action.[26]

Statutory experience was already being obtained in respect of hydroelectric development, primarily for industrial purposes, in the Scottish Highlands. Although the word 'legislation' is almost invariably perceived in the negative sense of regulation – as a restraint or prohibition – Acts of Parliament may also provide opportunity for achieving something not otherwise possible. Most Public and General Bills are enabling measures, establishing a broad framework within which ministers and their officials, with 'expert' advice, may draft more precise guidelines upon which 'the administrative decision' can be made. Legislation has an even more explicitly constructive role in both local government and the former utilities of water, gas and electricity and so forth, namely what is called Local and Private Legislation founded upon the broad constitutional principle of ultra vires. Put simply, the local councils and utilities are permitted to act only in so far as permitted by Parliament.

The incremental nature of most legislation may be illustrated by reference to the so-called amenity clause. It was initially developed as a response to the outcry against the ambitious civil engineering schemes located within some of the most picturesque countryside in Britain, namely hydroelectric power. The Lochaber Water Power Act of 1921 established the precedent whereby an undertaker was required to have 'all reasonable regard' for the preservation of 'the beauty of scenery', both in the interests of property owners and the public. The Grampian Electricity Act of 1922 and subsequent measures included provision for the appointment of amenity committees to advise on how the obligation might be discharged. The powers were generalised under the North of Scotland Hydro-Electric Development Act of 1943, establishing the North of Scotland Hydro-Electric Development Board to promote further development.[27] Precedent was set for such protective powers as included the North Wales Hydro-Electric Bill of 1955, which enabled the Ffestiniog pump-storage and Rheidol schemes to proceed.

Whilst none doubted the exceptional quality of the Highland and North Wales scenery, there was a growing feeling that more should be done to safeguard the country at large from the rapid and complex advances in industrial development. Even if the nuclear power stations proposed for the remoter parts of the British Isles could be accommodated with minimal impact, there was no concealing 'the spidery trail of pylons'. Those of the 275 kV supergrid were each almost as high as Nelson's Column. During the debates on the Electricity Bill of 1957, there was parliamentary pressure for a declaration of principle, giving general effect to what had already been achieved in the Highlands and North Wales. The outcome was a government amendment whereby both the industry and the Minister,

> having regard to the desirability of preserving natural beauty, of conserving flora, fauna and geological and physiographical features of special interest, and of protecting buildings and other objects of architectural or historic interest, shall each take into account any effect which the proposals would have on the natural beauty of the countryside or on any such flora, fauna, features, buildings or objects.[28]

Section 37 of the Act became a benchmark for the electricity industry and the model for what might be achieved in the coal industry (the Opencast Coal Act of 1958), The scope of the 'clause' was further widened as the peculiar circumstances of the particular industry were considered. So as to make it explicit that Parliament intended 'to improve and enhance' the towns as well as the countryside, the words 'beauty or amenity in any rural or urban area' were included in the relevant clause of the Water Bill of 1973.

Critics of Section 37 of the Electricity Act of 1957 pointed to how the 'clause' was notably silent on enforcement. Was it conceivable that it could ever prevail over Section 2 of the same Act, which spelt out the now familiar injunction 'to develop and maintain an efficient and economic system of supply of electricity'? It would however be misleading to dismiss the effect as entirely symbolic. Engineers within the industry were in no doubt that a new era had dawned. Previously officers of the industry had to demonstrate the greatest possible pressures, whether of a hostile or more positive kind, when justifying to their Accounting Officer expenditure on any concession to visual amenity, wildlife, or recreational interest. The 'amenity clause' provided the necessary justification. Officers in the industry could now respond

48   *John Sheail*

without risk of being accused of acting ultra vires. Whatever was decided, it could be represented as conforming with the prescribed objects of the industry.

Demonstrably, amenity matters had to be taken fully into account at the earliest stages of planning. It was not enough to design a power station and to 'apply' amenity as a cosmetic afterthought. As a statutory duty, the making of informed assessments, whether of visual amenity or pollution control, could not be left to external advisors. At public inquiries, the Board had to provide a team of witnesses thoroughly versed in the complex issues at stake. The distinguished architect and planner, Sir William Holford, was appointed the first part-time member of the Board. Under his tutelage, the CEGB became a principal patron of architecture and landscape design.

Whilst there was much criticism of the vagueness of the requirements placed on industry, within the amenity clause the same quality conferred much needed flexibility in responding to hazards which had hardly bulked in the views of Parliament and voluntary bodies as they promoted and debated the clause. As officers pointed out, first to the CEGB and then to the Treasury, in the 1980s the issue of acid rain fell squarely within the obligation imposed on the industry to produce electricity economically and with due regard to the environment. As the CEGB reiterated, in evidence to a House of Commons committee, the industry must not only secure a proper understanding of the implications of its activities on public health and the environment, but it must also ensure that whatever it did to protect the environment was effective. This meant tailoring not only solutions to the situation, but defining the extent and seriousness of the problems which the controls were intended to eliminate. In many cases, the industry itself became a leading patron and practitioner of the particular fields of environmental science.[29]

Set-squares and concrete

To mark the Queen's coronation, the BBC Home Service broadcast a series of talks by those of her generation, who included the politician Anthony Wedgwood Benn and the Olympic ice skater Jeannette Altwegg. Another was the chartered civil engineer, Dugald Fraser, the resident engineer of the North of Scotland Hydro-Electric Development Board's Gaur project. Where those with the requisite skills had been forced so often to look overseas, there were now faint signs of Scotland affording such employment. Through planning, there was 'a sense of "up-and-doingness" in Scotland today' – of bringing power into the glens:

> And to me, these pylons striding over the heather in all directions are a symbol. They are carrying on their shoulders a new power, an injection of fresh vitality, a blood transfusion. There is more to it than just a

mass of cables and wires and concrete. There is something you can feel, something you can sense.[30]

In Fraser's words, there was 'a creative thrill' at the Gaur station, when 'the dash-lamps glowed, the ammeter needles in the control panels flickered, and energy – clean as the water that made it possible – surged out on to the transmission lines.' There was an exhilaration that 'every time a Highland housewife plugs in an iron, or power is switched to Clydeside to avoid load-shedding, then my work is justified.'

Dugald Fraser concluded his brief talk, 'Set-Squares and Concrete', by remarking how they say that 'know-how' had far outstripped the will to apply it properly and that, 'in an age of plumbing life is too easy.' As one of the plumbers, he had even heard it said 'we are spoiling that Highland housewife by giving her an electric iron.' As an engineer and practical man, 'I believe you can only get the best out of people if the conditions under which they work are as good as you can make them.' That was his job, and indeed it might well have summed up what had been the ultimate responsibility of the industry as a whole.

Notes

1 R. Cochrane, *Power to the people. The story of the national grid*. London: Newnes, 1985.
2 Cochrane, *Power to the people*, pp. 28–29.
3 Cochrane, *Power to the people*, pp. 30–39.
4 D.G. Dodds, 'A new phase in electricity', *Public Administration*, vol. 36, 1958, p. 20.
5 E.M. Nicholson, *A chequered career*. Unpublished autobiography, chapter 10.
6 L. Hannah, *Electricity before nationalization. A study of the development of the electricity supply industry in Britain to 1948*. London: Macmillan, p. vii.
7 D. Howell, 'Herbert Morrison', in *New Dictionary of National Biography*, vol. 39, 2004, pp. 335–344; B. Donoughue and G.W. Jones, *Herbert Morrison: Portrait of a politician*, London: Weidenfeld and Nicolson, 1973, p. 355.
8 H. Morrison, *The peaceful revolution. Speeches by the Right Honorable Herbert Morrison*. London: Allen and Unwin, 1949, pp. 41–42.
9 Morrison, *The peaceful revolution*, p. 98.
10 Dodds, 'A new phase in electricity', p. 21.
11 Central Electricity Generating Board, *Pattern of power*, p. 11.
12 Parliamentary Papers, 1948–9, X1V, First Report of the British Electricity Authority (London: HMSO), pp. 77–81.
13 Dodds, 'A new phase in electricity', pp. 22–26.
14 Cochrane, *Power to the people*, pp. 36–42; Dodds, 'A new phase in electricity', pp. 26–28.
15 Ministry of Housing and Local Government, *Annual Report*, London, HMSO, 1966, p. 2, and 1968, pp. 7–8.
16 The National Archives (TNA), POWE 14/224, 849 and 1056.
17 TNA, POWE 14/224.
18 TNA, POWE 14/224 and 849.
19 TNA, POWE 14/849 and 1223.

50 *John Sheail*

20 TNA, HLG 71/1383 and POWE 14/849.

21 TNA, POWE 14/849, 1056 and 1223.

22 CEGB, GBEC minute 24 April 1963; GBFM 1195 and minute 28 October 1963.

23 B. Luckin, *Questions of power. Electricity and the environment in inter-war Britain.* Manchester: Manchester University Press, 1990.

24 H. Morrison, The elected authority – spur or brake? In: *Vitality in administration*, H. Morrison et al. (eds). London: Allen and Unwin, 1957, p. 14.

25 Parliamentary Debates, Commons, 233, col 513 and 525.

26 TNA, CAB 23/62, and CAB 24/206; J. Sheail, *Power in trust: An environmental history of the central electricity generating board.* London: Clarendon Press, 1991, p. 5.

27 J. Sheail, *Rural conservation in inter-war Britain.* Oxford: Clarendon Press, pp. 42–44; P. Payne, *The Hydro: A study of the development of major hydroelectric schemes undertaken by the North of Scotland Hydro-Electric Board.* Aberdeen: Aberdeen University Press.

28 J. Sheail, 'The "amenity clause"; an insight into half a century of environmental protection in the United Kingdom', *Transactions of the Institute of British Geographers*, vol. 17, 1992, pp. 155–165.

29 Sheail, 'The "amenity clause"'.

30 D. Fraser, 'Set-squares and concrete', *The Listener*, vol. 50 (1275), 1953, pp. 218–219; E. Wood, *The hydro boys: Pioneers of renewable energy.* Edinburgh: Luarth Press, 2002.

4 Lighting the landscape
Rural electrification in Wales

Richard Moore-Colyer

From the perspective of an over-illuminated early twenty-first century, where 'light pollution' is becoming a matter of growing public concern, the profound darkness of the countryside of two generations ago is sometimes difficult to imagine. As the sun sunk below the western horizon and the evening drew in, most rural activity came to a halt when people withdrew to their hearth sides and waited for the night. In earlier years, those requiring more light than that cast by the hearth itself had recourse to rush or tallow candles, or even the crude and rather dangerous benzoline lamp. By the end of the Great War, however, the single-burner flat-wick paraffin lamp supplied a murky and fume-laden light to many homes in the Welsh countryside, giving way eventually to more sophisticated oil lamps and burners. Meanwhile, the open hearth or iron cooking range yielded to the oil stove/oven combination, although in many households the hearth was still employed for some categories of cooking. Open hearths, candles and paraffin lamps may have provided light, but they concurrently produced smoke and fumes, were subject to the capricious effects of draughts, and above all presented a constant risk of fire. The harnessing of a source of energy and illumination free from these hazards and irritations would clearly have massive implications in terms of offering access to an enormous range of time- and labour-saving devices. But the eventual availability of electricity in the rural world was also of profound cultural significance. People were finally freed from the tyranny of night by the simple expedient of flicking a switch. So was twilight extended into the night by the availability of a reliable source of continuous light. The leisure hours between late afternoon and dusk had long been the only opportunity for working people seriously to engage in cultural pursuits, in craftwork or some other form of creative activity. Electricity in effect extended the hours of leisure and even if it meant little more than glancing at a newspaper or tuning in to the wireless (now no longer reliant on a rechargeable battery), the countrymen and women of Wales were liberated from the dreary hours of darkness. This chapter seeks to trace the process whereby this great boon was delivered to villages, and more especially farms, throughout the length and breadth of Wales.

52   Richard Moore-Colyer

For the best part of half a century the history of electrification was dominated by dispute and squabbling between private generators and municipal authorities, largely as a result of the rather ill-conceived Electric Light Act 1882.The latter gave a local authority the power to purchase a private electricity undertaking after twenty-one years (extended to forty-two years in 1888), besides establishing the right of municipalities to develop their own supplies. Not surprisingly this piece of legislation tended to restrict the growth of supplies by stifling the private sector whose areas of supply were in any case limited by the output of the slow horizontal engines which only produced direct current.[1] However, with the development of methods of generating alternative current in the late 1890s, it became technically feasible for generating companies to cover wider areas which might well embrace several local authorities.[2] Meanwhile, as the young power companies complained of the inefficiency of municipal supplies under the control of local authorities, the latter looked askance at the companies whose quasi-monopolistic situation offered the potential (if nothing more) for exploiting the community. This sort of mutual distrust led to serious delay in the electrification of some Welsh towns. In Abergavenny, for example, an electrification scheme had been drawn up in 1894, only to fall foul of the intransigence of the local authority–owned Gas Company which had no intention of allowing its very profitable gas business to be threatened by a private electricity generator. The argument rumbled on for years and so vigorously did the local authority resist all attempts to undermine the gas monopoly that the town was denied an electricity supply until April 1932.[3] Elsewhere in provincial Wales the relationship between generating companies and urban and borough councils was equivocal at the very least. In the last decade of the nineteenth century the firm of Bourne and Grant had won the tender to supply street lighting for Aberystwyth and to this end purchased land in Mill Street to build a coke-fired electricity generating plant. This firm, under the later guise of the Chiswick Electricity Supply Company, continued to provide the town's electricity until the enterprise was taken over by the Aberystwyth Corporation in 1936. Throughout the whole of this period, when the streets of the seaside town were lit both by electricity and gas, there existed not only an uneasy relationship between gas and electricity suppliers, but a mutual suspicion of the machinations of the Aberystwyth Corporation.[4]

Alongside companies responsible for street lighting by way of coal and coke-fuelled generators there were a variety of other means of obtaining electricity supplies in one form or another. As early as 1910 John Colman's 'Picturedrome' in Newtown was being powered by electricity produced from a dynamo which was itself driven by gas drawn from the municipal supply.[5] Meanwhile, along with engine-driven dynamos for charging bicycle, motor and lamp batteries, many of the larger private houses in both town and country had their own direct current generators. In north Wales, moreover, the development of hydroelectric schemes at Blaenau Ffestiniog, Beddgelert

Rural electrification in Wales   53

and Conwy between 1899 and 1910 was followed by the establishment of smaller hydroelectric enterprises elsewhere.[6] The year 1906 witnessed the commissioning of the Cwm Dyli hydroelectric station to service the nearby slate quarries, while the Aluminium Corporation set up the Dolgarreg station to power its aluminium works the following year. On a smaller scale, at locations blessed with a good head of water, local entrepreneurs sought to exploit hydro potential. By 1920 two Pelton wheels, driven by a 70-foot fall of water, were providing 240 volts direct current to subscribers in and around Llanuwchllyn. Villagers enjoyed their supply at low cost since the local engineer who had set up the system had managed to do so by using carefully adapted second-hand materials in what an admirer described as 'a good instance of private enterprise'.[7] The combination of water-powered turbines and a back-up diesel engine meant that by 1935 Dolgellau housewives could at last make use of the expanding range of electro-mechanical devices for cooking and cleaning, while the cumbersome and unwieldy battery operated wireless set now became redundant. A hydroelectric system powered by water from the Teifi had been up and running in Newcastle Emlyn since 1908, providing for the needs of a cinema and 170 subscribers who were still being supplied via the original turbines at the outbreak of the Second World War.[8] While there was growing incentive for entrepreneurs to establish electricity-generating capacity in the country towns of the Welsh heartland in the early decades of the twentieth century, the situation was rather different in the industrial and mining centres of the south where there was a tendency for industry to generate its own supplies. In fact, as late as 1930 some 60 per cent of all electricity consumed was generated by end users with obvious effects on the potential for expansion of the supply companies.[9]

As the Great War drew towards its close, it was becoming increasingly obvious that the confused and piecemeal state of the electricity supply industry was in need of urgent reform. Such was the vital importance of this energy source that its management and distribution demanded the development of some sort of national policy. Successive reports on the condition of the industry emphasised the need to move away from its localised character. The deliberations of a Board of Trade committee in 1917 and 1918 formed the backcloth to the Electricity (Supply) Act 1919, which established the Electricity Commission. The work of the Commission in turn led to the passing of the Electricity (Supply) Act 1926, whereby the newly established Central Electricity Board was empowered to concentrate generation at a selection of efficient stations and to create a single unified power zone by way of a national grid system. The Committee which reviewed the problem of electrical supplies in preparation for the 1926 Act brought the issue of rural electrification into special prominence, specifically noting the potential social benefits. Nevertheless, they could not avoid the conclusion that in view of the formidable logistical difficulties, the prospects of the more remote parts of Britain receiving electricity supplies in the foreseeable future were severely limited.[10]

But these various processes of rationalisation by no means precluded the continued growth of private generating companies and even individuals. The West Cambrian Power Company, for example, no doubt reflecting on the Central Electricity Board's interest in identifying 'efficient' stations, bought up most of the supply companies in Pembrokeshire and a number of those in Carmarthenshire and south Cardiganshire in 1931.[11] In the remote west of the latter county water turbines were still being installed at Talybont and diesel generators fitted up at Borth and Bow Street. Mr G. Jones of Bow Street attracted thirty subscribers to his supply and throughout the Second World War his diesels provided both the local Women's Land Army headquarters and the Home Guard station with light and power. In 1948, however, Jones and the rest were absorbed by the North Wales Power Company, whose cable system now extended south from its original limits at Barmouth.[12] During the depressed years of the 1930s the government had given loans to electricity companies at highly favourable rates as part of a scheme to promote employment while concurrently accelerating the build-up of rural electricity networks.[13] At the time the potential significance of rural electrification was at last becoming appreciated among politicians and officialdom. Although references to the uses of electricity on the farm had been 'almost wholly facetious' during the parliamentary debate on the 1926 Electricity Act, the subject was nevertheless firmly on the political agenda. Conservative activists stalked the country with an 'electro-farming' film which they showed in village and town alike, both Labour and Liberal land policy embraced rural electrification, while organisations like Montague Fordham's Rural Reconstruction Association urged the electrification of the countryside as a matter of prime importance.[14] But to a growing appreciation of the benefits which would accrue to the rural economy from the provision of reliable electricity supplies was allied the embarrassing realisation that Britain lagged behind many countries in developing this facility. In Sweden, for example, as much as 40 per cent of the arable regions of the country had been connected to public electricity supplies by 1924, a time when the issue was largely ignored in Britain.[15] France and Denmark too were far in advance of the United Kingdom from the standpoint of rural electrification, with three out of five Danish farms linked to a public supply.[16] By 1930 there remained 30,000 square miles of Britain with no access to low-tension distribution wires which, in effect, meant that upwards of four million country people awaited a supply along with all but 25,000 of the 388,433 farms in England and Wales.[17] In Wales herself some progress was being made so that the North Wales Power Company could boast that its transmission lines had been extended from 110 to 1,077 miles between 1923 and 1936, while numbers of consumers had advanced from 2,344 to 34,665. But most of these were urban consumers. The West Cambrian Power Company reckoned that by 1935 it had been able to connect 13,000 out of 17,000 premises within 'reasonable distance' of the main lines,

Rural electrification in Wales 55

comparable figures being reported by the South Wales Power Company being 34,000 out of 42,000.[18]

By the outbreak of the Second World War almost 30 per cent of the farms in England were connected to a public electricity supply, although the National Farm Survey of 1941 indicated that only 8 per cent of Welsh farms were so served. Others, however, had their own petrol-driven generators so that in Carmarthenshire, for example, of the 10 per cent of farms using electricity, nine out of ten generated their own supplies.

Even where supplies were available, it appears from contemporary studies undertaken by economists at the University College at Aberystwyth that, despite the availability of a variety of deferred payment schemes, the uptake of the new technology was inhibited by what many farmers regarded as excessive cost. In an important survey of fifty-seven electricity-using farms in south Wales carried out in 1932, twelve employed electricity fully in the farmhouse, for power, heat and light, eighteen for heating and lighting and twenty-seven for lighting only. Although economies of scale operated to the extent that the unit cost of wiring declined with the number of lamps and power sockets installed, many farmers were chary of getting 'wired up' any more than they felt to be absolutely necessary. Even on those holdings which used electricity for purposes other than lighting, the range of modern appliances adopted was severely limited. Of twenty-five farmhouses, eight had electric cookers, and twenty-two had electric fires, yet the investigators found only three vacuum cleaners and a couple of water heaters. As with refrigerators and washing machines (which were completely absent on these farms), most domestic appliances were available on the hire-purchase system.[19]

The concern over costs which limited rates of adoption of electricity even where supplies were available left the Central Electricity Board with something of a conundrum. The thinly distributed population of rural Wales (at 150 people per square mile compared to 4,600 in urban areas) inevitably meant that the capital cost of providing power lines to isolated villages and farms in the countryside was, pro rata, far higher than in the towns. This in turn meant that to justify the expense of high-tension cables, service lines, distribution lines and transformers (to say nothing of the growing problem of negotiating way leaves), not only would rural charging tariffs need to be higher, but a supplier would need to be convinced that his efforts would be rewarded with a high level of demand. This, of course, was by no means guaranteed and many contemporary reports and surveys stressed the importance of farms, shops, institutions and industries in the countryside adopting electricity thereby encouraging suppliers and reducing unit costs. Farmers, in particular, urged one report, should consider the farmhouse and the farm itself as one since 'women have important duties on the farm [and] the lighting of their household tasks may have definite economic importance, altogether apart from the general improvement of domestic conditions.' On the

56   Richard Moore-Colyer

face of it rather patronising, this comment highlights the growing role of farm women in the non-domestic quotidian activities of the farm.[20]

To reduce costs and stimulate supply, farmers were cajoled to adopt electricity for as many practical purposes as possible. By the 1930s it was technically possible to replace with electrical equipment both the horse gins and steam engines (which had dominated the farmyard since Hanoverian times) and the more recently developed static petrol engines. Ten years earlier a great deal of interest had been generated by the idea that crop growth on a field scale could be stimulated by the application of electricity. Studies by Sir Oliver Lodge and others had seemed to indicate quite dramatic increases in crop yields where a high-tension electrical discharge was passed into the soil by way of an overhead wire network. This gave rise to a lengthy series of experiments conducted under the auspices of the Ministry of Agriculture with funding from the Development Commission. But eventually the whole idea was quietly dropped on the grounds of hopeless impracticality and the realisation that general developments in plant breeding and agronomy would be likely to bring about the improvements claimed by the electro-agriculturalists at a fraction of the capital cost. Nonetheless, a whole range of farm operations lent themselves to electrification. Food preparation, chaff cutting, pulping root crops for housed livestock, sheep shearing and wood sawing were just some of the jobs which could be readily mechanised with a single- or three-phase electric motor. The environmental control of livestock buildings, crop stores and glasshouses also lent itself to electrification and electricity was widely adopted by the expanding poultry industry along the north Wales coast and in the vales of Glamorgan and Monmouth. Here eggs could be incubated with more precision and new-born chicks could be kept warm without the need for the suffocating and fire-prone paraffin lamps previously in use. Besides, with reliable artificial illumination egg production could be sustained throughout the winter months when egg prices tended to be higher.[21] But from a purely Welsh perspective it was within the dairy sector, which expanded rapidly between the wars, and was to prove the salvation of many a farming family in the depressed years of the 1930s, that electricity really came into its own.[22] As the Welsh dairy industry adjusted from a traditional mode whereby butter in wooden casks was sold to the mining valleys of the south, to one by which in 1930 more than three-quarters was marketed in liquid form, dramatic changes in equipment were required. The newly established Milk Marketing Board set rigorous standards both of hygiene and nutritional quality so that production methods needed to be scrupulously clean and the old wooden dairy utensils replaced with readily cleaned stainless steel. No longer could a farmer wash his churns and milking equipment in the farm pond or a nearby stream (unquestionably the source of much urban enteric disease in the past); now all churns, buckets and other milking impedimenta had to be steam-sterilised daily. Once again, economic studies from Aberystwyth demonstrated the benefits in terms of cost of adopting the electrically operated milking machine and

Rural electrification in Wales 57

abandoning the old coal-fired steam cleaning equipment in favour of electric sterilising and cooling devices. A typical study of 1940 revealed that cost per gallon could be slashed from 1.25d. to 0.48d. by following these measures.

In Britain as a whole the number of on-farm electric motors fed from a public supply increased from 11,000 to 253,000 between 1939 and 1960. Yet throughout this period the rate of farm connections to public electricity varied widely from area to area while rate of adoption varied from farm to farm. The 1941 National Farm Survey starkly revealed the overall backwardness of upland Wales in this regard. Thus it was that whereas 30 per cent of farms in Glamorgan were connected to some form of public electricity source, the corresponding figure for Anglesey, Cardigan, Radnor and Montgomery was a mere 2 per cent. Individual parish studies also reflect a countryside where daily life began to close down as the sun disappeared. At Llanfihangel yng Ngwynfa in north Montgomeryshire a small hydroelectric plant supplied the local mill by 1949, but all the farmsteads and cottages in the area remained entirely reliant upon paraffin lamps for lighting.[23] In 1957, several years after the Mid Wales Investigational Report had emphasised the importance of electric lighting as a means of allowing farmers the chance to read in their leisure time and so to improve their technical knowledge, a study showed that on sixty Welsh farms there were no more than thirty-four pieces of equipment powered by electric motor.[24] A decade or more before the publication of the Mid Wales Investigational Report, Lord Justice Scott's Committee on Land Utilization in Rural Britain had recommended the rapid provision, free of charge, of electricity to all occupied agricultural holdings in the country.[25] In so doing, the Scott Committee echoed the views of the Welsh Reconstruction Advisory Council, which saw the delayed extension of supply lines to the more remote reaches of Wales in terms of socio-economic exclusion. Indeed, Caernarvonshire representatives on the Council reckoned that the development of various hydroelectric schemes in Wales, far from solving the problem of rural areas, would merely contribute to the resolution of the national grid's peak load difficulties. They suggested, accordingly, that a single Welsh electricity board be established to oversee the development of electrical schemes in Wales and thereby to safeguard the interests of people living in the country. The Caernarvonshire proposal was rejected, however, by a majority of representatives of other local authorities, who divined the idea of a single electricity board for Wales as a precursor to the Nationalist commitment that Wales be treated as a separate entity, administrative and otherwise.[26] But the issue refused to disappear. After villagers in some south Cardiganshire parishes had been advised in 1957 that they would be unlikely to be connected for at least the next fifteen years, the local MP, Roderic Bowen, hinted at the desirability of a single Welsh electrical authority.[27] Gwynfor Evans, a leading figure in the Welsh Nationalist movement, was far more forthright and regularly vented his spleen over the vexed issue of the net export of electricity from Wales into the national grid. He raised the matter in the House of Commons in 1968, but the Labour government

58   Richard Moore-Colyer

took little notice, the Ministry of Power refusing to be drawn on the matter of the administrative structure of the electricity industry.[28]

Political debate, argument and rhetoric would do little to resolve the issue of electricity supply which continued to be a matter of concern for another two decades. County Development Plans, required by the government under the terms of the Town and Country Planning Act of 1947, lay heavy emphasis on the vital need for the rapid spread of rural electrification. The plans for Flint and Merioneth (1951) embraced schemes whereby supply lines would be developed, the Brecon plan (1954) emphasised the 'sad neglect' of the electrification of the countryside, while the Carmarthen plan (1954) noted that though it was unreasonable to expect the provision of electricity to resolve the problems of the rural world, it would nevertheless 'do much to raise the standard of living of country folk'.[29]

The twelve regional Electricity Boards, established under the 1947 Electricity Act, were charged to secure as far as possible the extension of cheap supplies of electricity to the countryside of Britain. But few involved with the newly nationalised electricity industry had any illusions about the financial and logistical difficulties involved. In 1950 the provision of a single carriageway 'A' road cost around 30 shillings per linear yard, and mains water supply some 12 shillings. By comparison, high-tension electricity cable was priced at 50 shillings per linear yard, amounting to £4,000 per mile.[30] Given that the Merseyside and North Wales Electricity Board alone would need to erect more than 3,000 miles of high-tension cable on steel pylons if every village, hamlet and farm were to be reached, it was an awesome undertaking. Besides, setting up the 132,000 volt cables was merely the overture to the complete work. Sequences of transformers on distribution and supply lines were required to step down voltage before it reached the consumer, hundreds of thousands of poles and insulators had to be secured, way leaves had to be negotiated, compensation for disturbance paid and recalcitrant and disputatious land owners pacified. With the cost of connection to individual houses and farms being estimated in 1948 at between £200 and £400, it was inevitable that rural provision would initially be unremunerative for electricity boards in north and south Wales and the enterprise would have to be subsidised by revenue from urban consumers. Return on the heavy investment would only accrue as consumption increased and, perhaps not unnaturally, there was a tendency for the two Welsh boards to concentrate their efforts in rural areas of greater population density. Thus it was more feasible for the South Wales Electricity Board to push out into rural Glamorgan (sixty-seven people per 100 arable acres) and Monmouth (sixty-nine), or the Merseyside and North Wales Electricity Board to extend its activities into the Flintshire countryside (eighty-nine), than for the latter to move into Ceredigion, Montgomery and Radnor whose populations amounted to little more than eight or nine people for every 100 acres of arable land.[31]

The massive project was further hampered by the post-war credit squeeze and the insistence by government that Electricity Boards maintained expenditure within strict limits. With tedious regularity questions to Ministers regarding the slow rate of rural electrification in parts of Wales and elsewhere were countered with the riposte that developments in this area could only proceed when the country could afford the capital resources. With real term cuts in capital expenditure imposed in 1949, the Ministry of Fuel and Power had no choice but to announce that rapid progress in rural electrification would be 'impossible in the immediate future'.[32] To the chagrin of many, the South Wales Electricity Board was asking for capital contributions from individual villages towards the cost of linking the community to the mains. Raising the issue in the House of Commons late in 1954, Tudor Watkins, Member for Brecon and Radnor, pointed out that while the villages of Nantmel and Gladestry had been asked to pay £160 and £625 respectively, places like St Harmon, Llanwrthl and Pantydwr had not been approached for contributions. In response, the Parliamentary Secretary to the Minister of Fuel and Power, David Joynson-Hicks, explained the apparent anomaly by indicating that Boards could levy charges where revenue from use did not meet (or was anticipated as not likely to meet) annual charges and interest on installation costs. If only Watkins could persuade his constituents to use more power, he observed, then both connection charges and overall tariffs would decline.[33]

Desperately keen to stimulate consumption to satisfy government insistence that annual revenue met expenditure, the Boards went to enormous efforts to persuade farmers and other country folk of the benefits of electricity and the wide range of its application. The Boards were no tyros when it came to propaganda, the British Electrical Development Association having been set up for the purpose of promoting domestic consumption as early as 1919.[34] Advertising space was bought in farming and trade magazines and lectures and demonstrations were held throughout Wales as farmers, blacksmiths, garage proprietors, quarry owners, factory managers, shopkeepers and others were urged and exhorted to make full use of public supplies once they became available. Nor did the Welsh countrywoman escape the attention of the Boards and their seductive advertising activity. The Electrical Association for Women, which ran from 1924 to 1986 and sought to modernise the British household by educating housewives about the uses of electricity, played little part in Wales, where the coal-fired iron range of Victorian vintage had long been deemed sufficient for most households.[35] Even so, the two Welsh Boards targeted housewives in their forays to school and church hall, where dedicated demonstrators exposed the wonders of electrical cooking methods to a sometimes sceptical audience. Indeed, these intensive campaigns of the 1950s and 1960s could be hard going for the lady demonstrators who journeyed into the depths of the Welsh countryside. As they tried to persuade audiences of the virtues of electrical appliances as against the iron range, the smelly paraffin-oil cooking stove, the flat iron and the wet battery powered wireless, they came up against some resistance. Many women, delighted to replace their candles or 'Aladdin' oil lamps with

60   Richard Moore-Colyer

electric lighting, were chary of spending scarce disposable cash on electrical gadgets which could revolutionise kitchen life. The 'electric kitchen', pioneered at the Columbia Exhibition in Chicago in 1893, had been emulated by the City of London Electric Light Company the following year when six electric ovens were enlisted to feed 120 guests who sat down to the world's first all-electric banquet.[36] The early cast-iron electric cooker, expensive and ugly though it might have been, at least offered the chance of accurate temperature control and thus more culinary precision. Yet these were to have little real impact on the Welsh country kitchen for many years as women kept faith with their range, coal-fired 'Rayburn' or 'Aga', only turning to electricity (perhaps in the form of the 'Baby Belling', available by 1935 at £4 per cooker) when cooking temperature needed to be carefully controlled.[37]

The adoption of electricity in household and on farm presupposed the availability of a supply and while there had been some progress in parts of south Wales and the countryside of the north-east, the situation in the rural mid-Wales counties remained poor. Starved of capital investment, decent road infrastructure and piped water supplies and bedevilled by the running sore of depopulation, the farmscape of Ceredigion, Radnor and Montgomery remained largely free of public electricity supplies into the mid-1950s. The figures in Table 4.1 starkly reveal the situation in sample parishes.

Table 4.1 Electricity supply to farmsteads, 1955 (number of farms).

Parish	No supply	Wind	Water	Oil	Engine	Private	Public
Blaenpennal	60	0	0	2	1	0	66
Caron is Clawdd	88	0	2	7	0	20	117
Caron uwch Clawdd	27	0	0	2	0	13	42
Cwm Rheidol	58	0	4	4	10	0	76
Gwnnws issa	32	0	0	1	0	0	33
Llanddewibrefi	75	0	0	3	0	11	89
Lower Lledrod	49	0	0	4	5	0	58
Gwnnws uchaf	45	0	1	2	0	14	62
Llanfihangel y Creuddyn	55	4	4	3	5	1	72
Upper Lledrod	32	0	0	4	0	0	36
Ysbyty Ystwyth	21	0	1	0	0	23	45
Llangurig	133	1	6	5	1	0	146
Abbey Cwmhir	29	0	0	2	1	32	
Beguildy	48	0	1	5	0	8	62
Llananno	27	0	0	0	0	0	27
Llanbadarn Ffynydd	35	0	1	1	0	0	37
Llanbister	92	0	0	3	0	0	95

Parish	No supply	Wind	Water	Oil	Engine	Private	Public
Llanddewi Ystradenni	47	1	0	1	0	4	53
Llansantffraid Cwmdeuddwr	45	0	0	4	0	1	50
Nantmel	107	0	1	4	0	12	124
St. Harmon	72	0	1	3	0	4	80
Rhayader	0	0	0	0	0	2	2
Total	1180	6	22	60	23	113	1404

Source: *Mid Wales Investigational Report*, HMSO, 1955, Cmd. 9631.

Table 4.2 Analysis of work in mid-Wales on approved schemes under the Hill Farming Act and the Livestock Rearing Act (as at 30 June 1955).

	Proposed	Completed and claimed
Farm buildings	£154,711	£59,594
Farmhouses	£143,192	£60,430
Water supplies	£33,321	£11,098
Electricity supplies	£22,074	£8,254
Fencing	£101,915	£31,174
Lime, reseeding etc.	£181,216	£39,550

Source: *Mid Wales Investigational Report*, HMSO, 1955, Cmd. 9631.

Among the various pieces of legislation designed to promote the expansion of post-war British agriculture as a means of saving on the balance of payments account (and collaterally of helping to feed a starving Europe), the Hill Farming Act 1946 and the Livestock Rearing Act 1951 were of profound importance to Wales. In essence, the two Acts ushered in grant aid at the level of 50 per cent for schemes of capital investment involving the improvement of farmhouses and buildings and the laying on of water and electricity supplies. In parallel ran non-comprehensive production grants for the purposes of drainage and fencing, grassland improvement and renovation, the application of lime and other means of boosting the output of the pastoral landscape. The official returns suggest that alongside these various demands on taxpayers' capital, electricity was accorded relatively low priority by farmers (Table 4.2).

Over the course of the following decade, progress throughout Britain as a whole was rapid, and as the National Farmers' Union lobbied government in the hope of securing additional funding for the Electricity Boards in the interest of rural electrification, the Minister of Fuel and Power finally ordered relaxations on capital expenditure restrictions. He concurrently announced

62   Richard Moore-Colyer

a structured programme of rural electrification which would ensure that 85 per cent of all farms in England and Wales would be connected by 1963.[38] In the event this target was achieved eighteen months ahead of schedule and by March 1964 over 90 per cent of potential farm customers in England and Wales were supplied from the grid compared to 33 per cent in 1947–1948. But, yet again, Wales, or at least the essentially pastoral counties of mid-Wales, remained a relative backwater as returns from the Annual Reports of the two Welsh boards reveal (Table 4.3).

Within two years of the publication of these figures, the South Wales Electricity Board was confidently able to assert that by the end of March 1964 85 per cent of all farms would be connected, while the Merseyside and North Wales Electricity Board claimed that this level would be met by late March 1963.[39]

Within two years, 94 per cent of Welsh farmsteads enjoyed mains electricity.[40] There remained, however, serious problems for the relatively impoverished mid-Wales region, in particular for occupiers of distant upland farms where low incomes and inadequate amenities had long been a cause for concern. After the 1963 Select Committee on Nationalised Industries had recommended that the Electricity Boards set a limit to their contribution to the cost of supplying remote farms, government directed that such holdings should only be connected 'at an economic rate'.[41] In other words, the government continued to repeat the mantra that each Electricity Board should earn a return on project investment consistent with agreed financial objectives, which meant that in the case of rural electrification farmers would have to contribute significantly towards the cost of connection. However, limited capital reserves and low annual incomes meant that whatever the advantages of a reliable electricity supply may have been, farmers in the central upland counties thought very carefully before committing themselves to the supply as it became available. As Table 4.2 implies, they were probably more inclined to invest their own or borrowed capital into projects likely to have an immediate and tangible effect on income than the mere provision of electricity. They had, after all, farmed in the darkness for generations. In any event, by the winter of 1969, 1,200 farms in the five mid-Wales counties

Table 4.3 Percentage of farms connected to public electricity supplies between nationalisation in 1948 and 31 March 1961.

County	Number of farms	% connected on 1 April 1948	% connected on 31 March 1961
Brecon	1,881	0	56.0
Radnor	1,353	0	40.0
Cardigan	4,595	3.2	60.7
Merioneth	2,116	4.2	53.3
Montgomery	4,379	3.7	58.4

Rural electrification in Wales 63

remained unconnected although all had been offered terms by the Electricity Boards and virtually all were eligible for grant aid under the Hill Farming and Livestock Rearing Acts.[42]

Although the Electricity Boards frequently bemoaned the low rate of uptake of electricity by British farmers throughout the 1960s, distribution lines from the grid continued to snake their way into the more remote areas.[43] Barn machinery, crop and forage drying systems, intensive livestock units and glasshouse crops benefited enormously and holdings with these sorts of enterprises were enabled to embrace a plethora of new technology. Rural electrification was indeed an essential component of the unprecedented advances in agricultural productivity characteristic of the 1960s and 1970s. But much of the countryside of Wales and almost all of the hills and uplands were hardly in a position to exploit much of the new technology. Factors of climate, soil type and elevation, juxtaposed with the theorem of comparative advantage, predicated that much of the country remained the province of livestock, notably sheep and cattle. While the availability of an electricity supply yielded massive benefits to the dairy farm, took a great deal of the sweat out of the annual task of sheep shearing, and eased the difficulties of managing in-wintered livestock, its application was strictly limited by the nature of the enterprises practiced on the Welsh farm. As Manweb and Swalec extended their activities and the final tentacles of the grid reached all but the most distant farms by the late 1960s and early 1970s, the Electricity Council continued manfully with its drive to persuade Welsh farmers to consume more kilowatt-hours thereby to reduce unit costs. But as Table 4.4 suggests, once farms were equipped with a basic supply of electricity for house, barn and milking shed, little more was required and annual consumption hardly altered between the mid-1960s and 1980. It should be noted that the decline in quinquennial averages of farm numbers after 1961–1965 was due essentially to a rise in farm amalgamations resulting from retirements or from farmers leaving the industry.[44]

Cliché it may be, but it is no bad thing for historians to walk their battlefields. More often than not, a few hours at the location of an event can reveal more understanding and insight than a week of archival research or a

Table 4.4 Mean numbers of Welsh farms (thousands) connected to public electricity supplies and annual electricity consumption (millions of units), 1949–1980.

	1949	1950–1954	1955–1960	1961–1965	1966–1970	1971–1975	1976–1980
Farms	6.2	10.0	26.5	43.6	43.0	31.2	28.9
Consumption	17	31.8	106.0	200.0	261.2	260.6	259.3

Sources: Digest of Welsh Statistics, 1954–1980, London: HMSO; Electricity Council, *Annual Reports*, 1964–1972, London: HMSO.

64   *Richard Moore-Colyer*

similar time spent foraging among official documents. On this basis, anyone with any doubts as to the immediate, obvious and dramatic advantages of electric light in particular to the livestock farmer should set out on a wet and windy March night to attend to a sick animal equipped only with a hurricane lantern or a less than reliable acetylene torch. Or he might care to round up and drive a herd of recalcitrant cows from field to byre on a winter's morning and set about milking them by hand in semi-darkness. Light alone was of enormous practical benefit. Moreover, there were additional and more subtle advantages to be gained from the availability of clean, safe and reliable power. In the sense that a man could go about his winter farm tasks without the fear of stumbling in darkness, or missing some vital husbandry detail in the encircling gloom, the electric light offered a tremendous psychological boost. And if the electric motor removed much of the physical effort from many farmyard tasks, it might even be argued, without stretching the point too far, that it went some way towards promoting greater domestic harmony. If a man could complete his work rather earlier in the day, walk into his kitchen without being totally exhausted and enjoy the company of his wife and family for a few hours of the evening, an essential element of home life would be fulfilled. This would be of growing importance over the decades as servants and farm labourers declined in number and farmers became increasingly reliant on the input of their wives.[45] On the lonely and isolated hill or upland farm where a man might spend days or even weeks working entirely on his own, a convivial domestic life was of the first importance. Electricity, by easing the lot of both the farmer in his barn and the wife in her kitchen, may have gone some way towards promoting it.

Yet if rural electrification carried such advantages, why was it not adopted with boundless enthusiasm once supplies became available? Whether or not a single Welsh authority devoted to the interests of Wales rather than the demands of the national grid would have more effectively ensured a supply of power to rural areas, the fact is that, by the late 1960s, the overwhelming majority of farms had access to a public supply. In the arable vales of Glamorgan, Clwyd, south-eastern and eastern Wales, where forage and cereal crop drying was of importance and where poultry and intensive livestock units were common, farmers were keen to secure mains electricity even where they had to contribute to the cost of bringing supplies to the holding. The relatively high gross output of these farms per unit area, and, in the case of intensive poultry and pigs, per unit of electricity, totally justified the costs of installation. But in the hills and uplands and the distant valleys of the heartland the situation was entirely different. The low value of outputs from the extensive livestock farm, the inherent inefficiencies and uncertainties of hill farming and the chronic undercapitalisation of that sector of Welsh farming engendered a cautious and conservative view of potential change. For generations, the upland farmer – proud, fiercely independent and physically isolated by dint of poor communications – had been chary of innovation.

Rural electrification in Wales 65

To invest scarce capital, or to borrow money to plough into projects of dubious merit (which he and his ancestors had noticed to have been the practice of 'fashionable' gentleman farmers of the past) seemed to him to be a highly questionable exercise. The low level of uptake of grant aid in mid-Wales in the first few years after the passing of the Hill Farming and Livestock Rearing Acts is indicative of the widespread sense of caution abroad in the upland farming world. Electricity may well have offered all the benefits mentioned earlier, but these came at a price, and a price which went beyond financial considerations. When the Mid-Wales Investigational Report of 1955 implicitly attributed the conservative perspective of the hill farmer to his concern at the possibility of the disintegration of a centuries-old tradition, it hit upon a basic truth. Whereas in Britain as a whole, and indeed in much of lowland Wales, farming had by now become essentially a business with the pursuit of profit as the principal motivation, this was far less so in the hills and uplands. Of course, only a fool would deny that he farmed to make a surplus, yet few would claim to be interested in profit maximisation. On the other hand, these windswept, lonely holdings were the repositories of an older way of life which emphasised independence, self-sufficiency, respect for the past, concern for the longer-term future, a passionate sense of attachment to the land and a deep suspicion of the short term 'quick fix'.[46] To many denizens of the hills, moreover, the conservation of the Welsh language (at serious risk in the 1950s), the completion of a poem, or winning the local *eisteddfod* was every bit as important as enhancing the efficiency of the farm. Besides, local cultural prominence carried with it a status in society that the possession of mere money could never deliver.

The preservation of older values (still raised from time to time in the early twenty-first century as a justification for Treasury or European Community support for the Welsh hills and uplands) was all very well, but was hardly compatible with post-war agricultural policy which demanded the maximum output from every available acre. From today's post-productivist viewpoint, when environmental, amenity and ecological issues appear to be accorded more importance than food production, it is easy to forget the vital role of the Welsh hills in the complex structure of British agricultural systems in the immediate past. The hills and uplands provided the breeding stock which formed the basis of the British sheep farming industry and a high proportion of the cows which bred calves to feed in to the lowland beef sector. The essential importance of the upland regions in these respects was recognised by the generous financial aid available under the Hill Farming and Livestock Rearing Acts which, in addition, helped to reduce the haemorrhage of people from the upland areas of Wales.[47] Moreover, lobbyists from various sectors of the political spectrum recognised that the rate of rural depopulation would decline with the increased productivity of agriculture which itself would be enhanced with the development of decent communications, clean and reliable water supplies and electrical power. Electrification was just one strand of a complex web of economic and structural developments which

66   Richard Moore-Colyer

were necessary to prevent the virtual desertion of the more isolated parishes of the mid-Wales area in particular.

If there were still a few who clung to the belief that in the wake of the electric light would follow every conceivable species of villainy and evil, the overwhelming majority of the upland farming community embraced the technology as it became available. Throughout the 1960s and 1970s, a raft of economic and fiscal measures helped promote a growth of agrarian prosperity and stimulated widespread agronomic improvements, all of which became feasible once the rural infrastructure was in place. But for all this, the hills and uplands continued to represent a system of communities existing within a closely knit framework of meaningful social relationships underpinned by a mythic tradition, itself arising from the rhythms of the farming world. Respect for language, tradition, history and community eventually remained keystones of upland agrarian life. Technologies might have come and gone, economic circumstances might have changed, yet the bonds which linked the hill farmer of Wales to his locality and community were as deeply rooted as ever.

Acknowledgments

An earlier version of this chapter was published as 'Lighting the Landscape: Rural Electrification in Wales', *The Welsh History Review*, Volume 23, Number 4 (2007), pp. 72–92.

Notes

1   R. H. Morgan, 'The development of the electricity supply industry in Wales to 1919', *Welsh History Review*, vol. 11 (3), 1983, p. 317.
2   R. H. Morgan, 'The development of the electricity supply industry in south Wales to 1939', in C. Baber and J. Williams (eds), *Modern Wales: Essays in economic history.* Cardiff: University of Wales Press, 1986, p. 223.
3   A. Jones, 'The introduction of public electricity to Abergavenny', *Gwent Local History*, vol. 92, 2002, pp. 67–83; Jones, 'The old chestnut: The introduction of electricity to Abergavenny', *Transactions of the Newcomen Society*, vol. 72, 2000–1, pp. 127–145.
4   T. Evans, 'Electricity comes to Aberystwyth', *Ceredigion*, vol. 13 (4), 2000, p. 75.
5   D. Pugh, 'Electricity in Newtown', *The Newtonian*, vol. 15, 2003, p. 17.
6   D. W. Thomas, 'Historical notes on hydro-electricity in north Wales', *Caernarvonshire Historical Society Transactions*, vol. 50, 1989, p. 88.
7   Electricity Council, *Electricity supply in the United Kingdom: A chronology from the beginnings of the industry to 1985.* London: The Council, 1987, p. 37; C. D. Whetham, 'Electric power in agriculture', *Journal of the Royal Agricultural Society of England*, vol. 85, 1924, p. 265.
8   D. Slyfield, 'Dolgellau and its electricity supply, 1935', *Journal of the Merionethshire Historical and Record Society*, vol. 12, 1994–7, pp. 197–198.
9   T. Boyns, 'The electricity supply in south Wales to 1949', *Welsh History Review*, vol. 15, 1990, p. 79.

Rural electrification in Wales   67

10 *Report of the Committee appointed by the Board of trade to consider the question of the Electrical Power Supply* (1918), Cmd. 9062; *Report of the Committee appointed to review the National problem of the supply of Electrical Energy, 1925*. London: HMSO, 1927.
11 Baber and Williams, *Modern Wales*, p. 236.
12 Evans, 'Electricity comes to Aberystwyth', p. 79.
13 A. W. Gray, *Electricity supply in the rural areas*. London: Eyre and Spottiswoode, 1968, p. 5.
14 R. B. Matthews, *Electro-Farming; or the application of electricity to agriculture*. London: Ernest Benn, 1928, p. 6.
15 D. G. Turner, 'Rural electrification and the pioneering schemes of the Hereford Corporation, 1919–28', *Transactions of the Newcomen Society*, vol. 51, 1979–80, p. 124.
16 Parliamentary Debates (Commons), vol. 184, 1924–5, p. 74.
17 E. W. Golding, *The electrification of agriculture and the rural districts*. London: English Universities Press, 1937, p. 56.
18 W. H. Jones, *Development and uses of electricity in rural Wales*. Aberystwyth: University of Aberystwyth, 1938.
19 A. W. Ashby and W. H. Jones, 'Light, heat and power in rural areas: Uses of electricity in South Wales', Welsh Housing and Development Yearbook. Cardiff: Welsh Housing and Development Association, 1933.
20 W. H. Jones, *Light and power on farms: A study of the uses of electricity in South Wales*. Aberystwyth: Department of Agricultural Economics, University College of Wales, 1932.
21 Jones, *Development and use of electricity in rural Wales*.
22 R. J. Moore-Colyer, 'Farming in depression: Wales between the wars, 1919–1939', *Agricultural History Review*, vol. 46 (2), 1998, pp. 177–196.
23 A. D. Rees, *Life in a Welsh Countryside*. Cardiff: University of Wales Press, 1975, p. 48.
24 J. Slater and M. Jones, 'A survey of Welsh hill farm mechanisation', *Journal of Agricultural Engineering Research*, vol. 2 (3), 1975, pp. 222–234.
25 *Report of the Committee on Land Utilisation in Rural Areas*, Cmd. 6378, 1942.
26 National Library of Wales, ex. 24, Association of Welsh Local Authorities.
27 Parliamentary Debates (Commons), 578, 1957–8.
28 Parliamentary Debates (Commons), 760, 1967–8.
29 County Development Plans, 1951–1954.
30 *Mid Wales Investigational Report*, Cmd. 9631, 1955.
31 A. D. Hooper, *Rural electrification and the farming community in Wales*. Aberystwyth: Department of Agricultural Economics, University College of Wales, 1952.
32 Parliamentary Debates (Commons), 470, 1948–9, p. 427.
33 Parliamentary Debates (Commons), 529, 1953–4, pp. 560–588.
34 H. Self and E. M. Watson, *Electricity supply in Great Britain: Its development and organisation*. London: George Allen and Unwin, 1952, p. 71.
35 C. Pursell, 'Domestic modernity: The Electrical Association for Women, 1924–86', *British Journal for the History of Science*, vol. 32, 1999, pp. 47–67.
36 A. Byers, *Centenary of service: A history of electricity in the home*. London: Electricity Council, 1981, pp. 24–29.
37 S. M. Tibbott, 'Going electric: The changing face of the rural kitchen in Wales, 1945–55', *Folk Life*, vol. 28, 1989–90, pp. 64–72.
38 Electricity Council, *Electricity supply in the United Kingdom: A chronology from the beginnings of the industry to 1985*. London: The Council, 1987, p. 58; National Farmers Union, *British agriculture looks ahead*. London: NFU, 1964, p. 70.

68   *Richard Moore-Colyer*

39 *Report of the Committee on Depopulation in Mid-Wales*, Ministry of Welsh Affairs, June 1963.
40 Parliamentary Debates (Commons), 741, 1966–7, p. 673.
41 Parliamentary Debates (Commons), 728, 1966–7, pp. 182–183.
42 Parliamentary Debates (Commons), 787, 1968–9, pp. 318–319.
43 Electricity Council, *Annual Report*, 1964–5, London, 1965.
44 This, in fact, was merely the continuation of a trend which had been going on since the end of the war, to the effect that total holding numbers declined from 55,692 in 1948 to 31,996 in 1978.This trend was officially encouraged and even assisted by various forms of grant aid in the belief that the larger the farm, the more efficient its operation. While economies of scale can be exploited on the larger unit, the advantages of the larger farm are at present being seriously challenged on sociocultural and environmental grounds: See P. Midmore and R. J. Moore-Colyer, *Cherished heartland: Future of the uplands of Wales*. Cardiff: Institute of Welsh Affairs, 2005.
45 J. Lees and R. J. Moore-Colyer, *Hill farming in Wales: Manpower and training needs*. London: Agricultural and Horticultural Industries Training Board, 1973.
46 Which remains very much the case today: See Midmore and Moore-Colyer, *Cherished heartland*.
47 J. Saville, *Rural depopulation in England and Wales, 1851–1951*. London: Routledge and Kegan Paul, 1957.

5 The electrification of Highland Scotland

David Fleetwood

Introduction

Scotland has a proud international history of being at the vanguard of engineering and infrastructure on a global scale, and it is not only through the ships built on the river Clyde that Scottish engineering and technology has had a worldwide footprint. Scotland was also at the forefront of the creation of infrastructure from the nineteenth century onwards, both in developments at home, such as the Loch Katrine water supply system taking clean drinking water to Glasgow, and internationally such as the water supply system in Taipei designed by William K. Burton. Scotland also played a pioneering role in the development of electricity, in particular from hydro power, and it was the introduction of this technology in particular which had a radical effect on the country, bringing electrical power to communities throughout the country and overcoming the not insignificant challenges of the nation's topography.

The history of the development of the electricity supply industry in Scotland and related infrastructure for the transmission of this power across the country both to heavy industry in the central belt and to the smallest settlements in the North and West of Scotland is one which includes state intervention, international technology breakthroughs and a uniquely Scottish approach to the role which infrastructure development could have in transforming lives across the country.

This chapter will consider this history, focusing on the provision of power to rural communities in Highland Scotland. By providing a snapshot of the Scotland which existed before the onset of national infrastructure projects and contrasting this to the Scotland which emerged by the latter half of the twentieth century, in particular following the great national project for the development of Scotland's water power resources for hydroelectric power, the chapter will examine the social changes delivered. However, by largely focusing on the story about Highland Scotland this chapter only includes a passing reference to the story of the large rural areas of Southern Scotland, primarily in the Borders and Dumfries and Galloway. These areas also have a fascinating story to tell about the role infrastructure played in driving

70   *David Fleetwood*

rural development, some of which is shared with the story of Highland Scotland. However, this would require a more comprehensive research project to give more than a cursory overview at this stage. This development was perhaps most dramatic in the Highlands and West of Scotland, where what had once been remote rural settlements were transformed into industrial societies, and in many cases this was accompanied by an influx of new faces to communities across North and West Scotland, including many from abroad. This chapter will focus on the radical phase of development across Highland Scotland for industry and electrical power and contrast this with the social and economic position of Scotland before these developments.

The powerful transformative force of electricity and industry on Scotland has shaped the nation we know today, and in particular the national project for the development of the nation's hydro power resources after the Second World War remains a key part of Scotland's national identity.

Highland Scotland before electricity

The development of electricity supply and industry throughout the North and West of Scotland in particular transformed what had previously been an area of the country challenged by difficult topography and characterised by relatively dispersed rural settlements, large landed estates and coastal communities. Whilst there was not a total absence of industry, which included coal mining at Brora in Sutherland, this tended to be of a relatively small scale. In many areas there had been limited changes to the structure of society from the nineteenth to twentieth centuries, making the coming of electricity to these areas even more radical a change when it eventually occurred.

During the nineteenth century the Highlands remained traditional and had few connections to the Scottish Enlightenment or the emerging industrial revolution in the south of Scotland, focused in particular on the central belt.[1] Wealthy landlords were intent on protecting their income from Highland estates, focusing on the development of a sheep-based economy and eroding away the patriarchal structure of society which had existed in earlier periods. Ultimately this resulted in the highland clearances with landowners displacing tenants from their Highland estates in favour of sheep which offered a better economic return.

Following the removal of tenants from the highland landscape during the clearances, alongside the high levels of emigration and men enlisting for military service, a new class emerged in the Highlands, that of the crofter.[2] These poor families lived on marginal land, with small rented plots providing a subsistence on growing potatoes and harvesting kelp. The condition of crofters was a perilous one, and as in Ireland the failure of the potato crop had disastrous effects. In 1851 such a failure of the crop led to disastrous conditions across the Highlands, Sir John MacNeil observing that 'the inhabitants of these distressed districts have neither capital enough to cultivate the extent of the land necessary to maintain them if it could be

The electrification of Highland Scotland 71

provided, nor have they land enough were the capital provided to them.'[3] This 'central dilemma of the crofter economy' pervaded well into the twentieth century.[4] It was the impact of the fundamental failure of the socio-economic system on the people of Highland Scotland that the development of industry and electricity supply set out to tackle. Clearly for society to be radically changed by the development and supply of electricity in Highland Scotland, a very significant socio-economic shift was required.

Early development of electricity supply

The early history of the use of electricity for both domestic and industrial supply is intrinsically bound up with the development of hydro power, as this provided an accessible form of generation. However, in the absence of the technology and capacity to transfer electricity over significant distances supply was always close to the area of consumption. Despite the challenging social conditions, or perhaps partly because of them, it was Highland Scotland which was at the forefront of the development of electricity supply from the late 1800s. Whilst larger-scale power generation was increasingly common in England and in the central belt of Scotland, mainly based on thermal power generation using coal, this was not the case in Highland Scotland where there are no significant reserves of coal. Instead, Scotland followed the model developed in alpine and Nordic nations, using the steep topography and high rainfall to generate power from the abundant supplies of water. These early developments also illustrated the social conscience of the industry from an early stage, with supply being extended to local communities, as far as technology would allow.

One of the earliest developments in Scotland was at Fort Augustus on Loch Ness, where an 18-kilowatt scheme was developed as early as 1891. The scheme used the water from the river Tarff and was developed by the Augustinian monastery to power its electric organ and the lights of the village. The local legend suggested that when the monks played the organ the lights of the village went two shades dimmer!

There was a range of similar small developments across the Highlands. In Strathpeffer the Raven's Rock Hotel advertised the novelty of its frontage being lit by electric light from 1903. However, this particular scheme illustrated the problems of the widespread adoption of electric power through the Highlands. The market for the power, outwith the façade of the hotel, was limited. Many of the surrounding communities were still relatively undeveloped, with some houses no different from those described by authors in the nineteenth century and hardly suited to electric light. The scheme failed in 1920 and was only resurrected when it was absorbed into a large scheme after the Second World War.

Before 1930, it was not the use of electrical power for domestic supply which revolutionised the Highlands, but the localised generation of Direct Current (DC) power for the electrochemical industry, namely the production

72   David Fleetwood

of aluminium. The production of aluminium removed the barriers to development which had challenged the Raven's Rock development, as there was no requirement for significant transfers of power and the market was assured through the presence of an industrial consumer on the same site. In 1894 the British Aluminium Company (BAC), then newly formed, purchased the British and colonial rights to the Hall Heroualt smelting process, which required large amounts of DC power for electrolysis. The topography which proved so challenging for the development of infrastructure was advantageous for BAC as it provided them with access to cheap electricity through the use of high-head hydro.

The development of the Foyers scheme, also on Loch Ness, from 1894 onwards was the first of three major schemes developed by BAC which revolutionised parts of the Highlands and saw the development of new industrialised communities in what had previously been undeveloped rural communities. As early as 1895 the potential for electrical power to radically change the social and economic conditions of the Highlands was widely recognised. An article in the *Northern Chronicle* suggested that 'the founding in the Highlands of manufacturing or other industries calculated to develop local resources and provide employment and increase a resident population is deserving of the warmest encouragement and support.'[5]

Alongside the development of a power station and smelter at Foyers, BAC also created a small community with houses for workers and other social infrastructure including a school. By the standards of the surrounding rural settlements the houses were of a high standard and powered by electric light and appliances. This approach, both to the creation of social infrastructure and the high quality of architecture and design developed by BAC for the Foyers scheme, set the pattern for future developments across Highland Scotland. By 1905 the scheme was producing over 5 per cent of the worldwide output of aluminium.

The BAC expanded the concept which they had pioneered at Foyers, with a hugely ambitious development at Kinlochleven with an Act of Parliament in 1904. The creation of the 13 km long Blackwater reservoir through one of the earliest examples of a reinforced concrete dam, which stopped the river Blackwater, provided the water for a scheme which was completed in 1909. Such was the scale of the Kinlochleven development that it received international attention on its completion. Along with Foyers there was nearly a third of worldwide aluminium production coming from Highland Scotland. Much like the development at Foyers, the creation of the Kinlochleven scheme was accompanied by the creation of social infrastructure with a range of housing for engineers and workers as well as lodging for visitors and a school and medical provision. All of this was created at the head of a loch which had previously been home to a tiny rural community. Clearly, electricity had the power to revolutionise the socio-economic position of Highland Scotland.

The government also recognised the potential for electricity to have a significant impact on the prosperity of the Highlands. However, despite the successes of the BAC schemes, the problems of the necessary number of consumers willing to pay for power and the challenges of transmitting power to remote consumers remained. To this were increasingly added concerns of landowners and early tourist operators about the impact of development on the scenic amenity of the landscape.

A Board of Trade Committee was established in 1918 to investigate Britain's water power resources. The committee was chaired by Sir John Snell who was strongly persuaded by the opportunity presented by hydro power to shape a modern and forward looking society which would significantly change the way people lived across Britain. Snell's vision was a far-reaching one, which had a significant impact on later developments. He outlined a pattern of development focused on the use of multiple power stations throughout a single catchment which provided power both to their local community, and, when aggregated on a national scale would prove revolutionary on a national scale. Snell shared this vision of the socially transformative power of electricity in the Highlands with the chief engineer for the BAC schemes. In 1935 William Murray Morrison wrote in a letter to a friend, Dr Lachlan Grant, that 'it is a most pleasing recollection in my career that I have been able to do some practical and lasting good to my beloved Highlands.'[6]

Development of the national grid

Whilst the transformative effect of the introduction of electricity to the Highlands of Scotland had been proven by the BAC schemes, and validated by the vision of Snell, endorsed by government, the practicalities of delivering this vision across rural Scotland was still a significant problem, something which for some areas of the Highlands and Western Isles would last into the 1990s.

The BAC schemes had demanded a high level of technical skill and innovation in order to deliver the breakthroughs represented by these schemes and equal innovation was required to overcome the technical challenges required to deliver Snell's vision across Highland Scotland. Two Scottish engineers were critical to this vision being achieved these men were Edward (later Sir Edward) MacColl and James T. W. Williamson. MacColl had long experience with electrical power, having worked on the electrification of the Glasgow tram system, a project which required electricity transfer over a wide metropolitan area. MacColl was also chief technical engineer of the Clyde Valley Electrical Power Company which developed two hydro power stations on the Falls of Clyde just outside Glasgow. At the same time James Williamson was working with landowners in Kirkcudbrightshire in the far south-west of Scotland on a proposed hydro development of a quite significant size. However, what led the coal industry to nickname the Falls of Clyde

74   *David Fleetwood*

Scheme 'MacColl's folly' and for Williamson's development to fall through was the lack of an effective grid infrastructure to transport the power from sources of production to areas of consumption.[7] Whilst the electrochemical industry had solved this problem by locating supply and consumption on the same site, by far the largest market was in the domestic and industrial consumers of the central belt of Scotland. These areas were largely served by thermal power stations and a fragmented system of local grids which were ineffective. This dispersed approach, largely driven by privately financed developments, left large tracts of rural Scotland with no electricity supply at all, and no prospect of one. Apart from those small areas adjacent to industrial developments in the Highlands, or benefiting from a landowner like the monks of Fort Augustus, supplying power was simply uneconomic.

The proof of concept for the development of a national grid was located not far south of the Scottish border, in the work of Charles Merz, of the Merz & McLellan consulting partnership. At his Neptune Bank Power Station near Newcastle upon Tyne the three-phase high voltage supply system pioneered by Nicola Tesla in his work for Westinghouse was employed.[8] This opened in 1901 and by 1912 had developed into the largest integrated power system in Europe.[9]

It was another Scot who took the development of the grid to the next level when in 1925, the British government asked Lord Weir to solve the problem of Britain's inefficient and fragmented electricity supply industry. After consulting with Merz on the potential for the development of a national integrated grid, the Electricity (Supply) Act 1926 was passed by Parliament, which recommended that a "national gridiron" supply system be created. The 1926 Act created the Central Electricity Board, which set up the UK's first synchronised, nationwide AC grid, running at 132 kV, 50 Hz.

The national grid began operating in 1933 as a series of regional grids with auxiliary interconnections for emergency use. There were no plans to link the grids in the short term, but after some unauthorised trials by engineers at night in 1937, by 1938 the grid was operating as a national system. The growth by then in the number of electricity users was the fastest in the world, rising from three-quarters of a million in 1920 to 9 million in 1938.[10] However, whilst the challenges of developing the grid in England and Wales were significant enough the transmission of power across the topography of Scotland was a further challenge to the newly formed grid. MacColl was appointed to the Central Electricity Board in 1927 and immediately began work on the technical challenge of the transmission of power over long distances, something which was critical to the supply of power across Scotland and also to the realisation of the potential for power generation infrastructure, including hydro, to be developed in Northern and Western Scotland. McColl pioneered the MacColl protective system which is a form of protective system used on electric power networks; it operates on the balanced principle embodying biased beam relays.[11] This technical breakthrough allowed for the transmission of power over longer distances and opened up the potential for the development of grid infrastructure throughout Scotland. There were some subsequent developments of the grid in the period in the run-up to the Second World War, but in Scotland this phase of development was largely concentrated on urban areas and the connection of the central belt.

The onset of the Second World War changed the priorities for the development of grid infrastructure, with the emphasis on connecting areas of strategic importance such as new barracks and military bases and maintaining the infrastructure damaged by attack from the air. This saw the construction of some 500 miles of new grid during the war.[12] For large areas of rural Scotland the prospect of a reliable connection to the grid had never been further away, despite the fact that by 1944 two out of every three houses nationwide had a connection.[13]

Nationalisation

The vision of one man changed this situation significantly, both through the development of a concerted national programme to create grid connections and also in a diversification of generation capacity away from coal and towards hydro power. The parallel development of hydro power and grid infrastructure was critical to the development of a robust system of electricity supply to rural Scotland, as the majority of the hydro power stations to be developed were in the Highlands and so the grid infrastructure was not only required for supply purposes, which would still have been uneconomic, but also to connect new centres of generation to the larger markets of southern Scotland.

The special status of the rural north of Scotland for the purposes of electricity supply was recognised from an early point in the post-war development of Britain's national grid. On 1 August 1948 the British electricity supply industry was nationalised. The British Electricity Authority (BEA) became responsible for the generation of electricity and its bulk transmission to fourteen separate statutory Area Electricity Boards. The board was also responsible for the co-ordination of the supply of electricity at a national level, with one notable exception – the north of Scotland. A very different story would develop here, with a strong social element and based on the overriding vision of one man who believed passionately in the role of electricity generation and supply in transforming societies in some of the most remote parts of the UK.

When Churchill reformed his cabinet in 1941 he made Tom Johnston (1882–1965) secretary of state for Scotland. Johnston was a long-standing supporter of the hydro power industry and believed in the potential of Scotland, and particularly the Highlands, for its development. Johnston made his appointment to the role as secretary of state subject to the establishment of a Commission under Lord Cooper to look at the potential of using Scotland's resources for hydro power and the wider issues associated with this,

76   David Fleetwood

including concerns over the impact on the landscape of any developments and also the necessary grid infrastructure.

The report was published on 15 December 1942 and presented a compelling vision for the development of the Highlands. It opened with a broadside against the competing visions which had stifled pre-war developments and the detrimental impact of this on the development of the Highlands in particular.[14] The report showcased how the provision of grid connections to areas of Invernesshire and Easter Ross had begun to transform communities in this area and also described the signs of economic recovery which accompanied this. The critical report that the committee made was that grid connections to these areas of the Highlands were simply impossible to conceive of through the traditional thermal power generation system which Scotland was largely reliant on in this period. Whilst this may suit the needs of the central belt, the committee was convinced that the only way to electrify northern Scotland was through hydro. The clear focus of the Cooper Report on the transformative potential of hydro power and the key role it would play in providing not only additional power resources to the south of Scotland, but also in connections for local communities throughout Highland Scotland and the Hebrides, was to have a very significant effect on how the recommendations of the Committee were implemented.

Johnston's ability to influence the agenda was coupled with the strong political will for the solutions to the issue of the economic deprivation of the Highlands and this saw the recommendations of the Cooper Committee become law by 1943. The Hydro Electric Development (Scotland) Act set the foundation for the state to develop hydro power throughout the Highlands and to use the availability of power as a transformative force in communities across the north of the country. It also formed the North of Scotland Hydroelectric Board (NoSHEB) which had responsibility for the development of hydroelectric power and the supply of power across Northern Scotland. Lord Alness, speaking for the government in the House of Lords during the passage of the Act, affirmed that the first duty of the Board was 'to provide supplies of electricity required to meet the demands of ordinary consumers in such parts of the North of Scotland District (including isolated areas)'.[15] This proved to be an enduring legacy of the Act.

Johnston's vision, now enshrined in the creation of the North of Scotland Hydroelectric Board through the 1943 Act, was heavily influenced by his own interests and his previous involvement in considering the use of industry to stimulate economic redevelopment. He had been involved in the commissioning of a polemical report from 1941 by Alan Reiach and Robert Hurd titled *Building Scotland* and was also strongly influenced by the Norwegian experience, where from 1945 a state policy was put in place to reconstruct the internal economy and assist in exports.[16] Critical to this approach was the provision of widespread electrical power generated through hydroelectricity.[17] He spurred NoSHEB into activity quickly, utilising compulsory purchase powers in the Act to buy land and begin developments. Aware

The electrification of Highland Scotland 77

of the need to quickly establish revenue generating schemes to support the delivery of the wider social vision, the first development at Sloy on the banks of Loch Lomond was well placed to provide power to Glasgow and act as the first in a series of income generating schemes.

Despite rapidly embarking on the vision established by the Cooper Committee and the Act, Johnston and NoSHEB faced an early challenge in continued debates around the future of electricity supply in Great Britain. Gwilym Lloyd George, then Minister of Fuel and Power, was amongst a number of parliamentarians who were quick to identify the scale of the challenge that NoSHEB had taken on. Speaking in 1944, he pointed out:

> The only district in Great Britain in which the Central Electricity Board, the owner of the grid, does not operate is the North of Scotland, which is covered by the provisions of the Hydro-Electric Development (Scotland) Act, 1943. The area of this district is about 23 per cent. of Great Britain and its population about 1½ per cent. Inside the grid area, however, there are numerous small rural districts which do not receive a public supply. I am unable to say exactly what percentage of the total population is at present within the area of public supply of electricity, but I am advised that it is certainly in excess of 90 per cent.[18]

Not only did Lloyd George see the challenge which NoSHEB had taken on, he also had ambitions to overhaul the national grid more comprehensively, including taking over the responsibilities which NoSHEB had for electricity supply in Northern Scotland. Johnston argued strongly against these proposals, making much of the special case for northern Scotland, which Lloyd George himself had also commented on in debates including those quoted earlier. Johnston suggested that he was

> quite satisfied that a central generating board of the kind suggested by your committee would not be able to command the confidence which the new Board [NoSHEB] has secured and that if you were to replace that Board on the generating side all the old controversies and difficulties would come to the fore once more.[19]

Johnstone's decision to simply begin building had been vindicated and NoSHEB survived the planned changes and was able to concentrate fully on delivering the more than 100 individual schemes which had been identified in its initial development plan.

Electrifying the Highlands

It is hard to comprehend the scale of the development which NoSHEB planned, and some of the evaluation of the success of this great national project has focused on what was not delivered. Certainly, the pioneering social vision which Johnston and his colleagues held with such conviction was perhaps not achieved to the extent they dreamed of. However, it is easy to underestimate the effect that the major construction schemes across the Highlands had between the first scheme built by the board in 1943, to their last major scheme at Ben Cruachan in 1965. Throughout this twenty-two-year period there was employment in a range of locations for a workforce that was at the top of its field internationally, illustrated by the number of tunnelling records which are accounted for by Highland hydro schemes. Thirty-four of the dams constructed during this period are also significant enough to feature in the World Register of Dams and attracted international attention on their completion. A comparative view of the other visions of a post-war future from the same period as the NoSHEB vision was being developed also show that other areas fell well short of delivering the full extent of what were often very utopian visions. We only have to look at the modern view of the idealised communities established in post-war high-rise developments to find a comprehensive parallel.

Whilst it is easy to assert that the vision for the transformation of the Highlands through the provision of electricity was not achieved when considering the work of NoSHEB at a national level, it is by considering some of the schemes in more detail that the true transformative effect can be more fully understood. Two schemes, one based on a remote part of the Hebrides in the mountains between Harris and Lewis and one North of Inverness, in their own ways demonstrate the impact of the electrification of the Highlands.

The Affric Beauly scheme was developed as part of NoSHEB's initiative to use the income generated from large schemes whose power was exported to the south of Scotland to finance smaller schemes for local supply in areas where this would otherwise have been uneconomic. However, as can be seen from an account of the development of the scheme, these initiatives also had a powerful transformative effect on society. The scheme utilises the upper tributaries of the Beauly River to the north-west of Inverness. Three dams and two power stations were constructed between 1952 and 1963, giving the scheme a total output of 168.4 MW. The scheme also contains the Monar Dam, which is unique in Scotland as a double arch dam.

Construction on the scheme transformed local society and employed over 2,000 people. Besides a large number of Highlanders, Lowland Scots and men from all corners of the UK were joined by Irish, Poles, Czechs, Canadians and even German ex-prisoners of war – particularly when tunnelling skills were in short supply.[20] The workers were housed in two camps, the main centre at Cannich and another at Cozac, near the Mullardoch Dam, with most accommodation housed in Nissen huts and reminiscent of a military camp. The development of such a significant settlement was a major contrast to the small settlement that had existed previously. In addition to domestic accommodation there was an administration building, large workshop, canteen, sick bay, general store and post office. A temporary generating station was established to provide power to the camp and immediate locality during construction work, delivering power to some parts of the local community for the first time without reliance upon costly and unreliable individual diesel generators. The settlement still has a legacy in the village, with the present village hall having been originally constructed as the canteen and mess room for the construction workers. Permanent housing was also required for the people who would maintain the scheme long after the construction workers had gone. Just as the power station at Fasnakyle was faced with locally sourced stone, new houses were constructed in the village of similar materials. Aptly, MacColl Road was named after the chief executive and vice chairman of NoSHEB from 1943 to 1951, Sir Edward MacColl, whose contribution to the success of the hydroelectric schemes throughout the country was immense.[21]

By contrast to the scale of the scheme at Beauly the Chilostair and Gisla schemes on Harris and Lewis in the Outer Hebrides were of a radically smaller scale. However, they still brought an additional eighty men into a small island community for the year that the scheme took to construct from 1959. In addition to the extra income this brought to the community, the main long term benefit was the provision of reliable electricity supplies for the first time. Whilst there had been some electricity on the island before the introduction of the Chilostair scheme it was mostly supplied by individually diesel generators, or at the best generators covering a group of a few houses. The generators were unreliable and very expensive to run, requiring the import of diesel by boat. The development of a reliable supply of electricity allowed power-based devices to be employed for both domestic and agricultural work. Electric refrigeration and washing machines were imported to the island for the first time and electric saw mills were used.

Quantifying the social change

The Chilostair scheme was one example of a number of similar initiatives of NoSHEB throughout the Highlands. The 1955 film *Crofter Boy*[22] shows the impact of the development of the Kerry Falls hydroelectric scheme, in a similarly remote location to the Chilostair scheme, but this time on the Scottish mainland near Gairloch. Kenny, the main subject of the film, describes the impact of electricity on the time, focusing on how much cleaner electric light is compared to the smoky oil lamps which were the main source of light before the town was connected. The film goes on to describe how the electricity has allowed the women of the local crofts to take advantage of modern conveniences like washing machines. Whilst there are not many shops in the village the NoSHEB mobile showroom visits, it demonstrates the latest electrical devices for home and croft and allows residents to order these for delivery. It is hard to imagine the impact that this kind of change must have had on society.

80   David Fleetwood

In an audio extract a Caithness crofter also describes the impact of electricity coming to the area. Electricity reached most of rural Caithness in the later 1940s and early 1950s through the work of the North of Scotland Hydro-Electric Board. Ninety per cent of crofting households were connected to the national grid by the early 1970s. The subject of the interview compares this to his early life on a Highland croft:

> I wis born in 1912 at Aimster in e parish o Halkirk an my father wis a – worked on farms an we were at Lynegar then, for eleven year an Ah left the school then, started work on the farms, ye know? Then Ah came here as a crofter in 1940. An I've been croftin ever since. There been a lot o changes in crofts in my lifetime. In 1930s you could live on a croft of thirty acre or less. You lived by the produce of the croft. You kept two or three cows an reared the calves; one cow for milk, for the household. You made your own butter an cheese. You grew your own potatoes, turnips, an you kept a score o hens, so you had eggs for your own use. You also hatched your chickens; the females you grew into hens an the males made a nice pot o broth. You had a pig which you fed on kitchen waste. It was killed an salted, an you made your own ham. Your fire was peat from the – you cut from, an dried an cut from – the hill. The houses were all but n bens with thatched roofs, warm an cosy, no mod cons, no bathrooms. The womenfolk did the work on the – at home, the men got part-time work on bigger farms; ditchin, drainin, no machinery, it was hard graft. You had a horse which you shared with a neighbour, an your light wis oil lamps. In the fifties the Hydro Board power came to the country. With power an light, you got washin machines. Before that the washin was done by hand on the scrubbin board. The watter had to be carried in an out – no sinks. Then the Regional Watter Board put watter all through the county an life became easier on the farm, or the crofts. Tractors replaced horse, an everythin became mechanised. Crofts still remains as crofts, just as a home. The man all ave to have other jobs. You could not make a livin on a croft today.[23]

The social change which was delivered by the overtly developmental policy pursued by NoSHEB during the development of Scotland's water power resources revolutionised many rural communities throughout Highland Scotland through the thirty or so years between 1943 and the early 1970s, after which the number of new grid connections in some of the remotest parts of Scotland began to decline.

Conclusion

The legacy of NoSHEB in electrifying Highland Scotland has been much examined and its success long debated. However, it is hard to overlook the impact described by both Kenny and the Caithness Crofter in the changes which electricity brought to their lives and communities. Whilst it can be

The electrification of Highland Scotland 81

debated whether this was wholly positive, and the extent to which the wider social policies outlined by Johnston and others at the point of nationalisation were delivered, it is clear that there was a quantifiable benefit delivered to a large number of rural communities through the work of the board. In the Scottish Labour Party's *Plan for Post-War Scotland* (1941: 23), if the Highlander had 'electric light, radio and a garage; had it been in reasonable reach of a cinema and a good dance band' then he would not leave the region.[24] The work of NoSHEB certainly went a long way to delivering at least part of this vision and slowing the steep decline in the population of the Highlands, although not creating population growth.[25] Other historians have considered this aspect of NoSHEB's work to be its crowning achievement. Interviewed by Radio Scotland, Ewen Cameron said 'the schemes were extraordinarily successful in generating cheap power. However, they did not attract industry to the north as envisioned by the late Tom Johnston.'[26] But when considering if the Board had delivered a lasting benefit to Scotland then, 'in improving the domestic life of people living in crofting communities, that was absolutely the case.'[27]

Today, the approach taken by NoSHEB to the economic development of a peripheral area has set the pattern for new approaches to halting the depopulation of Highland Scotland. Whilst the whole of the Highlands is now connected to the national grid, it is the roll-out of high-speed broadband which is the stimulus for economic development. Hydro and other renewable energy also has its place, with some of Scotland's newest large-scale hydro at Glendoe located less than five miles from where it all began at Fort Augustus. Ironically, in some of the remoter parts of the Highlands and Islands communities such as those on the Isle of Eigg are returning to life before the grid and carving out their own sustainable approach to electricity by existing off grid through wind, solar wave and hydro power.

The grid remains a key focus too, with what national grid have described as one of the most significant civil engineering undertakings in modern Britain as they redevelop the grid infrastructure in Highland Scotland. The most high-profile element of this new national project has seen construction begin on a new national interconnector running from Beauly in Invernesshire to Denny in the central belt. What is different now is that the power is flowing south with the large-scale hydro and wind installations of Northern Scotland powering the energy intensive central belt, and contributing to Scotland's ability to export energy to the rest of the UK and beyond.

The great project to use electricity to transform the Highlands began in the early twentieth century and has had as many ups and downs as the fluctuating AC current upon which the whole experiment was based. Whether you judge it a success, failure or something in between, there is no doubt that it changed communities forever to an extent which had never been achieved before, and the fact that people throughout the region still refer to 'the hydro' when they talk about electricity is as good a measure as any of the scale of this change.

82 *David Fleetwood*

Notes

1 Malcolm Gray, *The Highland economy, 1758–1850*. Edinburgh: Oliver and Boyd, 1957.
2 M. J. Daunton, *Progress and poverty: An economic and social history of Britain 1700–1850*. Oxford: Oxford University Press, 1995, p. 85.
3 J. P. Day, *Public administration in the Highlands and Islands of Scotland*. London: University of London Press, 1918.
4 Eric Richards, *The Highland clearances: People, landlords, rural Turmoil*. Edinburgh: Birlinn, 2008.
5 *Northern Chronicle*, 27 March 1895, quoted in Andrew Perchard, *Aluminium in the Highlands*. Inverness: University of the Highlands and Islands Centre for History, 2007, p. 7.
6 Letter from William Murray Morison to Dr Lachlan Grant, 1st January 1935. National Library of Scotland Acquisition 1287/7 quoted in Perchard, *Aluminium*, p. 9.
7 Historic Scotland, *Power to the people: The built heritage of Scotland's hydroelectric power*. Edinburgh: Historic Scotland, 2009, p. 19.
8 Mr Alan Shaw, *Kelvin to Weir, and on to GB SYS 2005*, Royal Society of Edinburgh, 29 September 2005.
9 North Northumberland Online, 'Survey of Belford 1995'.
10 Gerard Gilbert, 'Power struggle: The national grid was created to provide energy for all – but that's when the problems really began', *The Independent*, 22 October 2010.
11 http://thesciencedictionary.org/protective-system/.
12 http://www.nationalgrid75.com/timeline.
13 http://www.nationalgrid75.com/timeline.
14 Peter Payne, *The hydro: A study of the development of the major hydroelectric schemes undertaken by the North of Scotland Hydroelectric Board*. Aberdeen: Aberdeen University Press, 1988, p. 39.
15 Hansard, House of Lords Debate, 9 June 1943, line 42.
16 Historic Scotland, *Power to the People*, p. 30.
17 Clive Archer, *Norway outside the European Union: Norway and European integration from 1994 to 2004*. London: Routledge, 2005.
18 Hansard, House of Lords Debate, 25 January 1944, line 63. http://hansard. millbanksystems.com/commons/1944/jan/25/electricity-supply# S5CV0396P0_19440125_HOC_63.
19 Payne, *The hydro*, p. 58.
20 http://www.glenaffric.org/heritage_hydro_story.html.
21 http://www.glenaffric.org/heritage_hydro_story.html.
22 http://ssa.nls.uk/film/0112.
23 Am Baile, *A Caithness crofter remembers life on the croft*, asset 41328. http://www.ambaile.org.uk.
24 J. Burnett and H. Storhaug, 'The Highlands and islands of Scotland as a "cultural museum", 1900–2000', *Immigrants and Minorities*, vol. 20 (1), 2001, pp. 35–70.
25 C. G. Brown, 'Charting everyday experience', in L. Abrams and C. G. Brown (eds), *A history of everyday life in twentieth-century Scotland*. Edinburgh: Edinburgh University Press, 2010, p. 20.
26 BBC News Online, Scotland, *Hydro failed to attract industry*, 10 March 2009, http://news.bbc.co.uk/1/hi/scotland/highlands_and_islands/7933118.stm.
27 BBC News Online, Scotland, *Hydro failed to attract industry*, 10 March 2009, http://news.bbc.co.uk/1/hi/scotland/highlands_and_islands/7933118.stm.

6 Electrifying farms in England

Paul Brassley

At the end of the 1930s a little more than 10 per cent of British farms were connected to a supply of mains electricity, and farm sales accounted for less than one-half of 1 per cent of total electricity sales; fifty years later the figure had reached as near to 100 per cent as it was likely to get, although sales still accounted for less than 2 per cent of the total. This chapter sets out to explore the process of electrification, to explain why it happened when it did and not sooner or later, and to make some assessment of its impact. It relies on existing evidence from national sources but also presents new evidence that relates specifically to South West England in an attempt to explore electrification at the level of the individual farm. From the perspective of the early twenty-first century the significance of electrification, both for the domestic comfort of the farm family and the working of the farm, is so obvious that it hardly needs to be stated. Yet it is important to remember that a century earlier, when electricity supply companies were first being formed, it was by no means clear that a supply of electricity was even desirable, let alone necessary, as far as most farmers were concerned. They had the power that they needed from horses, steam and stationary oil engines, and tried and trusted sources of illumination. Why, when the economics of farming were uncertain, invest scarce capital and incur additional running costs in a potentially lethal source of light and power of which they had no experience?

It is important to distinguish between *rural* electrification, which is concerned with the supply of electricity, mostly for domestic purposes, to relatively concentrated – although not so concentrated as in urban areas – consumers; and *farm* electrification, with which this chapter is concerned, which is about the supply of electricity for a mixture of domestic and commercial or industrial purposes to, in the main, a much more geographically dispersed population. To the extent that farmsteads were located within villages this rural/farm distinction was less important, but for most British farmsteads this was not the case. Ironically, for those areas of the country characterised by nucleated settlement, farm electrification would have been easier before enclosure, when many farmsteads would have been located within the village envelope, rather than after, when thousands of new

84   *Paul Brassley*

farmhouses and buildings were constructed so as to be within easy reach of their fields. While this dispersal made perfect sense as far as most aspects of farming were concerned, it clearly increased the costs of supplying such farms with electricity generated at a central source.

Although a conference on electricity supply in rural areas held in 1928 concluded that cost factors precluded the provision of supply for 'up to 50 per cent of the more sparsely populated rural portions of the country' for many years to come, by 1939 no village with more than 500 inhabitants remained unconnected to mains supplies. This meant, however, according to the British Electrical Development Association's evidence to the Scott Committee, that 'about one third of all dwellings in rural district areas were not yet electrified,' a large proportion of which were farms and farm cottages. Even where industrial development had brought an electricity supply it often remained 'too expensive for the countryman with his lower wages either to connect or to use'. In its recommendations the Scott Committee described electricity as an 'essential service' and made numerous suggestions for standardisation of voltages, fittings, regulations, tariffs, and expansion of services after the war. As in much else, Dennison's Minority Report disagreed with this view and pointed out that it would inevitably involve some kind of subsidy.[1] By the outbreak of the Second World War, therefore, the problem of connection to mains electricity supplies in rural areas of the UK was largely confined to farms and isolated houses and cottages. Only about 50,000 farms (which Hannah calculates to be 12 per cent of the total) were connected to the mains, and only a derisory 0.3 per cent of electricity sales went to farming in 1940. Even these figures represented some improvement over the beginning of the decade, when, according to Moore-Colyer, only 25,000 of the 388,433 farms in England and Wales had a public supply, and 30,000 square miles of countryside had no access to low-tension distribution wires.[2] As far as historical analysis is concerned, therefore, the task is to explain why farms were *not* electrified before the war, and why they were after it.

Farm electrification before the Second World War

Clearly the main reason why most farms were not connected to public electricity supplies before the war is that they were not given the option, for the reasons of cost discussed earlier. Yet even where a public supply was available, as in villages, the demand for connection was not always forthcoming. As in the towns, potential consumers would have had existing arrangements for heating and lighting, and would have faced both expensive and disruptive installations and possibly higher running costs than those to which they were accustomed, in order to gain access to unfamiliar appliances with, perhaps, uncertain or unproven safety records.[3] Nevertheless there were a few farmers – 200 in 1925 and 700 in 1928 – using electricity for farming as opposed to purely domestic purposes. These figures were produced by

Electrifying farms in England 85

Richard Borlase Matthews, the most prominent interwar advocate of what he called 'electro-farming'. Writing in the Country Gentlemen's Association's *Estate Book and Diary* for 1928 he produced detailed information on the sizes of motors required for such tasks as milk separation, butter churning, chaff cutting, threshing and so forth; the number of hours of light required to increase winter egg production by 15–20 per cent ('the cost of light works out at that of one egg per bird per season'); and the advantages and limitations of wind, water, and internal combustion engines to power generators.[4] In the same year he produced a complete textbook on the subject, with numerous illustrations of electrically powered machinery on his own farm, and a chapter comparing the progress of farm electrification in Britain unfavourably with its uptake in other European countries together with Canada and Japan.[5] Despite his advocacy, the references to farm electrification in the parliamentary debates on the 1926 Electricity (Supply) Act tended to be 'facetious', and the reasons for this can perhaps be understood by considering in some detail the article written by C. Dampier Whetham for the 1924 volume of the *Journal* of the Royal Agricultural Society, in response to a request from the Society's Research Committee.[6] Whetham's article suggests that the use of electricity on the farm was beginning to enter a practical phase, and that a more experimental phase was ending, for he began by examining various 'specific' applications, such as the electrical treatment of seeds to improve yields, the use of electricity to heat silage in order to improve fermentation, the promotion of crop growth by overhead electric discharges, and the electrification of mouldboards to reduce draught in ploughing. None of them worked. This may not surprise a modern reader, but the fact that they were under investigation is revealing of the state of knowledge at the time Whetham was writing.

Most of Whetham's article, however, was devoted to examining the demand for electricity and its supply to villages and farms. He divided the uses of electricity on the farm into power, lighting and domestic purposes. Electric motors, he pointed out, could be used for all purposes for which stationary oil engines or waterwheels were currently used, such as chaff cutting, threshing, root cutting, wood sawing and pumping, and for several – cream separating, butter churning, sheep shearing and horse clipping – currently done by hand. There were also new applications, and he cited the example of Borlase Matthews, who had a hot air egg incubator and used an electric fan for crop drying. And 'electric motors, especially those for three-phase currents, are very simple and robust. They are cheaper and longer lived than oil or petrol engines.' To set against this, however, was the fact that 'nearly all farms now have an oil engine' and only use power for a few hours each week, and

> when a farmer's only requirement is to use occasionally a good deal of power at one time to drive barn machinery, chaff cutters, &c., in one building, or other machines in a place to which a portable engine or

86 *Paul Brassley*

tractor can be taken, he may just as well drive direct from his engine, and not bother about electricity.[7]

He had no such doubts about electricity for lighting, which 'gives an easy, efficient, and economical method of lighting, which may safely be used where flame lights are dangerous or inadmissable', and would promote cleaner cow stalls, enable work to be carried on later, and could promote winter egg production if henhouses were lit in the evening. Lighting, he felt, was also the chief benefit of electricity in farmhouses and cottages, although how much light was involved is an interesting question. In considering typical installations, he thought that a typical farmhouse and set of buildings might install from twenty to twenty-five lamps, and each cottage three more. Since he also mentioned the 20-watt lamps used with generator plants, the average cottage perhaps remained fairly dark.[8] As far as power was concerned, 'an occasional electric iron is almost the only article which absorbs electric current for domestic heat or power on ordinary English farms,' although he admitted that vacuum cleaners 'may become common as time goes on', together perhaps with washing machines.[9] Overall, however, there was no doubt that electricity added greatly to the comfort and amenities of life in farmhouses and villages generally, and he regarded 'lighting as the chief function of electric current in country districts, and power as subsidiary'.[10]

Given the difficulty and cost of connecting to a mains supply, and the prevalence of stationary engines on farms in the 1920s, it is not surprising that Whetham also considered the possibilities and economics of on-farm or private electricity generation. Water and wind power might be employed in suitable locations, but for most farmers the addition of a dynamo and battery to a stationary engine would be satisfactory. A half-kilowatt plant, suitable for lighting, could be installed for a capital cost, including wiring, of about £100; running costs, including interest and depreciation, would be about £20 per year. By the time he was writing, some manufacturers of these small generators incorporated what would eventually become the 'startamatic' principle, so that when a light was switched on the battery gave a current that was used to start the generator engine, which then ran until all the lamps in the circuit were switched off.[11]

By the 1920s, therefore, mains electrification of farming had made some progress, as Table 6.1 suggests, beginning from a base close to zero and extending to nearly 20 per cent of the farms in England and Wales by the beginning of the Second World War. Even by 1940, however, farm consumption accounted for less than 1 per cent of total consumption, and many more farms used electricity for lighting the house than for agricultural purposes.

A private supply of electricity would also become a possibility for some farms and a necessity for others. The increase in liquid milk sales as opposed to farmhouse butter and cheese production encouraged hygiene in milk production, and especially after the establishment of the Milk Marketing Board in 1933 the requirement for churns, buckets and other milking equipment to

Table 6.1 Mains electrification 1920–1940.

	Number of farms with mains supplies	Electricity sales to farms (million kWh)
1920	151	–
1925	3,430	2
1930	9,582	10
1935	20,684	32
1940	47,089	75

Source: See the statistical appendix.

be steam-sterilised gave an incentive to install electric water heating.[12] The interwar period saw an increase in the use of electricity in poultry farming, with electrically heated brooders and artificial lighting to manage day length and so prolong the egg-laying period, although it is worth noting that coal gas, Calor gas and oil lamps could also be used for this purpose.[13]

A survey of published statistics, mostly from census enquiries, on the sources of power available on farms in Great Britain gives some idea of the increase in the use of electric motors in the first forty years of the twentieth century, and their importance compared with stationary petrol and oil engines. These figures are given in Table 6.2, and to some extent confirm Whetham's view of the significance of stationary oil engines, although his claim that nearly all farms had one in 1924 is revealed as an exaggeration, since there were only 85,200 of them in Great Britain, perhaps a third of the total number of farms. The total horsepower in the final column of the Table includes that derived from steam and gas engines, tractors used solely for stationary work, and other stationary power sources such as wind and water, the total of which declined slightly from about 150,000 horsepower to 120,000 horsepower between 1908 and 1939. Therefor it is clear that the fourfold increase in stationary power in these thirty or so years was almost entirely due to the expansion in the number of oil engines. In percentage terms the expansion of electric motors was significant, but the numbers and horsepower involved were still only a tenth of the petrol and oil engine figures. The average power output of the two power sources in 1939 was roughly the same, at about 5 horsepower. However, it should be remembered that the presence of an electric motor on a farm does not necessarily imply that the farm had a mains power source, because the electric motor might have been powered by a private source of electricity, and the absence of one does not imply that the farm was not connected to the mains, because some farms employed electricity for lighting only. Despite these caveats, however, these figures illustrate the slow spread of electrification in the interwar period.

88 *Paul Brassley*

Table 6.2 Stationary power on farms in Great Britain, 1908–1939.

	No. of electric motors ('000)	Total H.P. of electric motors ('000)	No of petrol and oil engines ('000)	Total H.P. of petrol and oil engines ('000)	Total stationary power ('000 HP)
1908	0.2	1	10.5	66	213
1913	0.4	3	24.2	146	293
1925	1.1	8	85.2	472	630
1931	3.5	23	97.1	536	695
1937	10.6	56	127.5	636	820
1939	13.0	62	139.2	671	854

Source: D. K. Britton and I. F. Keith, 'A Note on the Statistics of Farm Power Supplies in Great Britain', *Farm Economist*, vol. 6 (6), 1950, pp. 163–170.

The state of electrification in 1942

The National Farm Survey of England and Wales was carried out under the auspices of the County War Agricultural Executive Committees, and has become well known to rural historians as a prime source of data on the state, not only of agriculture, but also of rural social conditions, because it produced information on the condition of roads, water supplies and cottages, and an assessment of the management abilities of farmers.[14] Among the questions to be answered for each farm were several concerning the electricity supply. They asked if the farm was connected to a public electricity supply or had a privately generated supply, and whether this was used for light and/or power, and for household or farm purposes.[15]

The summary report published in 1946 analysed and reported the resultant data, and it is worth examining it in some detail. It revealed that there were some 78,000 holdings of over five acres in England and Wales with an electricity supply, which represented 27 per cent of the total of 290,000 holdings at that time. Of this 27 per cent, 24 per cent drew their electricity from a public supply, and 3 per cent, or about 9,000 holdings, generated it for themselves. The data were reported at a county level, and the range was enormous. Only 1 per cent of holdings in Radnor had a supply, nearly half of which generated it for themselves. In Surrey, at the opposite end of the scale, 62 per cent of farms had a supply, and only 7 per cent of those generated their own electricity. It is clear from Table 6.3 and Figure 6.1 that the main factor determining this variation was the proximity to urban areas. The most electrified counties were mostly those near London or near industrial areas, such as Nottinghamshire, Warwickshire, Derbyshire and Lancashire. The least so were all the Welsh counties, with the exception of Glamorgan in the south and Flint in the north, and the far western English counties, together with the Isle of Ely, all of them less urbanised or industrialised. It is also interesting to compare the extent to which counties were electrified and the

Table 6.3 Percentage of holdings with an electricity supply (of which % with private supply %P).

Under 15	%P	15–24	%P	25–34	%P	35–49	%P	50+	%P
Cornwall 14	17	Lincs Kesteven 23	6	Wiltshire 34	17	Lancs 49	3	Surrey 62	7
Devon 14	23	Cambs 22	8	Glamorgan 34	0	Leics 46	4	Herts 55	9
Hereford 14	36	Gloucs 22	26	Durham 33	10	Oxon 45	15	Middx. 52	4
I. of Ely 14	14	I. of Wight 22	11	Somerset 33	11	Warwick 45	8	Notts 50	3
Monmouth 13	14	W. Suffolk 21	30	Yorks WR 32	7	Bucks 43	6	W. Sussex 50	26
Carm'then 12	8	Flint 21	22	Soke of Peter'brgh 31	2	E. Sussex 42	15		
Denbigh 11	30	Salop 20	16	Staffs 31	5	Northants 41	8		
Caern'von 10	36	E. Suffolk 19	16	Cambs 29	12	Cheshire 39	7		
Merioneth 10	44	Lincs. Holland 17	7	Rutland 29	4	Beds. 38	6		
Brecon 8	12	Lincs. Lindsey 16	11	Yorks NR 29	9	Derby 37	2		
Pembroke 6	26	North'd 16	24	West'm'd 27	8	Hants 36	17		
Montgomery 5	62	Hunts 15	15	Worcs 27	12	Berks 35	20		
Cardigan 4	38			Yorks ER 26	4	Essex 35	22		
Anglesey 3	40			Dorset 25	20	Kent 35	10		
Radnor 1	44			Norfolk 25	12				

Source: Ministry of Agriculture and Fisheries, *National Farm Survey*, p. 107.

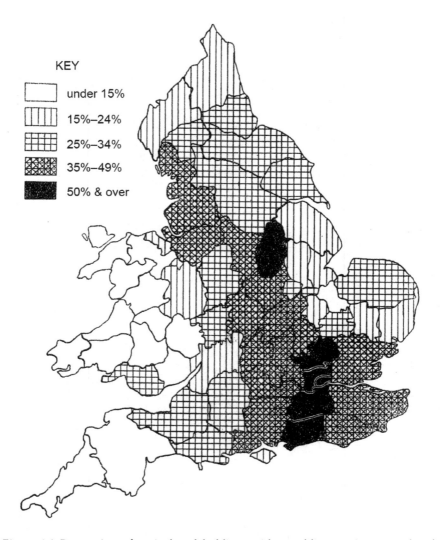

Figure 6.1 Proportion of agricultural holdings with a public or private supply of electricity in each country of England and Wales in 1942.

Source: Ministry of Agriculture and Fisheries, *National Farm Survey of England and Wales: a summary report*. London: HMSO, 1946, map 6.

likelihood of farms generating their own electricity. As Table 6.3 also shows, in all but five of the counties with less than 15 per cent of their farms electrified, more than 20 per cent of the electrified farms generated their own supply. Conversely, in only four of the counties with more than 25 per cent of their farms electrified did the level of private generation reach or exceed the 20 per cent mark. As the MAF report on the NFS also demonstrated, the bigger a farm was, the more likely it was to be electrified. Of farms with between 25 and 100 acres, 22 per cent had a public and a further 2 per cent a private supply. Of those with more than 700 acres, 43 per cent had a public supply and a further 16 per cent a private supply. This appears to reflect the higher living standards of the larger farmers more than their desire to electrify their farms, for 38 per cent of all farm consumers used electricity only for lighting the farmhouse, and a further 15 per cent for light and power in the farmhouse. In other words, less than half of the farms with an electricity supply used it for farming purposes. There were a few farms – 2.8 per cent of the total – that used electricity only for farming purposes and had no farmhouse connection, and the NFS report suggested that these were more likely to be in the east and south-east of the country, where the scope for applying electric power to barn machinery was greater. Having said that, farms with dairy herds were also more likely to be connected: 64 per cent of herds with more than 100 cows had a supply to the farm buildings, as opposed to herds with twenty to twenty-nine cows, only 25 per cent of which did so, and smaller herds had even lower figures.[16] The larger dairy farmers presumably agreed with the electrical engineer C.A. Cameron Brown. Writing in the Ministry of Agriculture's journal in 1945, he argued that

> whatever may be the general assessment of the place and value of electricity in agriculture generally, there can hardly be any doubt of its worth on the milk-producing farm. There may occasionally be some uncertainty on economic grounds, but there can be none on the technical merits of electricity in the various processes involved in producing and handling clean milk. . . . It is well known that all bodies interested in the upgrading of milk production would like to see electricity available in every dairy farm.[17]

To summarise the position in 1942, only about a quarter of the farms in England and Wales had an electricity supply, and less than half of them used it for farming. The number that did have a supply for the farm buildings – 47 per cent of 78,000, or about 37,000 holdings – is of the same order of magnitude as the 29,000 electric motors listed as being on farms in 1942 by the Britton and Keith (1950) survey. It is also worth noting that their figures for Scotland suggest a slightly slower pace of change there. And the likelihood of connection had little to do with farming requirements and much more to do with urban proximity and farmhouse amenity, all of which tends to confirm that wisdom of Whetham's predictions that lighting, primarily, and household appliances, secondarily, would be the main attractions of electrification.

Electrification in the Second World War and after

The expansion of production and increased labour costs during the war gave a boost to labour-saving devices such as electric fences. The wartime editions of the *Journals* of the Royal Agricultural Society regularly contained

92   Paul Brassley

advertisements for electric fencing equipment made by firms such as Wolseley of Birmingham and the Harvest Saver and Implement Company of London, both of whose units cost £7.14s., battery extra. They emphasised that these units worked from battery power and required no mains supply. The same *Journals* also ran advertisements for the small stationary engines made by Petters of Loughborough and Listers of Dursley (Gloucestershire) for powering electric generators, among other uses.[18] Farmers became more familiar with the use of electricity during the war, as the increase in the number of electric motors on farms, from 13,000 in 1939 to 69,000 in 1948, suggests.[19] In part this reflected the increased use of on-farm generators, but the mains network also expanded, as is confirmed by the figures for mains connections reported in Table 6.4, which show the number of farms with mains supplies doubling in the 1940s.

The Ministry of Agriculture and Fisheries used the National Farm Survey data, with some additions, for its internal report on *Farm Water and Electricity Supplies* at the end of the war.[20] The low levels of provision of both services in many parts of the country, as highlighted by the NFS, was a matter of concern to a Ministry charged with increasing agriculture's output and efficiency. The report pointed out that higher labour costs and higher prices of alternative fuels had increased the farm demand for electricity. More farmers wanted a supply, and those already supplied were using more. Yet supply problems remained. In fact, the report argued, the capital cost of supplying the greater part of the rural population was not substantially greater than that of supplying urban areas, because overhead lines, which could be used in the countryside but not in towns, were cheaper to install than underground cables, up to the point at which about 70 per cent of premises were connected. The main difference between villages (which for the purposes of this argument included premises within the surrounding quarter of a mile) and urban areas was in the concentration of consumers

Table 6.4 Mains electrification 1940–1970.

	Number of farms with mains supplies	Electricity sales to farms (million kWh)
1940	47,089	75
1942	57,701	–
1945	71,848	140
1947	86,801	215
1950	113,936	439
1955	176,397	987
1958	214,909	1,497
1961	243,418	1,923
1966	253,100	2,531
1971	255,745	3,014

Source: See the statistical appendix.

and the lack of industry. Village supplies might therefore need some subsidisation from existing consumers, but not necessarily at a very high level.[21]

The principal difficulty lay with the remaining 30 per cent of premises, many of which, if not most, were farms. The report identified problems with both capital and running costs. As far as capital was concerned, the main problem was the connection cost. The pre-war cost of a low-tension line was about £750 per mile; a high-tension line was cheaper, at £500 per mile, but a transformer costing £100 was needed at the end of it. The cost of wiring the farm buildings once a supply was available, on the other hand, was not excessive, at about £50 on average at pre-war prices, although that might remain a problem for small farmers. The average cost of connecting and wiring a farm was estimated at £250, so the total cost of bringing electricity to the 215,000 farms still to be connected was nearly £55 million.[22] A cartographic survey of the Swindon area had found that three-quarters of the farms already connected to a public supply were either within a village or hamlet, or close to one, but that many farms within a short distance of a distribution line remained unconnected. Bringing a supply to these easily connected farms would, it was estimated, add another 65,000 to the total of electrified farms. There were perhaps 20,000 holdings that were too far from a supply ever to be connected to the mains, so any reasonable farm electrification plan would need to cope with about 130,000 farms for which the cost of connection would be higher, probably significantly higher, than previous connection costs. However, farmers themselves could help the programme by minimising wayleave costs, and the National Farmers' Union Machinery Committee was now enthusiastically supporting electrification, in marked contrast to the union's obstructive attitude before the war.[23]

A bigger problem was the relatively high cost of electrical equipment. It remained high because demand was low, and demand was low because the cost was high. It was estimated that twenty cows was the minimum economic dairy herd size for machine milking, and only one-quarter of herds had that many cows. In 1944, only 30,500 of a total of 160,000 dairy herds were machine-milked. While electricity was cheaper than alternative power sources for low-power work such as shearing or bottle washing, and had been increasingly used for grinding and crushing mills and poultry lighting, it remained more expensive than coal for heating. Moreover, there were still large numbers of stationary engines already installed on farms, and the number of farming operations suitable for electrification was limited, although further research should increase the number of applications. One of its big advantages was that electricity was reliable, clean, and easy to handle.[24] On the whole, therefore, given the high capital costs and low usage, it was 'by no means certain that the present organisation of the distributive industry will enable the widest possible distribution of electricity to be carried out'.[25] In other words, widespread farm electrification was difficult to justify in strict accounting terms and would require a radical change in the organisation of the electricity supply industry to bring it about.

94 Paul Brassley

By the end of the 1960s the electrification of farms was virtually complete (see Table 6.4). Having started so slowly in the interwar years, it ended in a rush, as the radical organisational change took effect. From nationalisation in 1948 farm electricity consumption increased more than tenfold by 1970 while overall national consumption increased only fivefold in the same period, although farm consumption still represented less than 2 per cent of national consumption by 1970.[26] It is interesting, but hardly surprising, to see that electricity sales to farms increased more than the number of farms receiving supplies, because most farmers would take some time after being connected to the mains to invest in electrically powered machinery, or to introduce enterprises that depended upon an electrical supply for their efficient working. It is also worth noting that some isolated farms still remain unconnected today. The Warren House Inn, in the middle of Dartmoor, relies on its own generator, as do half a dozen neighbouring farms, and the neighbouring small village, Postbridge, was only connected in the 1980s.

The principal reason for the post-war expansion of mains electricity supplies to farms was the subsidisation of the cost of connection, but there were also several subsidiary factors.[27] To begin with, before nationalisation, as we have seen, the provision of electricity was the responsibility of companies or local authority undertakings, both of which tended to charge higher prices for rural electricity since the costs of supplying it were greater. Furthermore, the plethora of boundaries between these numerous small organisations made efficient zoning of supply extensions difficult. Nationalisation overcame these problems. It came into effect on 1 April 1948, under the provisions of the Electricity Act 1947, and transferred the responsibility for supplying electricity from 560 private and municipal undertakings to fourteen Area Boards. The boundary problems disappeared and the local political pressure for higher rural prices was reduced. More importantly, during the Act's passage through Parliament the Conservative opposition, supported by rural pressure groups, had successfully proposed an amendment to the Act requiring the Area Boards to 'secure, so far as practicable, the development, extension to rural areas and cheapening of supplies of electricity'. To assist in this process, a government White Paper referring to the Act, and published in the same year, accepted the principle of all consumers in a Board area bearing the cost of rural electrification. Addressing an international conference on agricultural electrification in 1968, A. W. Gray argued that 'this removed the barriers to full electrification which would have been present if rural electrification had had to be justified on economic terms.'[28]

In the immediate post-war years there were shortages of some of the necessary supplies such as poles for overhead lines, and government cuts in capital budgets, both of which delayed the expansion of supplies. Despite the 1947 White Paper the argument over who should subsidise rural consumers was still going on in 1951, when Sir Henry Self, at that time deputy chairman of the Central Electricity Authority, considered that subsidisation by 'the general body of consumers' would be 'unreasonable'.[29] High costs and low tariffs produced a deficit in the accounts of the South West Electricity

Board, which had one of the largest rural populations. Its chairman, Stanley Steward, supported by his Consumer Consultative Council, on which there was effective rural representation, put pressure on both the government and the Central Authority for a subsidy. It was not forthcoming, but there was increasing pressure from Conservative MPs with rural constituencies to promote electrification, and less pressure on capital resources. There was pressure from other directions too. In the autumn of 1951, during the Korean War, the president of the National Farmers' Union (NFU), Sir James Turner, wrote to Sir Thomas Dugdale, then Minister of Agriculture and Fisheries, arguing that if the agricultural industry were to respond to requests for maximum food production it must have the tools for the job, and those included electricity.[30] By December of that year the Minister of Agriculture was using this NFU pressure to argue against the Chancellor of the Exchequer's proposals to suspend all rural electrification. And the union maintained the pressure. Turner wrote again to Dugdale in March 1953 asking for a meeting with him and the Minister of Fuel and Power, the Home Secretary and the Welsh Secretary, to push the rural electrification programme.[31]

With the end of the war in July 1953 the NFU's line of argument changed. When Mr Greig of the NFU met Ministry officials in September 1953 he explained that the Union regarded the amenity value of electricity as important in preventing the loss of labour from the land. It also recognised that it was difficult for Area Boards with a high percentage of rural consumers to pay their way, and suggested that their obligation to do so should operate at a national rather than an individual board level.[32] It was certainly the case that there were differences between area boards, both in the ways in which they calculated connection costs and in the percentage of farms connected. In March 1953, for example, over 60 per cent of farms in the Southern and North Western board areas had a public supply, whereas in the South Western, North Eastern, and Merseyside and North Wales areas the figure was less than 40 per cent. In South Wales only 19.2 per cent of farms had a supply.[33] The dialogue was wider than a purely NFU/Ministry of Agriculture matter. In December 1953 the Chancellor of the Exchequer faced questions about the high level of capital contributions required for farm connections when addressing the Dunmow Farmers' Club in Essex, and earlier that year, in April, a deputation from the Rural District Councils Association met a Ministry of Agriculture official, Mr Wilcox, who explained to them that there was no policy to restrict rural electrification, although there was a general shortage of labour and materials, and that electricity charges could not 'be used as instruments to tax the urban areas in order to pay a subsidy to the rural areas'.[34]

At a meeting of the Central Authority and Area Board chairmen in July 1953 it was decided to establish a committee to formulate a rural electrification policy. The committee, with Sir Henry Self in the chair, met at a hotel in Moretonhampstead in Devon over a weekend in October 1953 and eventually agreed a plan for rural electrification. The plan required 85 per cent of farms to be connected by 1963 (there does not appear to have been a target for the number of rural connections in general) in a two-stage process. The

96   Paul Brassley

first stage was to take five years, to 31 March 1958, and result in the connection of 57,000 farms, and in the second five-year period a further 43,000 farms were to be connected. The total cost was estimated at £130 million, and *annual* losses at £4 million, to be borne by consumers in general. Their bills, estimated Hannah, were increased by about 2 per cent.[35] ' "So far it has not been possible to secure an adequate financial return on rural electrification schemes," noted a Mr Peirson in his paper to the Institution of Electrical Engineers,' 'and if the capital resources of Area Boards are to be employed to the best advantage, a fuller use of electricity for farms is essential.'[36] An estimate made after the programme had been completed put the capital expenditure incurred at £145 million, with continued annual losses, but made the point that 'one must, however, judge this loss against a total annual revenue from all urban and rural consumers of over £1,000 million.'[37] Hannah's justification of the policy was slightly different: since the rural electrification subsidy came not from the Treasury but from the Area Boards and their consumers, 'arguably their rural subsidies went no further than a prudent private enterprise firm would have gone in recognizing clearly-felt social and political priorities in the community in which they operated.'[38]

As the target of 85 per cent of farms connected, set in 1953, was achieved in the early 1960s, and more remote farms came into the electrification programme, the cost pressures increased rather than diminished. The 1963 Select Committee report on the industry quoted an average annual loss per area board of £500,000.[39] The electricity industry, supported by the Ministry of Power, was reluctant to invest money in connecting the 'hard core' of still-unconnected farms, many of them in the hills and uplands, some of which might be abandoned.[40] The NFU's argument for continued electrification changed from its importance in maximising output or preventing the loss of farm labour to emphasising amenity. Writing about the hard-core areas in the South West and South Wales to the Minister of Power in June 1964, the NFU president, Sir Harold Woolley, argued that it was 'unreasonable to expect this section of the community to be deprived of what in this modern age is recognised as an essential service'.[41] At a subsequent meeting the NFU delegation brought the argument back to labour supply. Mr Gummer, of the Ministry of Power, observed that the NFU's main interest in rural electrification was not mechanisation of agricultural processes but the enjoyment of the same amenities as would normally be available to an urban population. If, they said, 'farms did not have television, the younger generation would abandon farming'. At a further meeting at the Ministry of Power a few days later, a delegation from the Devon branch of the NFU also emphasised the social importance of electricity rather than its impact on agricultural efficiency.[42]

The need to strike a balance between economic efficiency and social responsibility was one of the themes of a film about the electrification of the village of Widecombe on Dartmoor (Devon).[43] It was made for the South West Electricity Board (SWEB) in 1962, mostly celebrating the technical achievement of overcoming the problems of taking 11 kV power lines over difficult terrain. It is worth noting, though, that it also examined the implications of electrification for consumers and the environment. It asserted that women were the first to appreciate the advantages of electrification, and included shots of a couple examining electrical appliances in a showroom as well as those of new milking machines being delivered to a farm. From an environmental viewpoint it emphasised the landscape impact of the line. It pointed out that planning approval was required, and that the engineers planning its route had to balance practicality with making it as inconspicuous as possible. To avoid disturbing the skyline in the National Park a section of the line over Aish Tor was put underground, at a cost six times higher than that of an overhead line. This concern for the landscape impact of electrification in National Parks can be traced back to 1955, and probably earlier. On 26 July 1955 a meeting was held in London between the National Parks Commission and representatives of the Park Planning Authorities, for which Devon County Council, which played an important part on the Dartmoor National Park Committee, produced a briefing paper on 'electricity problems'. The paper recognised that there was a conflict between the 'right' of National Park inhabitants to receive electricity and the impact of overhead lines on natural beauty. Under the SWEB rural development scheme the extra cost of undergrounding was charged to the Board's area as a whole rather than to the individual consumers concerned. Nevertheless, the paper contended, since National Parks were for the benefit of the entire nation, the nation rather than any particular region should bear the extra cost. This specific line of argument may not have been successful, but, as Sheail points out in chapter 3, section 37 of the 1957 Electricity Act required electricity undertakings to have regard to natural beauty when instigating new proposals. It was presumably this legislation which allowed the Aish Tor underground section.[44]

It is important to realise that farms were only a small part of the total rural demand, which itself was less than 20 per cent of the total load at the end of the war. In addition to quantifying the number of farms, Peirson also gives figures for the number of other rural consumers from 1920 to 1958, from which it can be calculated that farms were always a small minority of rural consumers, as Table 6.5 shows.

Table 6.5 Farms as a % of all rural consumers.

Before 1935	Less than 4
1936–1942	4–6
1943–1949	6–8
1950–1954	8–10
1955–1958	10–12

Source: G. F. Peirson, 'The development of rural electrification: A review of progress', Proceedings of the Institution of Electrical Engineers, vol. 108, part A, 1961, pp. 114–115.

98   *Paul Brassley*

Although both Hannah and Gray measure the impact of the rural electrification schemes by quoting the numbers of farms, or the percentage of total farms, which were electrified at various dates, the data in Table 6.5 make it clear that it is not possible to distinguish between the costs of electrifying farms and those of connecting other rural premises. It is likely that the cost of supplying a farm set in the middle of its fields would be greater than that for a house in a village, but the small number of farms in comparison with village houses meant that they must still have accounted for the minority of rural connection costs.

The new post-nationalisation electricity boards recognised that extending rural electrification brought problems that either did not occur or were not serious in towns. H. W. Grimmitt, in his chairman's address to the Transmission Section of the Institution of Electrical Engineers in 1945, discussed various problems with overhead lines, fuse gear and transformers, and suggested that 150,000 transformers, varying in size from 5 to 25 kVA, would be required if all farms were to be given a supply. There was also the question of whether all farms required a three-phase supply or could manage with single-phase, which would be 10 to 15 per cent cheaper.[45] A subsequent paper to the institution, discussing the development of rural electrification; mentioned problems of insulators, isolators, switchgear and television interference;, and illustrated an early post-hole borer mounted on a former US Army truck that could excavate a 20-inch diameter hole to a depth of five or six feet in four minutes, once it was in position.[46] Even when supplies were in place, meter reading and servicing were more expensive in rural areas because the personnel involved had further to travel, while rural consumers, with the possible exception of farms, tended to consume less than urban consumers.[47] In response to this the Area Boards could make an additional connection charge to rural consumers. The South Western Electricity Board (SWEB) instituted a Rural Development Contribution (RDC) Scheme in 1954, and revised it as the electrification programme reached into more remote areas in the 1960s. From 1 April 1965 the charges for farms that could be connected for £400 or less was a basic RDC of £1.5s. per quarter plus a further shilling per quarter for each acre of crops and grass up to a maximum of £8.15s. Thus a farm of 175 acres or more would pay the full £400 over ten years, whereas smaller farms would be subsidised to a varying extent depending on their sizes and connection costs. More remote farms with higher connection costs had higher charges.[48]

Not all farmers, especially in the immediate post-war years, were convinced of the value of electrification. A textbook published in 1951 described electricity as a 'modern slave' but bemoaned the fact that few farmers made full use of it, 'often because they do not understand electricity and perhaps more often because of the cost of installation'. Both connection and wiring costs were high, it argued, but also many farmers did not know what running costs were likely to be, so it went on to explain the relationship between volts, amps and watts.[49] Writing two years earlier, however, the editor and assistant editor of the periodical *Farm Mechanisation* suggested that farmers had been 'indifferent' to the availability of supply until ten or twelve years previously, whereas 'there now exists a rural demand which cannot be met by the supply authorities.'[50] Both books then went on to survey the various uses for electricity on the farm, emphasising in particular its role in milk production, water pumping, poultry production and powering barn machinery, and not forgetting the its importance, on family farms, for mechanising household tasks. Ministry of Agriculture officials shared this ambivalent attitude in the 1950s, when it is clear from their files that they had no clear idea about whether farm electrification was economically worthwhile, although by the 1960s, when the Ministry's Regional Controller based at Reading quoted a cost of 3d. per unit for electricity from an on-farm generator, as opposed to half that as the cost from a mains supply, they were more convinced of its value.[51] The area boards were exasperated by the limited extent to which farmers used electricity in the 1950s: 'The average annual consumption of farms connected in the South West amounts to about £26. This is little more and sometimes less than we expect to get from a small all-electric Council House in towns,' wrote a board official in 1954.[52]

By the end of the 1960s, however, sales per farm had doubled in comparison with the mid-1950s as farmers acquired more electrically powered equipment (see Table 6.4). In 1967 Claude Culpin, the National Agricultural Advisory Service's chief mechanisation adviser, observed that 'electricity is almost essential for efficient mechanisation of work about the buildings' and that electricity was the most economical of the available power sources.[53] He could assume by then that most farms would have a public supply, and that the wiring costs had also been met. Wiring costs were clearly a significant consideration for many farmers, but they were so variable that it is impossible to give any meaningful average figure for them. At one extreme, some farmers almost certainly fixed up some domestic lighting in the farmhouse for themselves; at the other, big farms making major investments in grain drying and storage, or milling and mixing equipment, needed the services of electrical contracting firms over several weeks. There was also the question, on tenanted farms, of who should pay for the costs of electrical installation. As it was part of the fixed equipment, the landlord would be expected to pay for it; whether this was always the case is a question that requires further research.

Ruth Janette Ruck vividly conveyed the delays and eventual rewards involved in electrification in her account of life on a hill farm in Snowdonia. It had no mains supply, or generator, until 1965:

> For years we had been happy enough with oil lamps but now, all of a sudden, we were impatient for electricity to come. It would save time and also allow us to work in the sheds and barns after dark.

100 Paul Brassley

After the supply reached the nearest village 'everyone watched television,' and her father, who lived with her and her husband, was keen to do so, too. They were prepared for the arrival of a supply, having had the farmhouse and buildings wired, part of the cost being met by a Ministry of Agriculture Hill Farming grant. They also had a cottage, for which no grant was available, but her husband wired that himself. 'He was no electrician, but he studied the do-it-yourself manuals and had advice from a friend who worked in atomic power.' After a way leave problem had been resolved, they received a supply in the spring of 1965.

> Huge tractors churned over the muddy fields and a line of poles appeared. The poles were an eyesore but there was no alternative. . . . then the current was switched on and [her husband's] wiring of the cottage worked perfectly. Now we could shear by machine; now I could attack dust and dirt with a vacuum cleaner and now my father became an ardent televiewer. We were moving with the times.[54]

The electricity supply industry itself went to some lengths to inform and educate farmers on the possibilities of electric power and lighting. The commercial engineers employed by the Area Boards were in day-to-day contact with farmers. To support them, the Electricity Council's research centre at Capenhurst, near Chester, had a section specialising in agricultural and horticultural problems by the mid-1960s, and when the new Royal Showground at Stoneleigh in Warwickshire opened in the early 1960s it had an Electro-Agricultural Centre dedicated to providing events, exhibitions, publications, films, and training and conference facilities.[55] There was also an Electrical Development Association, among whose publications between 1955 and 1965 was a series of farm electrification handbooks, substantial booklets of 70 to 100 pages covering such topics as electric water pumps, farm lighting, electricity in the dairy, grain drying, milling and mixing, greencrop drying and automatic feeding.[56] At a more local level, the South Western Board produced a handbook for Young Farmers' Clubs and sponsored a quiz competition based on it. Ninety teams took part in 1965.[57]

In the twenty years between 1950 and 1970, therefore, the bulk of the country's farms had been given the possibility of adopting a range of new electrically powered equipment. The following section uses data from the south-west of England to examine the effect this had on farmers and their families.

Rural electrification in South West England

As the 1942 National Farm Survey revealed (see Table 6.3), the more industrialised or urbanised an area was by the 1940s, the greater the chance of farms being connected to the mains. This remained the case into the 1960s. In the North Western Electricity Board area 97 per cent of the farms in

Lancashire were connected by 1962, whereas only 85 per cent of the farms in the Lakeland part of the Board's area were connected by that time. Similarly, the far south-western counties of Devon and Cornwall were among the least electrified, with Dorset being somewhat better off (see Table 6.3). As the *Annual Report* of the South Western Electricity Board (SWEB) for the year ending 31 March 1953 pointed out, the problem lay 'in the sparsity and location of the population'. Half of the area contained only 7 per cent of the population at an average density of 56 per square mile, and the density of population over the SWEB area as a whole was the lowest of any of the board areas.[58] In 1948 only 18.5 per cent of farms in the area had a mains supply, and SWEB began a deliberate policy of accelerating rural electrification. By 1967 electricity had been brought to 92 per cent of the farms in the SWEB area, with an additional 1,424 farms being connected between April 1964 and March 1965. By 1967 the total of rural premises electrified since 1948, including farms, had reached nearly 140,000, at a capital cost of about £13 million. The map of the development of high voltage (33 kV and 11 kV) mains in West Devon (see Figure 6.2, which shows the area west of Okehampton and Bideford) shows just a few lines connecting the main towns and villages in 1950 (Figure 6.2a), but by 1967 it has become a tangled mass of small spurs and branches (Figure 6.2b).

The remainder of this section is concerned with the progress of electrification in Devon, Cornwall and Dorset, and the experiences of individual farm families in them. One source of information on electrification is the Farm Management Survey data held at the University of Exeter, the field books for which enable definite dates at which mains electricity was installed to be established for a sample of 125 farms spread over the three counties. The numbers electrified in various five-year periods are shown in Table 6.6, which suggests that the process reached a peak between the mid-1950s and the mid-1960s, and was virtually complete by 1970.[59] The pattern was the same for the South West Electricity Board as a whole. Warburton's figures show 5,674 farms connected to a mains supply between 1951 and 1955, 7,653 between 1956 and 1960, 7,413 from 1961 to 1965, and another 2,328 up to 1970.[60] Given the figure of 90 per cent of farms nationally electrified by 1964, this suggests that the south-western counties were not untypical of many rural areas in England and Wales. How did this affect individual farming families?

There is revealing evidence on the topic in the transcripts of oral evidence from farmers who participated in the survey (identified henceforth by farm code number).[61] Some farmers can still remember the days before they had electricity of any kind, and light in the house was provided by candles and oil lamps. Both Tilley and Aladdin lamps were mentioned as brand names (farms 669 and 782), and the same lamps were also used to provide light around the farm buildings. On farm 782, on Dartmoor, near Bovey Tracey, there are memories of milking by hand in the 1950s 'in the old shippon, we had two of the old Aladdin paraffin lights, hung one at each end of the

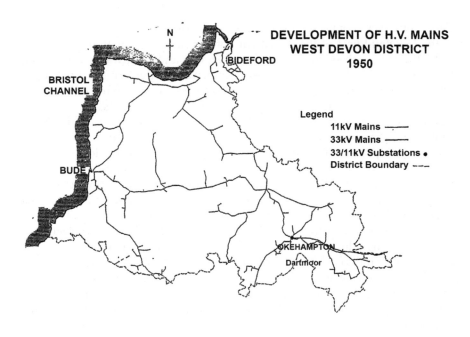

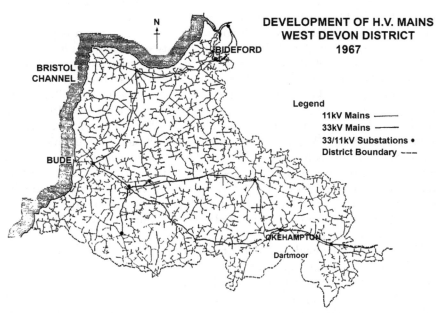

Figure 6.2 Development of high-voltage mains in the West Devon district, 1950 and 1967.

Source: SWEB, *Annual Report*, Bristol: The Board, 1967, pp. 13, 16–17. Maps reproduced by permission of Western Power Distribution plc, Bristol.

Electrifying farms in England 103

Table 6.6 Date of electrification of a sample of 125 farms in Devon, Cornwall and Dorset.

	Number electrified
1941–1945	7
1946–1950	12
1951–1955	15
1956–1960	39
1961–1965	40
1966–1970	8
1971–1975	4

Source: see text

shippon, and milk away, it was pretty primitive, in the semi-darkness.' On a farm near Hemyock (826) the farmer remembers that

> my father was a fairly traditional sort of farmer and long after electricity came [in 1935] he would still take his paraffin lamps out to milk his cows [by hand]. . . . The house of course was different because I didn't go to bed with a candle any more.

There was also gas lighting on some farms. At Hatherleigh in Devon there was a town gas supply, which reached some farmhouses on the edge of the town (e.g. farm 535), but farms further from a village might have Calor gas lamps. Farm 782, on Dartmoor, replaced Aladdin lamps with Calor gas lighting in the house before electrification: 'pull the chain down and light it with a match, that was a real novelty'. On dairy farms hot water was also needed for washing and sterilising milking equipment. On farm 7/8, near Fontmell Magna in Dorset,

> we had an old boiler that we had to fill up with wood, we used to put the wood on top of the boiler to dry it out, and occasionally it caught fire! We'd have to do that every morning.

In farmhouses and cottages heat and hot water were produced from solid fuel stoves, and there are vivid memories of coping with a young family on farm 570 near Bampton in Devon:

> I had two children and we managed with an Aladdin lamp, so that's why our expenses were so low. I had no heat except for the Rayburn, and used that for cooking, no hair dryer, no washing machine. I had an old enamel pan to boil the nappies up, on a gas ring, and that was the way of doing the nappies, it didn't matter about anything else. We had a wringer with big wooden rollers that my grandmother gave me, a mangle

104 *Paul Brassley*

it was called. The rollers were worn in the middle and I would put the nappies through and there would be all splinters in them. . . . We heated the house with an old Rayburn, and we burned logs and rubbish on it. Your grandma used to come and help us, she used to split the logs and things, she said 'If you soak the cardboard it'll last longer.'

Farms that used milking machines needed to produce power for the vacuum pump. This was often done with a small stationary engine ('a little engine in an engine house' on farm 7/8), as Britton and Keith's figures suggest (see earlier). For other power requirements, such as rolling or grinding oats and barley for livestock feed, farmers might use the power from a tractor pulley wheel or an old car. On farm 272, near Launceston, in the 1950s,

Father drove the mill off the back wheel of the car, with a belt. He had a man in Launceston who used to come out here a lot, an engineer, and he rigged up this business of driving the mill with the old car, old Austin, not the one we drove around in.

A few farms had windmills or water wheels. On farm 570 near Bampton a water wheel was installed at sometime around 1880 and worked until about 1950: 'there were twelve machines in the barn that worked from this water wheel . . . thrashing corn, . . . grinding it and rolling it, and they had a saw-bench sawing logs, and a reed comber'.

Farm 570's water wheel was also used, eventually, to generate electricity: 'it was stored in batteries, there were rows of giant glass batteries and it was stored in there,' but for most farms that wanted electricity before a supply was available from the mains, the alternative was an oil- or petrol-driven generator. About half of those interviewed had memories of generators, often of their sound: 'when you were milking you could hear the thing start up – bm-bm-bm' (farm 101); or of their parents listening from the bedroom window to hear if the generator was still working, because if it was it meant that a light had been left on somewhere on the farm (farm 787). Another farmer remembered 'the button at the top of the stairs to switch it off' (farm 139). One farmer's wife recalled the days

when every farm had a generator, and we were living in the cottage, we could stand outside and hear all the generators, they were all different speeds and sizes, you could tell whose generator was working, the one up at [. . .], it's only a mile and a half across the fields, and the game-keeper had a small one just for his house.

(Farm 570)

The Lister Startamatic (farms 101, 570, 669) and Petter (farm 273) were the firms usually mentioned as manufacturers of generators. On one farm

Electrifying farms in England   105

in north Devon (570) the farmer's son, newly married and living in a farm cottage, made his own generator:

> We went to a sale and bought an old farm baler engine, and a dynamo, for £5 . . . we fixed up this baler engine and we had a bit of string from the bedroom window to stop it last thing at night.

Generators often produced electricity at a lower voltage (often 110 V) than that of the mains supply, which could lead to problems later. Farm 570 again:

> It was very low voltage, and the interesting thing was that when the mains came my dad wasn't very good at wiring up plugs, he didn't bother about the red and the black, and on the batteries it didn't matter very much, but when the mains came I had a shock one day, I went up a ladder with an electric drill and I came down the ladder paralysed, because he'd been used to a low voltage.

In general, however, generators were felt to work reasonably well for farming purposes: 'they were very economical because they didn't use very much fuel' (farm 101), and 'did the job pretty adequately' (farm 162). Farm 570 put in a Lister Startamatic to extend the light period in their deep litter poultry houses in 1958. Other problems were more domestic: 'television was better with the mains – less voltage surge and drop' (farm 162), and 'when I went to primary school we did have a television but we couldn't watch it until they'd finished the milking because it was on the Startamatic, and there wasn't enough power for the milking machine and the television' (farm 787). Lack of power, in fact, was the principal problem. On farm 669 it was felt that the vacuum and water pumps were 'struggling with a 5 h.p. engine'.

By the 1950s, therefore, the means were available for many, if not most, farmers to satisfy their light and power requirements, to some degree at least, without having recourse to a mains supply. Nevertheless, when one became available, most chose to have it installed. When the farmstead was in the centre of the village it was usually electrified at the same time as the rest of the village, often before the war, as in the case of farms 842 and 3/1. Farm 826 was about a mile from a village in east Devon, and

> our neighbour back in the 1930s was the electrician in the milk factory, and he came to my parents and said if we put £50 in, it was the Culm Valley Electricity Company then, they would bring the mains up from the village to our two houses, which they did. We were on the mains from 1935. That was the deal, if we put £50 into the project he would wire the house for us, it was to his advantage too.

106 Paul Brassley

In other cases it might be part of a grant-aided improvement scheme, as in the case of farm 162, located outside a small village on the edge of Exmoor in an area that was relatively late in acquiring a mains supply, which went onto the mains in 1966. Farm 576, near Launceston in Cornwall, went onto the mains in 1960–1961:

> They did the village in the 1950s but we were outside the transformer area and they didn't think it was worth paying out so much money, because it would have meant a personal transformer, it would have been an expensive job, then in 1960 they had a scheme, so it was now or never.

Farm 744, near Ashburton in Devon, used an alternative arrangement in 1951, when they agreed to use at least £35 worth of electricity a year: 'you can't believe it, but we didn't have too many electrical things then,' apart from the milking machine. Not all farms found it easy to get the supply that they wanted. Farm 844, near Bampton in north Devon, described a 'battle' with the South Western Electricity Board (SWEB) in 1974, as did farm 929, also in north Devon, which was expanding in the early 1970s and developing a grain and intensive livestock enterprise:

> I had a good old battle with SWEB to get a three phase supply as opposed to single phase or split phase. They said I would never need more than split phase. Well within 12 months I'd outgrown that anyway, so having insisted I did get the three phase supply in there. I had to pay something towards it, on a ten year basis, as part of the electricity bill. The three phase was necessary for the drier and grinder for the pig meal all demanded powerful equipment, big powerful motors.

Farm 570 had a similar agreement to contribute to the cost of installation when they went on to the mains in 1967: 'you paid for the installation over ten years, forty instalments, interest free,' which meant £4 per quarter in their case.

The immediate effects of farm electrification varied. It was not always understood or appreciated by the younger or older members of the farming community. On farm 2/7 in Dorset, following the installation of mains electricity in 1948,

> 'I have this wonderful memory when I was about ten years old I thought I knew everything and it had just been installed, and I looked at the 15 amp plugs and I told my mother 'The hot air comes out of there.'

As the 1942 survey reveals, many farmers initially only had a supply to the house, and not the farm buildings. One farmer (535) remembers that when

Electrifying farms in England   107

electricity was first available in the farmhouse 'grandfather would only have it downstairs.' Others were excited by the possibilities of new electrically powered devices: 'the first electricity bill was paid in 1956. I was 21 at about that time, and I was given an electric razor which I couldn't use because the electricity hadn't been connected' (farm 7/8, Dorset). Some farms were also affected by the necessary infrastructure. On farm 2/9 in Dorset

> I know my mother never forgave my dad for letting them put the transformer in the garden, which she wasn't happy about, we've got this whacking great transformer in the garden which is not particularly aesthetically pleasing. You could have it moved but it would cost you a fortune. Dad was just pragmatic about these things.

For other farmers the supply lines were a small source of income. On farm 570

> there were poles all around, and my Dad said 'I don't want any poles on [the rented farm], stick them on . . . ours,' and now we get £700 income from the poles a year, wayleave. You don't get anything for the ones that are taking it to you, it's the ones that are taking it to your neighbours.

Opinions varied on the impact of mains electricity on the business of farming. On farm 162, a small dairy and livestock farm on the edge of Exmoor, 'I didn't notice much difference,' and similarly on farm 826 in the Culm Valley, 'It didn't make too much difference to the way we farmed.' Conversely, the advent of electricity to farm 576 near Launceston in 1960 meant that they no longer milked by hand, and so began to increase the cow numbers. Similarly farm 782, on Dartmoor, 'had the first milking machine in 1961 after the electricity came in, that transformed what you could do. Just the ability to turn on a switch and have light, in the buildings as well as the house.' On farm 669, in north Devon, electrification in 1964 improved conditions in the house, because 'we could have a washing machine, and with the lights on you could see what you were doing. Those were the two things we had at the beginning, the television and the washing machine.' But it did not initially 'make much difference to the way we farmed, because there was nothing running off electricity, other than the lights around the yard perhaps', but then the vacuum and water pumps went over to the mains, and

> gradually we installed more equipment that used electricity – the mill and mixer in 1969, as an attempt to bring down the feed bill. We still use that, several times a day. . . . that was a big saving, because we used to grind it before with an old engine down there, then carry it into the bin with a shovel and mix it, and that took hours and hours, so the mill and mixer was a big improvement, saving time and labour.

108 *Paul Brassley*

Similarly on farm 7/8 in Dorset it was felt that

> it made a big difference when we linked up to the mains, we could milk
> by electricity, hot water . . . we had light in the buildings as well as the
> house. It was a big wiring job . . . it was a big step forward. We used to
> grind our own barley in a grinder-mixer, we never had that before we
> had electricity. It was a major step forward, and quite an expensive one.

On farm 209, near Truro, which went on to the mains in 1947, electrification was included in the farmer's list of the most influential technical changes in his lifetime: 'a lot of the materials handling you couldn't do without electricity.'

Conclusions

This chapter has examined farm electrification mostly from the perspective of the individual farmer and the agricultural industry as a whole. It is important to remember that there is an alternative viewpoint, that of the electricity supply industry. At the peak period of farm electrification, in the 1950s and '60s, thousands of people were employed as field surveyors, engineers, wiring contractors, in drawing offices, construction gangs, the sales force, and as home service advisers and demonstrators, to take a mains electricity supply beyond the main centres of population, and make it effectively available to a new population of domestic and business consumers on farms and in farmhouses and cottages.[62]

Electrification took time to affect farms, because there were numerous sunk costs in existing machinery and systems of farming, but as new investments were made electrical equipment became more common. An oxy-acetylene welding kit might be replaced by an arc welder, or a rolling mill eventually fitted with an electric motor rather than being run off the tractor pulley, or, most commonly, the stationary engine powering the vacuum pump for the dairy might be replaced by an electric motor. The major question over electrification, for both farmers and electricity supply companies, was the balance between fixed and variable costs. For the suppliers, farms had a much bigger fixed cost than urban consumers, but there was always the possibility of industrial as opposed to domestic levels of consumption. For farmers, electrification could reduce variable costs and labour costs, but required capital investment. In addition, the fact that the household and the business are combined on most farms meant that domestic comfort and convenience entered into the equation in a way that they might not have done in an urban business, and it is certainly difficult, except at one point in time in 1942, to separate the number of farms that were connected for domestic purposes only from those that were using electricity for farming purposes too. It is all too easy to see electrification

Electrifying farms in England 109

now as something inevitable, but as Luckin points out, some of the crazier ideas about the application of electricity to agriculture were only just succumbing to scientific disproval in the later 1920s and early 1930s, and the scepticism of the ordinary farmer about the effect of electrical discharges on crop growth might well have affected his attitude to the use of electric light.[63] It should also be remembered that farmers were clearly reluctant to spend money on tried and tested inputs such as feeds and fertilisers between the wars, so something much less proven was that much less likely to be adopted. After the war things were different. Farmers were being encouraged to adopt new technology by a range of advisers and policies, and most of them responded. But what mattered most after the war was that the Area Boards made supplies available to them at prices that most of them could afford, subsidised by their fellow consumers. As Warburton argues, without nationalisation, many, if not most, farms 'had no chance of ever receiving a supply of mains electricity'.[64]

Appendix: Numbers of farms in England and Wales connected to mains electricity supplies

At first sight, quantifying the numbers of farms connected to the mains (in Table 6.4) would appear to be a simple problem, especially for the post-war or post-nationalisation period. Hannah, for example, tells us that 'the proportion of farms connected [presumably in England and Wales] rose from 32 per cent in 1948 to 47 per cent in 1953', and that 'by 1958 72 per cent of farms were already connected,' although he does not tell us how many farms would constitute 100 per cent.[65] Similarly the Electricity Council's report on the state of the industry at the end of 1972 tells us that in England and Wales 87,000 farms, or 33 per cent of the total, were connected in 1947–1948 (making the figure for 100 per cent 263,636 farms), while in 1971–1972 the figure had risen to 255,745, or 97.01 per cent of the total.[66] The problem is that the Electricity Council data does not cover all the intervening years, although its Handbook of Electricity Statistics also gives percentage figures for 1952 and 1961, apparently using the same 100 per cent baseline, from which it can be calculated that the number of farms electrified by those years were 126,545 and 224,091 respectively.[67] Data in the Ministry of Agriculture archives, derived from the Annual Reports and Accounts of the Electricity Council for 1956–1957 and 1962–1963 show 193,248 farms connected in September 1957 and 257,715 in June 1964.[68] Presumably the apparent decrease between then and 1966 (see Table 6.4) can be explained by the number of farm amalgamations going on at the time.

Peirson's article is the only source so far discovered which gives numbers of farms connected for each year (1920–1958) that it covers, but his figures are for England, Wales and South Scotland.[69] However, there are separate

110   *Paul Brassley*

Table 6.7 Number of farms connected to mains supplies in England and Wales.

	Peirson	*Electricity Council 1971*
1947	86,801	87,000
1952	133,200	126,545

data for the South of Scotland for two years in the Electricity Council (1973) report, from which it can be calculated that the England and Wales farms constitute 94.5 per cent of the total. Adjusting Peirson's figures by this factor and comparing the years for which the Electricity Council (1971) figures are available produces the results shown in Table 6.7.

Although there are only two years in which direct comparisons are possible, Peirson's figures agree with those of the Electricity Council Handbook to within less than 1 per cent and less than 5 per cent in those years. Luckin quotes a figure of 25,000 connected farms in 1936, and Ballin 30,000 in 1937, which compare closely with Peirson's 25,341 and 30,500 respectively for those years.[70] On the other hand, Matthews gives figures of 'about 4,000' farms in Great Britain in 1933 and about 8,000 in 1936 being connected to the mains.[71] Peirson's figures for those years are 14,487 and 25,341 respectively. Apart from the rate of increase being not dissimilar, there are clearly considerable discrepancies between these two sources. Unfortunately Matthews gives no indication of the evidence upon which his (perhaps suspiciously) rounded estimates are based, but Luckin makes it clear that Matthews was quoting figures only for those farms that used electricity 'for productive purposes' and omitted those that used it only for domestic purposes.[72] The other comparison point is the National Farm Survey figure for 1942, which found that 24 per cent of holdings, or about 69,000 holdings out of 290,000, were connected to a public supply.[73] Peirson's figure for the same year is 57,702, a difference of over 16 per cent, although if we take 24 per cent of 263,636 farms, that is 63,273 as the equivalent NFS figure, the difference is reduced to 8.3 per cent. And of course it is important to remember that some farms contain more than one holding, as defined in the NFS.

On the whole, therefore, it seems reasonable to take Peirson's estimates as being at least of the right order of magnitude. Unfortunately he does not reveal the source of them in his article, but it is presumably not unrealistic to assume that they are from a consistent source. And they have the great merit of covering the period from 1920 to 1958. From 1961 to 1971 there is a series of Electricity Council figures. The Council published data for total sales to farms and average sales per farm from 1960 to 1970, so dividing the latter into the former gives the number of farms for those years.[74] This calculation would give a total of 243,418 farms electrified in 1961, which does not agree precisely with the statement on the same page to the effect that

Electrifying farms in England 111

85 per cent of the country's farms, implying 224,091 farms, were connected by 1961. It is also unlikely, as pointed out earlier, that the Electricity Council series connects precisely with Peirson's series. However, in both cases the differences are less than 10 per cent, so as long as the data reported in Table 6.4 are used as an indication of the progress of electrification, rather than a precise record of it, they should not produce too much confusion.

Notes

1 L. Hannah, *Electricity before nationalisation: A study of the development of the electricity supply industry in Britain to 1948*. London: Macmillan, 1979, p. 190; Ministry of Works and Planning, *Report of the Committee on Land Utilisation in Rural Areas* (the Scott Committee). Cmd. 6378, 1942, London: HMSO, pp. 50–51, 109.

2 Hannah, *Electricity before nationalisation*, p. 192; R. Moore-Colyer, 'Lighting the landscape: Rural electrification in Wales', chapter 4 in this volume; C. Chant (ed), *Science, technology and everyday life 1870–1950*. London: Routledge/Open University, 1989, p. 94. In international comparison terms, it is interesting to note Chant's (p. 108) figure of 10% of farms in the USA electrified in the mid-1930s. There are more detailed figures in W. L. Calvert, 'The technological revolution in agriculture 1910–1955', *Agricultural History*, vol. 30 (1), 1956, pp. 18–27, who states that whereas in 1919 only 100,000 farms in the USA received electricity from power lines, the 1940 census revealed that 45.6% of farms had an electrical distribution line within a quarter of a mile, and by 1950, 77% of farms had electricity from a power line.

3 Chant, *Science, technology and everyday life*, p. 96.

4 R. B. Matthews, 'Electro-farming', in Anon (ed.), *The estate book and diary*. Letchworth: The Country Gentlemen's Association, 1928, pp. 324–328.

5 R. B. Matthews, *Electro-farming; or the application of electricity to agriculture*. London, 1928. The overall impression emerging from the book is that the author is at least an enthusiast and perhaps a fanatic. Matthews was born in South Wales in 1876 and educated at the Royal College of Science and the Central Technical College. After various jobs abroad, he returned to England in 1906 and practiced as a consulting engineer. In 1908 he claimed to be one of the first aeronautical consultants, and was attached to the Air Ministry when it was formed at the end of 1917. He was a fellow of the Royal Aeronautical Society and, from 1911, a Member of the Institution of Electrical Engineers. He had his own 640-acre farm at Greater Felcourt, East Grinstead, Sussex. He met a tragic end in August 1943, succumbing to heart failure after an unsuccessful attempt to save his younger son while bathing in rough seas at Port Darfach beach near Holyhead. See W.O.F., 'Obituary: Richard Borlase Matthews', *Journal of the Institution of Electrical Engineers* (henceforth *JIEE*) vol. 90 (1), 1943, p. 539.

6 Moore-Colyer, 'Lighting the landscape'; C. Dampier Whetham, 'Electric power in agriculture', *Journal of the Royal Agricultural Society of England*, vol. 85, 1924, p. 265.

7 Whetham, 'Electric power in agriculture', pp. 254, 267–268. It should be remembered that up to the 1950s many tractors incorporated a pulley wheel that could be used to drive large leather or fabric belts to power barn machinery, threshing machines etc.

8 A survey of 54 electrified farms in 1928 found that they had an average of 11.9 lamps in the farm buildings, with 15 lamps in smaller farmhouses and 25 in larger ones, at an average of 30 watts per lamp. See E. W. Golding, *The*

112   Paul Brassley

electrification of agriculture and the rural districts. London: English Universities Press, 1937, p. 31.

9 In the United States, similarly, electricity was first used mainly for lighting, but was subsequently employed for electric pumps, milking machines, ventilating systems, hay and grain dryers, silage unloaders, feed grinders, milk coolers and heat lamps for piglets, chicks and turkey poults. Farm household use by the 1950s included refrigerators, deep freezers, washing machines, dryers, irons, sewing machines, vacuum cleaners, food mixers, toasters electric blankets, air conditioners, radios and televisions, according to Calvert, 'The technological revolution in agriculture', p. 20.

10 Whetham, 'Electric power in agriculture', pp. 254–267.

11 Whetham, 'Electric power in agriculture', pp. 267–270.

12 Moore-Colyer, 'Lighting the landscape'.

13 K. Sayer, 'Battery birds, "stimulighting" and "twilighting": The ecology of standardised poultry technology', *History of Technology*, special issue, 'By whose standards? Standardization, stability and uniformity in the history of information and electrical technologies', 2008, vol. 28, pp. 149–168; W. P. Blount, *Hen batteries.* London: Bailliere, Tindall and Cox, 1951, pp. 31–38.

14 B. Short, C. Watkins, W. Foot and P. Kinsman, *The national farm survey 1941–1943: State surveillance and the countryside in England and Wales in the Second World War.* Wallingford: CABI, 2000.

15 Ministry of Agriculture and Fisheries, *National farm survey of England and Wales: A summary report.* London: HMSO, 1946, p. 108.

16 Ministry of Agriculture and Fisheries, *National Farm Survey*, pp. 67–69.

17 C. A. Cameron Brown, 'Electricity in clean milk production', *Agriculture*, vol. 52 (9), 1945, pp. 391–392.

18 *Journal of the Royal Agricultural Society of England*, vols 103 (1942), 104 (1943) and 105 (1944); see also A. S. Foot and J. F. Lovett, *Electric fencing*, MAF Bulletin 147, London: HMSO, 1951.

19 D. K. Britton and I. F. Keith, 'A note on the statistics of farm power supplies in Great Britain', *Farm Economist* vol. 6 (6), 1950, p. 167; Electrification may have expanded even more quickly in wartime France. Coal and oil shortages led the authorities to embark upon a campaign of electrification that saw 63,000 new electric motors installed between 1942 and 1944. By 1943–1944, 40% of the French harvest was threshed using electric power, compared with only 5% before the war, according to M. Cepede, *Agriculture et Alimentation en France Durant la Deuxième Guerre Mondiale.* Paris: Editions Genin, 1961, pp. 222–224.

20 UK National Archives, Kew (TNA), MAF38/695, Ministry of Agriculture and Fisheries, Economics and Statistics division, *Reports on the Economic Position of Agriculture No. 23: Farm Water and Electricity Supplies*, September 1945.

21 TNA, MAF38/695, *Farm Water and Electricity Supplies*, pp. 27–29.

22 TNA, MAF38/695, *Farm Water and Electricity Supplies*, p. 36. To put the £55 million figure in context, it was about 9% of gross agricultural output or 28% of farming income in 1945 – see H. F. Marks and D. K. Britton, *A hundred years of British food and farming: A statistical survey.* London: Taylor and Francis, 1989, p. 149.

23 TNA, MAF38/695, *Farm Water and Electricity Supplies*, pp. 37 and 40.

24 TNA, MAF38/695, *Farm Water and Electricity Supplies*, pp. 44–48.

25 TNA, MAF38/695, *Farm Water and Electricity Supplies*, p. 54.

26 The Electricity Council, *Handbook of electricity supply statistics, 1971.* London: The Council, 1971, pp. 53 and 70.

27 The following analysis essentially follows the account in L. Hannah, *Engineers, managers and politicians: The first fifteen years of nationalised electricity supply in Britain.* London: Macmillan, 1982, pp. 73–75 and 297, which is largely

Electrifying farms in England 113

based on unpublished sources in the files of government departments, the Electricity Council, and the various area electricity boards. Following the privatisation of the industry these records have been dispersed. Some are in the National Archives, some in the Museum of Science and Industry in Manchester (http://www.mosi.org.uk) and those (or some of them) for the South Western Electricity Board are in the archives of the South West Electricity History Society in Bristol (http://www.swehs.co.uk).

28 A. W. Gray, *Electricity supply in the rural areas*. London: Eyre and Spottiswoode, 1968, p. 6.
29 H. Self and E. M. Watson, *Electricity supply in Great Britain: Its development and organisation*. London: Allen & Unwin, 1952, p. 182.
30 TNA MAF 226/7, Rural Electrification Programme: Policy File, C.H.M. Wilcox (MAF) to M. P. Murray (Ministry of Fuel and Power), 5.11.1951.
31 TNA MAF 226/7 Rural Electrification Programme: Policy File, Turner to Dugdale, 20.3.1953.
32 TNA MAF 226/7 Rural Electrification Programme: Policy File, notes on a meeting with A. Greig, 25.9.1953.
33 TNA MAF 225/15 Policy of Area Boards on Connection Costs, 1951–1963; MAF226/9 Rural Electrification Programme: Policy File, extract from the Report of the Select Committee on Nationalised Industries: Electricity Supply Industry (1963).
34 TNA MAF 226/8 Rural Electrification Programme: Policy File 1953–61; MAF226/7 Rural Electrification Programme: Policy File, 1951–53, Notes for C.H.M. Wilcox, 22.4.1953.
35 Hannah, *Engineers, managers, and politicians*, pp. 73–75; G. Warburton, 'The story of SWEB's rural electrification', Supplement to *Histelec News* No. 17, April 2001, p. 3 (http://www.swehs.co.uk/tactive/_S17–0.html?zoom_highlight= rural+electrification).
36 G. F. Peirson, 'The development of rural electrification: A review of progress', *Proceedings of the Institution of Electrical Engineers*, vol. 108, part A, 1961, pp. 115–116.
37 Gray, *Electricity supply in the rural areas*, p. 7.
38 Hannah, *Engineers, managers, and politicians*, p. 143.
39 TNA MAF 226/9 Rural Electrification Programme: Policy File, extract from the Report of the Select Committee on Nationalised Industries: Electricity Supply Industry (1963), p. 144.
40 TNA MAF 226/9, Rural Electrification Programme: Policy File 1962–65, notes of a meeting at the Ministry of Power 18.4.62.
41 TNA MAF 226/9, Rural Electrification Programme: Policy File 1962–65, Woolley to Errol 18.6.1964.
42 TNA MAF 226/10, Rural Electrification Programme: Policy File 1965–73, notes of meetings on 4.11.1965 and 16.11.1965.
43 K. Pople, *Power comes to Widecombe*. Film. Devon: South Western Electricity Board, 1962. A copy is available in the archives of the South West Electricity History Society in Bristol (http://www.swehs.co.uk).
44 Agenda and papers for National Parks Commission, conference with Park Planning Authorities, 26 July 1955, in North Yorkshire RO, NYCC/P/YD, file of papers belonging to the Clerk of the Peace. I am most grateful to Richard Hoyle for providing a copy of the file.
45 H. W. Grimmitt, 'Considerations on some electricity supply problems', *Journal of the Institution of Electrical Engineers*, vol. 92, part 2, 1945, pp. 37–38.
46 Peirson, 'Development of rural electrification', pp. 119–123.
47 H. H. Ballin, *The organisation of electricity supply in Great Britain*. London: Electrical Press, 1946, p. 235; Grimmitt, 'Considerations on some electricity supply problems', p. 36.

114 *Paul Brassley*

48 South Western Electricity Board, *Electricity on the farm and in the house (guide for Young Farmers' Clubs)*. Bristol: The Board, 1964, pp. 3–4.
49 A. B. Lees, *Farming machinery*. London: Faber and Faber, 1951, pp. 158–160.
50 H. M. Hughes and A. C. Williams, 'The use of machinery on the farm', in J. A. Hanley (ed.), *Progressive farming*. London: Caxton, 1949, pp. 129–130.
51 TNA MAF 226/9, Rural Electrification Programme: Policy File, 1962–65, T. Marten to I.O.H. Lepper, August 1963.
52 TNA MAF 226/12, The Economics of Farm Electrification, 1953–55, W. J. Guscott to J. Tristram Beresford, 29.7.1954. Beresford farmed on a large scale in Wiltshire and was the Ministry nominee on the South West Electricity Consultative Council.
53 C. Culpin, *Profitable farm mechanisation*. London: Crosby Lockwood, 1968, p. 110.
54 Ruth Janette Ruck, *Hill farm story*. London: Faber and Faber, 1966, pp. 224–225.
55 Gray, *Electricity supply in the rural areas*, pp. 10–11.
56 Electrical Development Association (EDA), *Automatic feeding: Farm electrification Handbook No. 9*. London: The Association, 1964.
57 SWEB, *Electricity on the farm and in the house*, p. 7.
58 SWEB, *Annual Report*. Bristol: The Board, 1953, p. 6.
59 The field books are currently held in the Land, Environment, Economics and Policy Institute, University of Exeter, but will eventually be transferred to the University of Exeter library. I am grateful to Allan Butler for producing the raw data from which the figures in Table 6.6 were calculated.
60 Warburton, 'SWEB's Rural Electrification', Appendix II.
61 These transcripts are also held in the Land, Environment, Economics and Policy Institute, University of Exeter, and identified by farm code number.
62 Warburton, 'SWEB's Rural Electrification' provides a vivid account of this work.
63 B. Luckin, *Questions of power: Electricity and environment in interwar Britain*. Manchester: Manchester University Press, 1990, p. 78.
64 Warburton, 'SWEB's rural electrification', p. 1.
65 Hannah, *Engineers, managers and politicians*, pp. 74–75.
66 The Electricity Council, *Electricity supply in Great Britain: Organisation and development*. London: The Council, 1973, p. 43.
67 The Electricity Council, *Handbook of electricity supply statistics, 1971*. London: The Council, 1971, p. 71.
68 TNA MAF 226/4 Holdings connected to a public supply, 1957–1964.
69 G. F. Peirson, 'The development of rural electrification', p. 114.
70 Luckin, *Questions of power*, p. 75; H. H. Ballin, *The organisation of electricity supply in Great Britain*. London: Electrical Press, 1946, p. 231.
71 R. B. Matthews, 'Applications of electricity to agriculture', *JIEE*, vol. 78, 1936, p. 175.
72 Luckin, *Questions of power*, p. 75.
73 Ministry of Agriculture and Fisheries, *National Farm Survey*, pp. 107–108.
74 The Electricity Council, *Handbook of Electricity Supply Statistics, 1971*, pp. 70–71.

Part II
The effects of electrification

7 Electrification and its alternatives in the farmer's and labourer's home

Karen Sayer

Introduction

By 1928, when the national grid and the Central Electricity Board passed into law via the Electricity (Supply) Act 1926, the endorsement of electricity for agricultural purposes in Britain was already widespread.[1] Seven years before the national grid had been made fully operational, Borlase Matthews had already published *Electro-Farming: or the Application of Electricity to Agriculture* (1928) to encourage farmers to stimulate crop growth using electric cables, to light their poultry, and to heat and sterilise dairy equipment.[2] The Electrical Development Association encouraged rural demand in the context of the 1926 Act by finding new uses for electricity on the farm, including the farmhouse, and produced the *Practical Cinematograph Film on Rural Electrification: Showing How a Public Supply of Electricity in Rural Areas Can Be, and Is Being, Used*, to demonstrate the uses of electricity both on the farm and in the farmhouse.[3] However, expectations about the possible value of electricity in the countryside were already high among innovators and early enthusiasts, and tapped into wider discussions at home and abroad. In the case of illustrations such as those advocating the use of arc lighting to illuminate night-time harvesting in E. M. Alglave and J. Boulard's *La Lumiere electrique* (Paris 1882), or the rather more practical discussion of 'isolated installations' (i.e. factories and great country houses) in F. C. Allsop's *Practical Electric Light Fitting*, (first edn. 1892, and originally a series of articles in the *English Mechanic*), these ideas had long preceded the 1920s legislative framework designed to underpin the infrastructure of electrification,[4] and belonged to the wider early debate about what electricity was and what it was for.[5]

However, as becomes evident when we consider social commentaries such as C. S. Orwin's *The Problems of Rural Life* (1945), the promotion and supposed impact of electrification in rural areas must be set against the limited availability of electricity from the mains in the countryside (which continued until long after he wrote), the high cost both of initial connection and then of use in rural areas (which continued until the 1960s) and its questionable reliability. As historians of technology have argued, linear

118　*Karen Sayer*

models of electrification fail in the face of the evidence, along with those that see innovation as 'external to the normal business of human activity'.[6] Observers like Orwin focused on the adoption of electricity as a necessary precursor to looked-for modernisation of the labourer's and the farmer's home. However, their arguments made on behalf of the farm labourer, by emphasising the material failure to progress, serve instead to demonstrate that the process of electrification was far from straightforward, even once the basic premise that it would be beneficial in rural areas had been officially sanctioned. As will be seen in this chapter, there was a messy, non-linear, heterogeneous process at work regarding the everyday experience of rural electrification, based on multi-layered experiences ranging from election, to necessity and exigency, to constraint, that bore little relationship to the rhetoric.[7]

As was recognised in the Political and Economic Planning (PEP) *Report on the Supply of Electricity in Great Britain* (1936), published when only about 35,000 farms were receiving electricity through the still nascent national grid,[8] the countryside offered up some unique difficulties at the level of planning when it came to the implementation of this new piece of national infrastructure. As it said,

> In considering rural electrification it is necessary to bear in mind the peculiar conditions in which it has to be carried out. To mention some of the salient points, the problem takes different forms according to the different population density of different areas, to the type of farming carried on, the degree of prosperity prevailing, the extent and nature of factory or extensive industries developed, and the presence or absence of a strong suburban, residential, or holiday element in the life of the area. . . .
>
> [As a result] there is not a single rural electrification problem, but a mass of quite distinct problems, for each difference in population density and in social and economic characteristics involves a corresponding difference in electricity demands.[9]

The PEP report evidences a detailed understanding at the time among some of the structural and topographical complexity of rural life in interwar Britain, and its varied degree of interconnection with urban settlement and industry, which between them had led the way in the process of electrification in the UK. But, this statement also shows that though it might be useful to look at the promotion of rural electrification in order to understand how electricity was perceived at the time, how suppliers having generated it sought to make a persuasive case to landowners and farmers for electricity to be harnessed to agriculture in order to sell it, the texts associated with such an effort could never tell us about the actual extent of electrification within rural communities, demand or the occurrence and day-to-day use of use of electricity within farmhouse and cottage, let alone the understandings

Electrification and its alternatives   119

of electricity and electrification that existed on the ground. The more valuable sources in this case are those that capture the lived experience, such as the very many published and self-published local testimonies and memoirs written by the women and men who lived in rural communities at the time, such as Irene Megginson's *Mud on My Doorstep* (1987) and Paul Dunn's *Dunn and Dusted* (2005) (both about the north of England) that will be used here.[10] In parallel to this evidence, though electrification was often treated as one and the same thing as what came to be called 'modernisation', we also have the advertising aimed specifically at a category of consumer conceived of as 'the farmer's wife' in specialist publications such as the *Farmer & Stockbreeder* and *Farmer's Weekly*. This reveals that there were some very competitive alternatives to electrically powered domestic equipment that were represented by their manufacturers as equally 'modern'.

There are obvious difficulties at the quantitative level with this material. Whereas evidence for connection to the mains is quite clear cut, for example, it is much more difficult to judge the popularity of these alternatives, other than through their widespread, if unremarked, survival in rural areas. A substantive study of hardware shops' and ironmongers' sales and purchase ledgers, cash books and nominal accounts might be indicative of the extent of the adoption of solid-fuel ranges or paraffin, for example, especially if cross-referenced to local census data for information about where named individuals lived and of their work, agricultural or ancillary. A detailed quantitative analysis of this type is beyond the scope of the present study, but archived examples of ironmongers' and hardware stores' cash books and ledgers certainly record the sale of ranges and other domestic equipment, of replacement parts and of fuel, which gives a qualitative sense of the adaptation and sustained use of the different pieces of equipment. Through the personal testimonies, articles and letters in the home sections of the farming press, such as the *Farmer & Stockbreeder's* 'The Farmer's Home' that during the interwar period offered articles on, for example, wiring up private lighting plants to serve as power for the radio, 'Do it This Way' and 'Practical Hints Contributed by Readers' columns, and answers to readers' questions, we can then in addition gain some sense of the value of collective, manual labour within rural households (as another alternative source of power), the possible significance of repair, second-hand markets and informal exchange of goods, and of the importance of informal, everyday and individual adjustments to the built spaces of the home and its contents, such as rigging up switches and electrical cables to tap into the mains/lighting plants.[11]

The focus of this chapter is therefore the everyday aspect of rural electrification during the period spanning the interwar to immediate post-war period – the ways in which electricity and electric goods were presented to potential consumers by enthusiasts, (including suppliers, designers, commentators, politicians, and policy-makers), and the ordinary day-to-day negotiations involved in its adoption. That is, how electrical devices came to be absorbed into and adapted within the rural home, despite or

120   *Karen Sayer*

maybe because of its competitors. In addressing the ways in which electricity ought to be harnessed to country life, however, and by focusing on the material disadvantages in rural amenity experienced by farm labourers and their families, the commentators who focused on the failure of 'modernisation' (as solely dependent on electrification for power), it will be argued, unwittingly placed the labourer's home and 'the housewife' at the centre of policy-making.

All 'mod cons'

'Electricity brings its great benefits to the countrywoman, and earns her great blessings,' the British Electrical Development Association (EDA) asserted in its final chapter 'Electricity in Farmhouse and Cottage' in *Electricity on the Farm* (first issued 1947, revised edition 1954, reprinted 1956). 'No more lamps to fill,' it continued,

> no fire to light, and no doubts about the baking; electricity gives instant light or heat at the touch of a switch; it heats the oven and automatically keeps the temperature steady. It takes the drudgery out of washday, and gives the housewife far more time for all her other work.[12]

Having inadvertently provided evidence in this description of the daily household tasks undertaken by rural women, the EDA then went on to advise on items such as the choice of lights and light fittings, the probable costs of cooking by electricity, and the necessity of adequate wiring being installed throughout the home.[13] By writing on a level with, yet standardising 'the housewife' (in a caption: 'the wives of farmers and farmworkers alike'[14]), the EDA sought to establish the universal domestic value of electricity. In marketing electricity to her, in the 1950s the EDA simultaneously both detailed and smoothed out the spaces and work done in farmhouse and cottage, as if they were one and the same home, and used by people with access to identical resources. Farmhouses and cottages at the time were complex sites, each with their own varied and changing spaces and each of these spaces its own varied and changing uses: kitchen, 'back house' or scullery, and dairy; wash house; front room, living room, and parlour; bedrooms; toilet, outside privy, or bathroom; office, and so on. However, as Graeme Gooday has argued in *Domesticating Electricity*, 'an innovation will only gain a permanent footing in the home if its role is made meaningful and unthreatening,' and it is this process that we see at work in the pamphlet.[15] The EDA used a standardised rural home (constructed in text and image, but also seen in market-town showrooms and at exhibition displays), as a set or a stage on which the predicted use of electricity could be performed for a standardised (female) audience, and in this way made comprehensible, normal and therefore both safe and worth purchasing.

This was not, the EDA told its readers (who were, it supposed, farmers) in the pamphlet's preface, because electricity was not already in use. Indeed,

Electrification and its alternatives 121

'a large number of farmers are exponents of full electrification,' it suggested reassuringly, and went on to state that electricity had been 'in the fullest use for all purposes in the farmstead for a number of years'. Yet, it intimated, electricity had not been used to its fullest extent, and many installations therefore fell down in efficiency – this, in a post-war policy context of constant extortions to increased growth.[16] Indeed, as Newman has shown, earlier connection to the supply in Britain did not necessarily mean that electricity was being used on the farm for agricultural processes at all. Until the post-war period, 'farm electricity supplies had', Newman argued, 'been mainly used in the farmhouse.'[17] In order to smooth out demand, the EDA needed to encourage other uses in the countryside, which included the farm, but also (because of the then structure of the agricultural industry) the tied cottage.

Marketing electricity through the advice it provided, the EDA therefore went on to assert that 'a modern industry is not successful . . . unless its workers and staff are contented.' Electricity was, it argued, crucial to the maintenance of that content. 'To-day', it explained,

> farm workers prefer to work on farms equipped with electrical facilities, also with such working conditions allied to the very considerable value of a modern all-electric home in contributing to family comfort and happiness, the electrified farm is more likely to have contented and permanent workers.[18]

It was commonplace from the earliest days of electrification, as Gooday has argued, to make an idealised case for electricity based on its supposed safety and facility, and therefore modernity, just as we see here.[19] In an attempt to increase demand in the countryside, the EDA also adopted a specific interpretation of electricity that tapped into existing political rhetoric regarding agricultural production: concepts such as labour efficiency, ease in agricultural process and method, and increased output were essential in pushing those who had already gained access to the mains to use more power in the country, in order to smooth demand and load. In addition, the EDA also used arguments that fed particularly powerfully into long-standing national concerns about rural depopulation, and aimed these arguments squarely at the farmer. 'There can be no doubt that improvements in pay, hours and conditions of work would go more than half way to stemming the indiscriminate flow of workers from the industry,' agricultural economists A. K. Giles and W. J.G. Cowie wrote in the same period, based on a study of 500 labourers who worked or had worked on the land around Gloucestershire. 'In addition, however', they went on,

> it is equally obvious that some steps would have to be taken to ameliorate the problems of accommodation associated with tied cottages, . . . the long-term insecurity, the work-cottage tie, and the lack

122   *Karen Sayer*

of space and amenities of many cottages . . . impact . . . on the newly-married, amenity-conscious young workers and their wives.[20]

In an effort to end the longstanding problem of rural depopulation or what Giles and Cowie called the 'drift of workers' from agriculture, an electricity supply, along with other key components of amenity such as hot and cold running water and indoor sanitation, had already been introduced as key issues to the debate about the prospects for agriculture as an industry. For labourers, who were found at the time to be too low-paid to afford the rent due on council houses, much depended on the willingness or ability of their employers to connect their tied accommodation to the mains, and the condition of tied accommodation varied widely. A comment by Dr J. F. Duncan to the paper by Giles and Cowie, regarding Scotland, included the passing observation that if a cottage was not improved then farmers 'have difficulty in getting workers to go into them and much more difficulty in getting workers' wives to go into them'. In response, based on having 'questioned some wives', Giles and Cowie noted that

> there is no doubt that their reactions to the amenities of the tied cottage is vital. It was made quite clear to us that some farmers couldn't get workers to live in a given cottage simply because of the wife's reaction to this cottage and its lack of this, that or the other thing. There is no doubt that wives probably play a far more important part in this than the men.[21]

Though other factors were discussed, it becomes clear that there was at least an assumption at the time that the labourers' wives were crucial drivers in the search for improved living conditions, and that this included the availability of electricity. The EDA, sensitive to its audience, therefore drew on this context and argued that by harnessing electricity not just to the farm, but also to the farm labourer's home, the farmworker's happiness might be achieved via their family/home life, on the basis that it was thought necessary to maintain that happiness in order to keep them on the land and away from competing industries/the modern urban home.

The first condition to be met, if the land was to remain in good condition and fit for purpose, was the maintenance of skilled agricultural labour. This was an argument that had already gained currency in the interwar period. To keep the skilled labourer on the land, and therefore farming in a fit state for the nation (given the prospect of war), it was therefore widely thought necessary to improve the condition of the farmhouses and cottages. This was an argument that ultimately placed the home and family at the heart of a stable agricultural workforce, in the interests of the farmer/employer and the nation. As Sir George Stapledon put it in *The Way of the Land* (1942): 'There is hardly a district where housing conditions are *in toto* adequate or fit for a robust rural population. Something is always wrong.'[22] This

Electrification and its alternatives 123

'something' might be an absence/lack of cottages and therefore continuity of living in, which he says the farmers' wives and the labourers loathed, or the dire condition of both cottages and farmhouses. So, he stated of the investment required to maintain British agriculture: 'first the houses and cottages, then the workers and then the farming'.[23] The quality of housing and what the 'wives' thought of it was therefore an old chestnut, but one which regained currency following the war. Without modern amenities, it was argued, labourers who had either stayed on farms, or those who had deliberately moved to the countryside in order to labour on farms during the war, would leave. Viscount Astor and B. Seebohm Rowntree, in *Mixed Farming and Muddled Thinking* (1946), for instance, were absolutely certain that the provision of 'Water and Electricity Mains' were crucial to the improvement 'not only in the quantity and quality of the milk supply, but also in the health of the rural population generally'.[24] The net effect of these campaigns, unwittingly, was to place the labourer's wife centre stage, as it was the women, as suggested in the EDA pamphlet, who it was supposed principally had to tackle the daily/weekly round of cooking, cleaning and washing.

Little of the material just discussed contains direct evidence, however, of what the wives thought. What becomes clear from the testimony of farmer's wives (within a different social sphere) is that their experiences could vary quite dramatically depending not just on rural/urban location, but also the facilities put in or not put in by particular landlords. Irene Megginson, for instance, in joining a farming family in Yorkshire during the war, and helping her future mother-in-law with the housework, had to learn both how to undertake housework, and how to do so (having grown up in Hull) with what she identified when she wrote of the experience over forty years later: 'a lack of "mod. Cons." – amenities taken for granted by most townspeople then, and almost all country folk now'.[25] In describing the farm she notes that there 'was no electricity of course, and lamps or candles were our only illumination'. The radio had 'batteries that needed "charging" at a garage'.[26] They had a bathroom, but the number of baths was limited by the extent of 'pumping up' required – twenty minutes of hand pumping in the back kitchen to get the tank to the right level. They also used a copper for heating the water when washing laundry, and baked in coal-fired ovens.[27] The first tenancy that she and her husband took, for a neighbouring farm of 147 acres, had neither electricity nor mains water, initially, though it did have a 'Yorkist range in the kitchen', to which they added a back boiler – although wash days still involved boiling water in a copper.[28] Though she had help from her family when her children were born and in the house from her husband, it 'was quite difficult . . ., in lamplight, or carrying candles around with a baby under one arm, while keeping an eye on the toddler'.[29] It was only in 1956 when they finally moved 28 miles away to a new tenancy and began farming on the Yorkshire Wolds that they got access to mains electricity, water and sanitation. 'I was, of course, "over the moon",' she says, 'to think I would have not only "mains" electricity, but TWO proper toilets!'[30]

124 *Karen Sayer*

Megginson, who wrote occasionally for the home section of *Farmer's Weekly* in the 1940s and then regularly for the *Dalesman* from the late 1950s, described her domestic work in evocative detail. It is through testimony like this (as well as that contained in Brassley's and Shirley's chapters in this volume) that we can see which technologies farming families adopted and the qualitative difference that they made to those families. Megginson's testimony also reflects the ways in which the authors of memoirs like this seek to engage the reader's empathy, by stressing an expected gap in the experience of home life between author and reader. Straightforward jobs, she says, took a long time. Just going to and from 'the dairies' where the food was kept cold and the water was accessed, because there was no sink in the kitchen, made for 'a lot of walking'.[31] So, the introduction of relatively simple equipment like a portable oil stove,[32] or the purchase of a small bottled gas stove for cooking, could make a great deal of difference, as we see from the following observation:

> About this time [1943] we had a great improvement in our cooking arrangements. A two-burner Calor gas stove with a grill was bought and installed on a little table near the kitchen range with the cylinder sitting underneath. What luxury! It was such a joy to poach eggs and stir custard without the danger of smutts dropping in. The pans got so black on the fire too, and inclined to burn on one side. Now I could grill sausages or chops when we could get them, and that single little cooking stove was the most labour-saving gadget I'd ever had.[33]

In this instance, the work involved in cleaning dirty pans and the effects on the food produced of the older cooking technology are only made visible by the description of the new introduction.

At the same time, once their fourth child was born in 1947 (when they had 'four under five'[34]), she cut back on her indoor work by giving up on making her own bread and installing a hard-wearing carpet in the kitchen to reduce the amount of floor washing required and for the comfort of the children.[35] These unpowered changes may appear very remote from the process of electrification, but they made a difference to her daily labour, to the contentment of her young family, and conformed to existing advice provided in publications such as 'The Farmer's Home' supplement to the *Farmer & Stockbreeder*. 'Plain fawn, fitted hair-cord carpeting', the author of an article in 1937 stated, on moving into and adapting an old farmhouse, 'is proving most serviceable, as marks are easily removed, and it obviates the not inconsiderable work necessary to keep polished wooded or lino surround up to the mark'.[36]

At the same time, as part of this process the Megginson family also installed a lighting plant.

> Great excitement! The 'engine' was installed in a building near the back yard, and controlled by a button in the house. Of course we didn't press

Electrification and its alternatives 125

it in the daylight unnecessarily, but I could use the second-hand upright metal 'Hoover' and the electric iron, though it was usually dark before I got round to that job. Tilly lamps were still needed in the [farm] buildings, but how much easier life seemed when the 'chug, chug' of the generator filled the house with light. The power wasn't strong enough for any other labour-saving gadgets, though I would have liked a fire.[37]

This type of testimony gives us some sense of the significance of a new technology sought out and embraced by the household, and of the lived experience (the sound, the choices made of when to switch on etc.) when it was introduced. It also demonstrates the way in which electricity and electric devices were part of a mosaic of practical improvements to the farmhouse. Electrification was not transformative; rather, the transformation was the process of making the farmhouse 'attractive and serviceable at the same time' as set out in the *Farmer & Stockbreeder*.[38] Transformation was about a broader spectrum of improvement that was not exclusive to electrification. But, we see the priorities here, in reference to electricity as it was installed: light first, then cleaning/ironing and then heating.

It had long been assumed by observers that electric lighting would de facto be an improvement within any farm or farmhouse, and efficient artificial illumination became emblematic of modernity and prosperity. Though, for instance, the use of electric (along with steam) power for cultivation on small holdings and farms could still be dismissed very easily in discussions of increased labour efficiency in 1917, a national political consensus that electric light might be of real value to farmers had already emerged out of wider discussions of the use and value of electricity in general long before the First World War. The idea that tenants might create their own hydro-electric supplies for the purpose of lighting, and that this would inevitably constitute a material improvement to a farm that would deserve compensation, was for example raised in a discussion of the Land Tenure Bill in the House of Commons in 1906.

Artificial light had a wide range of agricultural uses, on and off the farm, and once electricity became available on a farm, the priority was, as the testimony suggests, always lighting.[39] As Dunn comments,

> People used to say to Mother, 'You will be able to have a TV, a washing machine and a fridge.' Mother used to say, 'If I get light that will satisfy me!'[40]

In the end they got a mains radio and a vacuum cleaner, 'followed by a washing machine some years later' and the pattern of acquisition of household appliances in this case seems typical.[41] However, electricity did not replace all of the previous technologies/fuels. Their cooking, even after electricity had come to New Leys, continued on the Aga – though these were ranges which could be adapted to new sources of fuel, which extended their use, even in its solid fuel form it remained an effective and efficient technology.[42]

126   *Karen Sayer*

At the farm on the Wolds, on the Halifax Estate, when the Megginson family finally accessed mains electricity, Irene Megginson was similarly later delighted to have an electric kettle, a cooker, 'rented from the G.E.C.', and other appliances. 'We were thrilled,' she reports, 'to be all electric, with washing-machine, fire and immersion heater.'[43] But, even then for a number of years they still had no fridge, and she observes that 'the dairy was cold, and there were plenty of vans to deliver our food' so that this did not really matter.[44]

It is telling that Megginson constantly refers to the concept of 'labour saving' in her earlier passages, a key component of the discourse of agricultural improvement as well as concepts of modernisation at the time, so that she frames her efforts in the same way as those of the farmers and the labourers. However, though electricity is referred to as labour saving, cooking and other tasks could, it seems, be improved by other means too. The introduction of the new forms of solid-fuel ranges, the Esse, Aga, Otto and Rayburn for instance, resulted in a very real enhancement to the quality of domestic life for those women who had access to them in the countryside. Modernity came in many forms. The Aga adverts directed at farmers' wives, which also used the phrase 'labour saving', for example, stressed that the Aga was a modern and efficient source of heat and hot water:

> To-day farmers' wives want their homes to be up to date. That's why they're changing to the Aga – they know it is the most efficient, labour-saving cooker. No fires to light – fuelling only twice a day. Cleaner kitchen. No fumes or smoke. Hot water any time – and a cosy kitchen always.[45]

The Aga is perhaps the best-known range today, but from 1946 Allied Ironmasters who made it also designed and sold the slightly cheaper Rayburn. The Rayburn was named after agricultural economist Dr John Raeburn (1912–2006), who as Secretary of the Home Agricultural Supplies Committee within the Ministry of Food had organised the 'Dig for Victory' campaign during the war and was one of the architects of the Agriculture Act 1947.[46] The Rayburn remained a rural favourite. Like the Aga it used solid fuel and advertised the same essential qualities within the 'modern' home.[47] So, by the post-war period the Aga was one of several ranges on offer (though it becomes a generic name, like Hoover for vacuum cleaner). 'I think it was in 1951,' Paul Dunn recollected, 'when we had our Aga cooker and a bathroom installed. Mother often said that she didn't know what she would have done without the Aga.'[48] However, even without the costs of installation, fitting a range was an expensive option.

The typical prices were often given in the advertising – including the cost of hire purchase. By using the wages established by the Agricultural Wages Board for England and Wales, which fixed the minimum rates of wages and other working conditions for agricultural labourers under the provisions of the Agricultural Wages Act (1948), alongside the advertising,

Electrification and its alternatives 127

it then becomes possible to consider the material significance to post-war rural households of the outlay involved in the adoption of these and other domestic equipment. For example, a manually operated Ewbank clothes washer from the mid-late 1940s, for which the water was heated elsewhere and poured in, was advertised as costing between £4.2s.6d. to £6.17s.6d.[49] Based on the idea that agricultural labourers needed a lower rate of pay than their urban counterparts, because of the provision of tied cottages and lower costs of goods in the countryside, they received roughly half of what other skilled manual workers were paid. At the beginning of the 1950s agricultural wages, as determined by the Agricultural Wages Board established through the Wages Councils Act (1947) and Agricultural Wages Act (1948), were set at £1.2s.6d. through to £4.14s. for the most skilled and longest-serving labourers. It is therefore clear that even a manually operated washing machine would only be accessible to the households of regularly employed skilled farm labourers or of farming families. Varying in price from £85 to £115, or a hire purchase rate from £2 a month, the Aga was thus, in comparison, a significant household investment, as suggested by the statement in its advertising that 'Fuel savings from the Aga finally pay its cost.'[50] As a result, only farming families such as the Dunns could afford that version of modernity.

As well as the Aga, the Dunn family had a telephone (from 1955) and, like most farming and labouring families, also a battery-operated wireless. The batteries for this had to be charged, and here we see the importance of ancillary services in the rural community, the ways in which hardware stores and garages worked with users in the assimilation of new technologies:

> I remember in the fifties we listed to the wireless quite a lot – that is if the battery was charged up! In those days wireless sets had wet batteries – or did they call them accumulators? You used to have to take them to Sid Wilson's up the High Street to get them charged up.[51]

Dunn's testimony also suggests that even with these technologies in place however, a lot of domestic work remained laborious:

> Mother must have been a very busy person at that time [c. 1955]. There were three men living in and a hungry, growing family to feed and no electricity! . . . Dad and Mam had to get up in good time on a Monday morning to get the copper fire on in the washhouse and Dad would use the peggy stick and dolly tub. I think Nicholas [the author's brother] was the chief lad for turning the clothes mangle before he went to school. Mother was quite a dab hand at making fruit cakes. It was a regular thing for us lads to beat the eggs – no electric mixers.[52]

In part, as with Megginson's testimony, this is written with the reader clearly in mind; a very deliberate and sharp contrast is thrown up through the understanding that though the reader might take electricity for granted, the

128   *Karen Sayer*

author's family had to manage without it. However, it is also clear from this that the farmer's wife called on the manual labour of all of the members of the household as and when she needed it, so that the farmer might be involved in the weekly task of washing alongside his wife, and that sons (not just daughters) might wash and cook with their mother.[53] It, along with Megginson's testimony, also evidences the continued use of much older technologies in the farmhouse. We see a mosaic of power forms, what was deemed 'modern' in daily operation beside what was old, and in throwaway asides, reservations are also observed:

> So what was my work? In Winter it was getting sticks [logs] and coals in, feeding my goats and lighting the Tilley lamps for the hens on a deep litter system. An old uncle of mine, commenting on this said, 'Pushing nature again. Poor old hens, can't thou let them have their proper rest? Thou's expecting them to dee ower time!'[54]

Following the expert advice of the period, Tilley lamps could be used to implement new step-lighting patterns to encourage the hens to lay longer, if not all year. Farming families did not wait on electricity to adopt new practices.[55] However, in the case of the Dunn household, the family wanted electricity, but were refused planning permission until 1959, because the pylons would look unattractive on the moor. 'Eventually', the author Paul Dunn says, 'after contacting our MP, plans were passed for electricity to come to New Leys.'

> It was a sore point with Mother that we, living in the country, were denied this necessity. She would often say when washing dirty lamp glasses, or when an Aladdin lamp mantle would get blackened or the Tilley lamp wouldn't work properly, 'If these Preservation for Rural England folk saw this lot they would change their tunes!'[56]

In other words, despite the enthusiasm of policy-makers, social and agricultural commentators, agricultural economists and rural families, there was enormous tension around the question of electrification, one which highlights the very different and competing perceptions of the countryside and rural life that emerged in the post-war period. As Alun Howkins has observed, there was 'a recognition that the countryside was to be something more than the site of agricultural production and that urban as well as rural voices were demanding a say in rural England and Wales'.[57]

As a result, on the one hand, there were those like Orwin who argued strongly for the need to introduce electricity and other modern amenities, such as piped water, to the countryside, in order to stem rural depopulation. On the other hand, as set out in the introduction to this collection, there were organisations such as the Council for the Preservation of Rural England (CPRE) who sought to protect the countryside from what it considered the visually destructive excesses of modern infrastructure, including electricity pylons. Wherever there is an attempt to stabilise meaning around debates like this, as geographer Doreen Massey established, there will be a political and social 'contest'.[58] Contests like this helped to create the dominant, public version of the post-war British countryside. But, they also clearly demonstrate the way in which rural electrification was never, even in 1959 – just six years after the 1953 decision to begin a planned programme of electrification, (in which it was determined to connect 85 per cent of all farms over the following ten years) – a foregone conclusion grounded in a linear model of increased efficiency, modernisation and progress.[59] In fact, the issue was already writ large before 1953 in terms of the likely conservation issues according to the evidence of the First Report of the National Parks Commission, carried out under the terms of the National Parks and Access to the Countryside Act (1949). Under the heading 'Electricity: Overhead Lines', it observed,

> Proposals by the various Area Electricity Boards for the extension of overhead lines in the prospective National Park areas have been troubling more than one Local Planning Authority anxious to preserve the characteristic beauty of their areas without, at the same time, denying farmers and others who so badly need it, the benefits of an economical supply of electricity.[60]

The Report noted particular difficulties being raised in reference to Westmorland and the Malvern Hills, in other words, areas of high landscape value that also came to be classified later under the heading 'Less Favoured Area' (in 1975) as particularly difficult to farm.[61]

While revealing the very clear-cut tensions surrounding the process of electrification just after the Second World War, we can also see how debates like this also framed electrification external to, as if 'impacting on', the countryside. But, it was never an external force for change in quite the way that bodies such as the CPRE presented it. Rather, as the testimony (and the sales of generators as described in this volume by Paul Brassley) suggests, electricity was sought by and made to fit into complex country lives, by country people, who did not necessarily have access to the powerful political voices needed to bring about the changes they wanted in a countryside that was increasingly torn between preservation and production.[62] The fact that in representing his mother's response to 'these Preservation of Rural England folk' thirty or so years after they sought the aid of their MP, Dunn highlights the work involved in managing the various lamps (Aladdin and Tilley, regarding glasses, mantle and making them work at all), is key to understanding the successful prosecution of their case. He is referring back again to the centrality of women at the heart of the commentaries on rural life and amenity. Indeed, what is perhaps most striking about Paul Dunn's testimony is that the author, who himself became a farmer, tells the story

130   Karen Sayer

through the lens of the home and from his mother's point of view, not the farm/farm work. He does go on to say, 'What an asset electricity was for the farm!' – citing infrared lamps to warm the young animals and electric power for the milking machine – but this is not his first port of call. Therefore, though the farm acquired mains electricity after the war – and joined the 80 per cent that were served by public companies by 1960[63] – this suggests that Leslie Newman's assessment that in the early days 'the emphasis placed on rural electricity was often that of increased amenity' may well have remained perfectly true in the post-war period too.[64] The net effect was to place the home, and therefore 'the farmer's wife', at the heart of thinking about and discussions of electrification.

Conclusion

Though it was seen at the end of the Second World War as almost a cure-all for the ills of rural society, electricity faced some very effective, equally 'modern', competition. Connection was at first piecemeal; even in the mid-1950s, if a neighbouring farm had an electrical supply, landlords often refused to pay for a connection to be made to the labourers' cottages. Tenants and those who were in tied cottages had no power to effect change at this level. Rather, alternative solutions (such as oil and paraffin stoves, solid-fuel ranges and bottled/Calor gas) that had already established themselves successfully in the interwar period, were more readily available, cheaper and more adaptable to farm and cottage than electricity/its appliances (or, might be adopted alongside it e.g. in the case of farms that used 10-volt DC generators), and were both sold and regarded as equally 'modern' components of home. Alternative technologies for heat and light were therefore widely adopted as perfectly practical solutions to the problems identified by social commentators, whose discussions, fears of and posited solutions to rural depopulation focused on home and family. What was wanted was a contented labourer, and that 'content' became dependent rhetorically on a modern home with amenities that included electricity. On this basis, at least one farming family successfully sought the support of their MP and a need for illumination, in order to tip the political balance in their favour in the context of a contested countryside in which electrification was framed as too modern, too transformative and too new.

Notes

1   L. Hannah, *Electricity before nationalisation: A study of the development of the electricity supply industry in Britain to 1948.* London: Macmillan, 1979; L. Hannah, *Engineers, managers and politicians: The first fifteen years of nationalised electricity supply in Britain.* London: Macmillan, 1982; B. Luckin, *Questions of power: Electricity and environment in interwar Britain.* Manchester University Press, 1990; R. Millward, 'Business and government in electricity

network integration in western Europe, c.1900–1950', *Business History*, vol. 48 (4), 2006, pp. 479–500; R.J. Moore-Colyer, 'Lighting the landscape: Rural electrification in Wales', *Welsh History Review*, vol. 23 (4), 2007, pp. 72–92; Leslie T. Newman, *The electrification of rural England and Wales*. Unpublished MPhil thesis, Institute of Agricultural History & Museum of English Rural Life, March 1991); M. Shiel, *The quiet revolution: The electrification of rural Ireland*. Dublin: O'Brien Press, 1984 (reprinted 2005); J. Sheail, *Power in trust: The environmental history of the central electricity generating board*. Oxford: Oxford University Press, 1991; J. Weller, *History of the farmstead: The development of energy sources*. London: Faber and Faber, 1982.

2   R. Borlase Matthews, *Electro-farming: Or the application of electricity to agriculture*. London: Ernest Benn, London, 1928). E-text at Cornell, http://chla.library.cornell.edu/cgi/t/text/pageviewer-idx?c=chla&cc=chla&idno=3143095&q1=electro-farming&node=3143095%3A4&frm=frameset&view=image&seq=3.

3   The film itself seems to have vanished, though its descendants, *Rural electrification drive aka way to plenty* (British Pathe, 1948) and *Power for the farmstead* (EDA 1959), are extant.

4   E.M. Alglave and J. Boulard, *La Lumiere electrique* (Paris 1882), reproduced in B. Bowers, *Lengthening the day: A history of lighting technology*. Oxford: Oxford University Press, 1998, and in William T. O'Dea, *The social history of lighting*, London: Routledge & Kegan Paul, 1958; F.C. Allsop, *Practical electric-light fitting: A treatise on the wiring and fitting-up of buildings deriving current from central station mains, and the laying down of private installations*, 7th edn. London and New York: Whittaker, c. 1915, pp. 128, 264–265.

5   For this earlier phase of electricity's history, see G. Gooday, *Domesticating electricity: Technology, uncertainty and gender, 1880–1914*. London: Pickering & Chatto, 2008.

6   S. Hinchliffe, 'Technology, power, and space – The means and ends of geographies of technology', *Environment and Planning D: Society and Space*, vol. 14, 1996, pp. 659–682, p. 661.

7   'Choice and contingency' were key. Hinchliffe, 'Technology', p. 662.

8   Weller, *History of the farmstead*, pp. 164, 169–171; N. Harvey, *A history of farm buildings in England & Wales*. Newton Abbot: David & Charles, 1984, pp. 211, 216.

9   Political and Economic Planning, *Report on the supply of electricity in Great Britain: A survey of present-day problems of the industry with proposals for re-organisation of electricity distribution*. London, December 1936, p. 84.

10 Irene Megginson, *Mud on my doorstep: Reminiscences of a Yorkshire farmwife*. Beverley: Hutton Press, 1987; Paul Dunn, *Dunn & dusted: Diaries and memories of North Yorkshire farmer Paul Dunn*. Helmsley: Paul S. Dunn, 2005.

11 As John Weller pointed out in his account of the history of the farmstead, many adaptations (cheap wiring and switches shoehorned in a practical fashion, into old timber-framed stalls) were potentially far from safe. Weller, *History of the farmstead*, pp. 169–173.

12 Anon, *Electricity on the farm*. London: British Electrical Development Association, 1956, p. 94.

13 Anon, *Electricity on the farm*, pp. 94–100.

14 Anon, *Electricity on the farm*, p. 98.

15 Gooday, *Domesticating electricity*, pp. 3, 38.

16 Anon, *Electricity on the farm*, pp. 94–100.

17 Newman, *The electrification of rural England and Wales*, p. 200.

18 Anon, *Electricity on the farm*, pp. 4–5.

19 Gooday, *Domesticating electricity*, pp. 9–35.

132 Karen Sayer

20 A.K. Giles and W.J.G. Cowie, 'Some social and economic aspects of agricultural workers' accommodation', *Journal of Agricultural Economics*, vol. 14 (2), 1960, pp. 147–169, p. 147; 'This quotation from a report [An Inquiry into reasons for "The Drift from the Land."] published in December 1957. . . . The drift of workers from the industry has continued', p. 147.

21 Giles and Cowie, 'Some social and economic aspects', pp. 153, 165, 168; NB, varying by region, they estimated 70%–85% of farm workers lived in tied housing in 1960.

22 G. Stapledon, *The way of the land*. London: Faber and Faber, 1942, p. 96; the book is based on lectures and presentations written/delivered over the period 1912–1942. The quote comes from chapter 8: 'The Land and the Nation', 'a paper read to the Autumn School of the National Labour Organization at Eastbourne, on the 6th November 1938'.

23 Ibid.

24 Viscount Astor and B. Seebohm Rowntree, *Mixed farming and muddled thinking: An analysis of current agricultural policy, A report of an enquiry organised by Viscount Astor and B. Seebohm Rowntree, written by F. W. Bateson*. London: Macdonald, 1946, pp. 124–125. It is quite telling that piped water supplies and mains electricity are linked here, as that often seems to be the case both in the rhetoric of commentators/campaigners, but also in those who report on their own experiences at the time.

25 Megginson, *Mud on my doorstep*, pp. 24, 31. Irene Megginson (1919–2007), while growing up in Hull, had holidayed on the same farm in the 1930s, spent 18 months training and working as a groom in Devon after leaving school in 1937, and went home in the summer of 1939. While visiting the old family friends, war was declared and she stayed on as 'part of the workforce'. That 'workforce' included the family plus two 'lads' who lived in. Her obituary appeared in the *Yorkshire Post* on Saturday 17 November 2007. http:// www.yorkshirepost.co.uk/news/community/obituaries/irene-megginson-1– 2476337.

26 Megginson, *Mud*, pp. 34.

27 Megginson, *Mud*, pp. 31–34.

28 Megginson, *Mud*, pp. 43, 46. The previous tenants had refused to have mains water, but they got it laid on quite soon after taking on the lease, pp. 43, 47, 49.

29 Megginson, *Mud*, p. 70.

30 Megginson, *Mud*, p. 96.

31 Megginson, *Mud*, p. 59.

32 Megginson, *Mud*, p. 70. 'We had a treasure of an oil stove, which made the bathroom warm.'

33 Megginson, *Mud*, p. 59.

34 Megginson, *Mud*, p. 77. First child was born in 1943, second born in 1944, third 1946, fourth 1947.

35 Megginson, *Mud*, pp. 77–78.

36 G. Moore, 'Transforming the farmhouse', The farmer's home' supplement to *The Farmer & Stockbreeder*, 21 December 1937, p. 7.

37 Megginson, *Mud*, p. 78.

38 Moore, 'Transforming the farmhouse', p. 7.

39 See Lord Bledisloe, The Government and Agriculture, HL Deb 07 May 1919 vol. 34 cc487–539, 502; Hon. Frederick Lambton, Land Tenure Bill, HC Deb 22 June 1906 vol. 159 cc498–560, 544; Even at a distance it was seen to be of benefit as it was considered essential in darkness to use it, rather than gas, to assess imported cattle for Foot and Mouth disease at harbours. Mr Hugh Barrie, 'Foot and Mouth Disease', HC Deb 08 February 1913 vol. 48 cc349–447, 355.

Electrification and its alternatives   133

40 Dunn, *Dunn & dusted*, p. 40.
41 Dunn, *Dunn & dusted*, p. 40.
42 'Well it's [the Aga] still going strong today although it now runs on oil and not solid fuel.' Dunn, *Dunn & dusted*, p. 24.
43 Megginson, *Mud*, pp. 96–99.
44 Megginson, *Mud*, pp. 99.
45 Aga, Advertising History: How AGA heat-storage cookers caught the world's imagination, 1950s, An Emerging Nation From the War Years. http://www.aga living.com/about-us/advertising-history.aspx.
46 These ranges have their heritage enthusiasts and popular accounts of the history of Aga and Rayburn can be found at 'Potted history of Rayburn solid fuel cookers post 1946', http://www.oilstoves.co.uk/webdocs/articles/History_of_Rayburn_ Solid_Fuel_Cookers.pdf, and http://www.agarangemaster.com/media/215514/ rayburn%20booklet_final_5th_march_lr.pdf.
47 Though in the war, Aga & Esse advertised together. Aga, Advertising History: How AGA heat-storage cookers caught the world's imagination, 1940s, Joint Advertising for Aga and Esse cookers. http://www.agaliving.com/about-us/ advertising-history.aspx.
48 Dunn, *Dunn & dusted*, p. 24. The author's parents married c. 1938. There were three boys (Christopher, Nicholas and the author) and a girl (Judith, the youngest child) living at home; another brother, the second eldest, with Down syndrome, was sent to live away at the age of 8, as 'a patient at Claypenny hospital, Easingwold, where he died in 1969' (p. 8).
49 E.g. see Ewbank advert: http://www.gracesguide.co.uk/images/a/ad/Im193904 22PP-Ewb.jpg. Assuming this was the price in 1940, in 2013 this would, based on the Purchasing Power Calculator, or £551.10 to £918.40 using the Labour Value of the commodity at Measuring Worth, http://www.measuringworth. com/, though this is probably an underestimate for an agricultural household as the wage indexes used for this calculation include urban as well as rural employment, and the agricultural wages were markedly lower than those for other industries. For more see Gregory Clark, 'The Annual RPI and Average Earnings for Britain, 1209 to 2010 (New Series)?', MeasuringWorth, 2011.
50 Ibid.
51 Dunn, *Dunn & dusted*, pp. 25, 27.
52 Dunn, *Dunn & dusted*, p. 26.
53 Their mother also insisted that they take 'cookery' in the last year at secondary school, even though 'we Dunn lads were quite domesticated,' and the boys in the class also learned how to iron. Dunn, *Dunn & dusted*, p. 33.
54 The gender mix also continues: There is a picture of his sister and a friend (girl) 'getting sticks in' c. 1959–1960 (p. 44); in the summer 'I would sometimes help Mam to collect eggs and wash them.' This was normally his mother's job, along with rearing the chickens. Dunn, *Dunn & dusted*, pp. 37, 40.
55 In the 1950s Blount noted that to stimulate hens to lay, 'coal gas, calor gas, or oil lamps' could be used if there was no access to electricity, or in a crisis such as a power cut, though these had to be well ventilated. W. P. Blount, *Hen batteries*. London: Bailliere, Tindall and Cox, 1951, pp. 31–38.
56 Dunn, *Dunn & dusted*, p. 40.
57 A. Howkins, *The death of rural England: A social history of the countryside since 1900*. London: Routledge, 2003, p. 189.
58 D. Massey, *Space, place and gender*. Cambridge: Polity, 1994, introduction.
59 Weller, *History of the farmstead*, pp. 164, 169–171; Harvey, *A history of farm buildings*, pp. 211, 216; Harvey notes that a survey showed that of 2,500 dairy farms in 1951, only half had electric light.

134   *Karen Sayer*

60   1950–1951 (26) National Parks and Access to the Countryside Act, 1949. *First Report of the National Parks Commission for the period ending 30th September 1950*, p. 509.

61   *First Report of the National Parks Commission*, pp. 509–510; They also noted worries about the proposal for hydro-electric generation in Snowdonia.

62   Hinchliffe, 'Technology', pp. 667–668; e.g. users 'subscribe' (or not) to a technology on offer, and its range of potential meanings, as offered up by designers and others who must predict their audience's interests, and redesign whatever fails; the technology becomes part of the dialogue.

63   Ibid., pp. 164, 169–171; see also Harvey, *A history of farm buildings*, pp. 211, 216.

64   Newman, *The electrification of rural England and Wales*, pp. xiv, 200. Certainly, as Newman argues, though farmers valued it for farm work after the war, until the post-war period, 'farm electricity supplies had . . . been mainly used in the farmhouse' (p. 200).

8 Pylons and frozen peas
The Women's Institute goes electric

Rosemary Shirley

In 1965 the rural women's organisation, the Women's Institute (WI), set its members that task of creating village scrapbooks as part of the celebrations for their Golden Jubilee.[1] WI chairman, Mrs Gabrielle Pike, declared that 'Each W.I. should enter the "Village Scrapbook Today" competition, which could well result in an "historic contribution towards the social history of this country".'[2] Emphasising that scrapbooks should provide a snapshot of village life in that year, rather than a chronicle of village history, she urged members to 'think 1965 – what you're wearing – what you're thinking – what you like and what you don't like, and without fail see that YOUR village is a link in this huge picture we hope to paint.'[3] Institutes across England and Wales took up the challenge and 2,500 scrapbooks were entered into the competition. An exhibition called *Scrapbooks of the Countryside Today* was held at London's Regent Street Tea Centre, showing the winning scrapbooks from each region together with the best one from each county.

The scrapbooks, now held in county archives or by the institutes themselves, provide a fascinating perspective on rural life, one that is constructed from multiple female voices and intimately involved in the detail of everyday life.[4] In contrast to more familiar accounts of rural living which often place agriculture at the heart of village life, the scrapbooks deal with everything from the geographical position of the village, to the daily school dinner menu, including sections on houses, work, school, church, pastimes, nature, village organisations, amenities, shopping, transport, food and drink, seasonal celebrations and fashions. Emerging from this wealth of detail is something of the complexity in how modernity has been felt in rural places, showing the dramatic yet uneven changes in the landscape, in consumption and in the home.

Inspired by the visual nature of the scrapbooks, together with the information they contain, this chapter will start by exploring the context of local and national tensions around the preservation and development of the rural landscape triggered by the installation of pylons and electrical wiring systems. It will then go on to focus on the domestic impact of rural electrification, specifically attending to the enthusiastic take-up of frozen food in rural places and the idea that rural women were targeted by manufacturers as

136   *Rosemary Shirley*

early adopters of deep freeze technology. In this way it attempts to animate the rural as an active site of modernity rather than as a passive victim of "the march of the pylons".

Many of the scrapbooks detail village electricity use in the 1960s, however the front cover of the scrapbook made by the North Hampshire village of Binsted is particularly intriguing as it makes a number of concepts which surround this subject visible. Using a type of sacking, known as a hop pocket (hops were a significant local crop), as the background material it features a design worked in appliqué and embroidery consisting of pictorial elements which relate to the village, its title is *A Collage to Suggest Binsted* (Figure 8.1). It includes things one might expect to find characterising a rural English village such as representations of agricultural crops like blackcurrants, hops, apple orchards and potato fields, together with elements from notable village buildings such as the church. However, more surprisingly, running through the centre of the design is a striking representation of an electricity pylon.

The inclusion of the pylon so centrally in the design perhaps points to the members' desire to show that they did not wish to shy away from the less picturesque elements of life in the countryside, and that theirs would be an honest representation of Binsted as it was in 1965. The presence of the pylon could also indicate its perceived newness to the village; it reminds us that at this point in time pylons were still something to be remarked upon, noticed and debated. In twenty-first-century Britain, pylons have widely become taken for granted and therefore, to some extent, an invisible feature of the landscape; its incongruous inclusion here has the effect of making pylons visible once more.

The pylon is at an angle, running diagonally across the background of the design, with its accompanying wires emanating out, spanning the width of the cover. Given the arguments voiced by prominent architects and writers of the time, asserting that electricity wires and masts were disastrously ruining rural landscapes – discussed further in the next section, it is significant that the pylon is fully integrated into the design as a whole and in effect forms the background. In this position it does not obscure the 'view' of the village, constructed by the rest of the collaged elements. This formal technique of building a composition using separate elements placed on top of each other – the pylon on the hop pocket, the appliquéd objects on the pylon – could be thought of as a process of overlay. This is also a concept used in understanding the history and development of landscapes. In his seminal text *The Making of the English Landscape*, W.G. Hoskins gives an account of the nation as a palimpsest of layered time, often drawing on aerial photography to reveal the impression of unseen structures, roads and field systems lying beneath the surface.[5] In a similar way George Ewart Evans uses this metaphor of overlay to highlight the presence of the past in twentieth-century rural beliefs, practices and architecture. In his study of

Figure 8.1 A Collage to Suggest Binsted: front cover of the Binsted scrapbook.

Source: Binsted Women's Institute Golden Jubilee Scrapbook, 1965, Hampshire Record Office, Binsted Women's Institute: 153M85/2.

138 *Rosemary Shirley*

East Anglian folk cultures, *The Pattern Under the Plough*, which is contemporary with the scrapbooks, he notes that

> just as the pattern of the ancient settlements is still to be seen in spite of years of repeated ploughings, so the beliefs and customs linked with the old rural way of life in Britain have survived the pressures and changes of many centuries.[6]

In the case of the Binsted cover this interplay of ancient and modern is reversed, with the more modern feature of the pylon forming the base layer with the more traditional layers in the foreground.

This process of overlay is of course central to the practice of collage, a technique used equally by artists and those who would not identify themselves as artists, to record, understand or critique the world around them.[7] As the title of the front cover indicates it was indeed thought of by its makers as a collage, a method which allowed for, or indeed encouraged, a collaborative approach to be taken with each contributor working in a medium in which they were skilled.[8] In addition to the cover, the scrapbooks themselves were essentially collages throughout, both in terms of their construction which utilised cuttings from magazines and everyday ephemera, and with regard to their content which (literally) glues together an encyclopaedic array of village detail. Collage is a method which is particularly adaptable to the juxtaposition of contrasting images or ideas. Art critic and writer Lucy Lippard cites collage as a strategy that allows alternative stories to be told: 'Obviously I mean collage in its broadest sense, not just pasted papers or any particular technique but the "juxtaposition of unlike realities to create a new reality." '[9] The scrapbooks show constant negotiation between different but simultaneous realities and times. They make visible some of the unevenness of rural modernity and technological progress such as electrification in a complex interweaving of ancient and modern.

There is some absurdity in rendering a pylon in thread. Embroidery is traditionally linked to a certain aesthetic which privileges feminine, 'pretty' subject matter. Rosika Parker, in her classic work *The Subversive Stitch*, demonstrates how over many centuries, complex networks of social and economic forces have worked to categorise embroidery as a 'feminine, domestic act'.[10] A pylon would seem to run counter to this aesthetic, as does the other element of modernity present in the *Collage to Suggest Binsted*: the tractor tyre, which is made from velvet with sequin embellishments. This fragment stands in for the mechanisation of agriculture, a process which was in full flow during the 1960s, with the push towards more intensive methods of farming and the replacement of manual labour with machines. Again here, rather than being marginal to the composition, the wheel is almost in the centre of the design; the treads – which look like little black heart shapes – are organised in such a way that the wheel appears to be moving, running towards the bottom left corner of the cover, a similar trajectory to that of the pylon.

In fact, the floating arrangement of all the elements in the collage gives an impression of movement or free flow, as if any element could be moved or exchange with any other. This impression is added to by the fractured nature of many of the collaged elements. For example, flowers are detached from plants, fruit is detached from trees, village buildings are represented by architectural fragments: the fascia from the railway station with its distinctive edging[11] and a window from the village's Wickham Institute building; part of an ecclesiastical archway has been drawn onto a scrap of paper. The paper itself forms the shape of an arrow which points towards the top left corner, this together with the pylon and the tractor wheel guide the viewer's eye in an anti-clockwise direction – again contributing to the feeling of movement here.

This visual representation of the village challenges the more prevalent cultural notion that the countryside is a place of unchanging continuity. In his writing on landscapes as national symbols, David Lowenthal argues that 'stability and order' are two central albeit constructed narratives which perpetuate the mythical status of the British countryside.[12] Here we can see that story disrupted, moving towards one in which flow and ambiguity are more appropriate themes. Further to this, in their collection of writings on the entangled relationships between nature and culture that texture experiences of place, *Patterned Ground*, Harrison et al. identify the concept of 'flow' as a key way of thinking about the landscape. Their concept moves beyond the idea of things being in constant motion, arguing:

> It is not so much that 'things' move in time and space, as if time and space were somehow a fixed template within which the world simply is. It is more that these flows – be they walkers on ridges or droplets of water in cycle – produce different forms of time and space: for example, cycles, channels, reversals, folds, scapes, interferences, inversions, convergences, divergences, expanses, details. And patterns.[13]

In his book *The Living Village*, which surveys the WI Golden Jubilee scrapbooks, Paul Jennings notes that 'there is a powerful sense of living in two times, in old and new Britain, with an awareness, an agility in effortlessly leaping from one to the other.'[14] This concept is certainly evident in the scrapbooks and will be considered here in terms of the flow of pylons and wires across the land; the folds and reversals encountered between the multivalent forces of development and preservation and the ancient and modern; and the different ways of experiencing time and space which electricity and its associated technologies such as home freezing brings.

Underground, overhead: wirescape tensions

In 1965 the issue of pylons in the countryside was hardly new. The national grid had been a familiar concept for almost forty years, however domestic and industrial electricity consumption was increasing exponentially, and the

140 Rosemary Shirley

existing system of supply was undergoing some radical changes, including the installation of taller pylons needed for the expanded 'super grid', as well as the increased presence of wooden poles and wire for increased local electricity use. Some of these changes were explained to the WI in an article which appeared in *Home and Country*, the WI's magazine, in 1964 shortly before the scrapbook project began. The article was called 'The Wirescape', and in it the author explained that

> the demand for electricity for factories, for public services like lighting and for use on the farm and in the home *now doubles in about seven years*. That means twice the amount of power plant every seven years, and twice the growth of the wirescape octopus.[15]

Clearly drawing on the familiar metaphor of the octopus as some insidious menace, used by Clough Williams-Ellis (1928) some thirty years earlier:[16]

> Don't look out the window. There may be a hideous monster creeping up on you (if you live in the country). Men, dwarfed by the structures on which they work, may be bringing steel latticework, pylons, later to be festooned with wires, right across the view from your windows. Before now, actual violence, including threats of shooting, has been offered to the unfortunate contractors who have to run overhead power lines, even recently, in the most peaceable parts of this country.[17]

After this initial outburst Sykes changes to a well-informed avuncular tone and explains that to meet this new demand more rurally based power stations were being built, and that the rural locations were being chosen out of pragmatism and not victimisation. This was primarily because they were sited within easy reach of the coalfields which provided the fuel they needed, and of the sea or rivers which provided the large amounts of water necessary for the cooling towers – the idea being that it is more efficient to transport the coal a short distance, and the electricity generated a long distance through the system of wire and pylons. This is an ideology which sees the rural spaces of the country as simply empty and ripe for utilisation. It is a position that also taps into a more ancient system of the country feeding the city, with farmers transporting their livestock and produce along ancient drove roads and later railway lines.[18]

In addition to *Home and Country* and the national press, the WI members may have been made aware of the debates around pylons and wire in rural landscapes through the Electrical Development Association (EDA) films programme. The EDA made a series of films promoting the use of electricity in the home and on the farm as part of its campaign to build support for supplies in rural and remote areas. An EDA brochure focusing on rural electrification lists a number of films 'which would be of particular interest to the WI', and could be hired out for meetings.[19] An apparently popular choice was the film *Power Comes to Widecombe*, which tells the tale of the electrification of the remote Devon village, which did not take place until 1962.[20] While Binsted, along with a large proportion of the British countryside, was connected to the grid many years before this date, the film in some ways acts as a propaganda device to generate support for the new super grid pylons. Even though these pylons are never mentioned in the film, the atmosphere of consensual democracy and collective future building is designed to communicate a feeling of pride in the part that rural places can play in the progress of electrification. In a similar way to propaganda films from the Second World War such as *A Canterbury Tale*, the star of *Power Comes to Widecombe* is the picturesque rolling hills, moorland and quaint cottages of the southern counties of England.[21] The effort to bring electricity to this remote village is portrayed as a heroic feat of engineering, manpower and cooperation between the regional electricity board, the land owners and residents. In scenes reminiscent of earlier Soviet cinema, men are filmed bare-chested, working in teams to lift wooden poles and unfurl giant reels of wire.[22] The recurrent theme of interplay between the ancient and modern is also accessed here, with a shot of another bare-chested man using a scythe to clear an area of ground by hand, quickly followed by a shot of a mechanical digger excavating a trench.

The successful connection of the village leads to much joy and celebration, pictured in the closing scenes of the film. The *Daily Telegraph*, September 21, 1962, reported that:

> Church bells will be rung and there will be dancing on the green. In the parish hall an oil lamp will be ceremoniously doused by Mr A. N. Irens, chairman of the South-Western Electricity Board. The parish council has written to thank the Board for bringing in the power lines without spoiling the village.

This last sentence would seem to illustrate *Power Comes to Widecombe's* primary purpose, to demonstrate the South West Electricity Board's (SWEB) commitment to what was called at that time 'landscape amenity', meaning a concern to preserve areas of 'rare and transcendent beauty' from what was thought of as the visual pollution of poles and wire.[23] The film is meant to justify the position of the SWEB – and of the Central Electricity Generating Board which was responsible for the large super grid towers –that cables could only be 'undergrounded' in exceptional cases, but that they were a sensitive organisation who would listen and respond to local concerns regarding this matter. In one scene the wooden poles and wire which scale a hillside are shown to fade into the background of trees and become unobtrusive; 'a new feature to the landscape yet one designed to merge as inconspicuously as possible', the voice-over tells us.[24] Ground is cleared manually

142   *Rosemary Shirley*

rather than with intrusive machinery which would be out of scale with the environment, and crucially we are shown and told that

> to avoid the ugliness of poles and cables breaking the moorland skyline this section of the line was laid underground but putting this kind of line underground costs six times more than overhead. Only in special sections of the route can the heavy extra cost be justified.[25]

The debate around the economic cost of undergrounding of cables versus what was often seen as the cost of the ruination of the landscape was often covered in the *Architectural Review*. Commentators were particularly vocal in calls for more consideration of the visual impacts on rural landscapes of the sighting of the new 160 ft. towers needed to carry increased tension lines. However, they were equally mindful of the local impacts of increased connection in rural places which necessitated extended networks of smaller wooden poles and wires. In 1965 the distinguished architect and town planner Lionel Brett published an article called 'Landscape in Distress', which detailed development taking place in the Oxfordshire area, highlighting the continued anxieties around what seemed like the inexhaustible spread of subtopia.[26] This term, used to describe the breakdown in distinction between town and country, was defined by fellow contributor to the *Architectural Review*, Ian Nairn, as:

> a mean and middle state, neither town nor country, an even spread of abandoned aerodromes and fake rusticity, wire fences, traffic roundabouts, gratuitous notice-boards, car-parks and Things in Fields. It is a morbid condition which spreads both ways from suburbia, out into the country, and back into the de-vitalized hearts of towns, so that the most sublime backgrounds, urban or rural, English or foreign, are now seen only over a foreground of casual and unconsidered equipment, litter and lettered admonitions – Subtopia is the world of universal low-density mess.[27]

Individuals and organisations come under fire in Brett's writing for contributing to this spread, including the electricity authorities. He argues:

> Our worry, in nearly every village and in many open stretches of country, has been the close-up wirescape – poles, insulators, transformers – which is often more obtrusive because always closer to the eye. The striking thing about this network is its cats cradle irrationality and confusion – nobody's fault, just an airborne diagram or paradigm of the growth process of a free-enterprise society.[28]

Brett calls for the Central Electricity Generating Board to triple its current grants to regional boards to enable them to underground a higher proportion of their low-tension wires. Echoing arguments that were being made by the Council for the Preservation of Rural England (CPRE) fifteen years earlier, he notes that large new housing developments are having their cables buried because the economic return from the large amount of new householders will repay the cost; presumably it was also less expensive to bury cables while the development was under construction.[29] Whereas the rural places that would most benefit from undergrounding cannot guarantee the return from such a small group of users, he notes that undergrounding 'does not happen because it is uneconomic, in the picturesque loosely planned villages that are characteristic of our area and most vulnerable visually. The places that need undergrounding most are thus the least likely to get it'.[30]

A pair of articles called 'Wires Underground" appeared in the *Architectural Review* in 1963 and 1964, making the case for undergrounding. In addition to the usual arguments about despoilation of the scenery, they put forward the case for undergrounding. First they cited the incredibly cold winter of 1962–1963 which caused many breakdowns in electricity supply, blamed on frozen fog settling on overhead wires, pylons and insulators, arguing that the cost of maintaining overhead wires should be added to the cost, which would decrease the disparity between the economic implications of underground versus overhead.[31] Second, coming less than twenty years after the end of the Second World War, they argue that undergrounding 'merits attention, if only because one would think that the burying of electric cable, after our experience of even the rudimentary bombing of the last war, had some strategic importance'.[32]

For his publication *Outrage*, which originally appeared in the *Architectural Review*, Ian Nairn made a journey from Southampton to Carlisle in order to identify and condemn all elements of what he called subtopia, in which he reserves some of his most venomous comments for the pylons and their accompanying strings of wire. He uses photographs of pylons and poles throughout the book to illustrate what he sees as the ill-considered corruption of open spaces:

> Wire obliterates the pattern of the countryside just as surely as though it were a blanket of semi-detached housing. The view becomes wire and pylon first and site second. In some cases it becomes wire and pylon everywhere and site nowhere.[33]

Nairn makes a clear distinction between wire and site: the wire is not part of the site or landscape; like all signs of modernity it is viewed as an aberration rather than a significant part of what rural modernity looks like. This is significantly different to the picture of the modern countryside portrayed in *The Collage to Suggest Binsted*, in which the pylon and wires are fully integrated into the village design. Importantly, for Nairn's arguments around subtopia, the wire is not simply something which is obscuring the view; it is something which is disrupting long-held ideas about what constitutes the

144 *Rosemary Shirley*

countryside, and disrupting the clear division between town and country. The wire physically and symbolically connects the rural to the urban, breaking down the distinctions Nairn is keen to preserve, yet the WI perceive to be already intertwined.

It is worth noting that Nairn and *The Architectural Review* in general did not automatically object to pylons. The magazine features images of examples where they felt that the dramatic nature of these structures augment that view rather than diminish it. This is in line with David Matless's observations that the preservationist rhetoric was somewhat ambivalent when it came to the idea of pylons. Some factions were pro-standardisation and saw the steel latticework towers as aesthetically pleasing modernist objects which were far more preferable than the ill-matched and badly designed collection of wooden posts which in some cases they replaced.[34] Matless's analysis also complicates the preservationists' position by showing that in some cases the preservation of rural villages was seen in their ability to become economically active, and that the picturesque quality of a village was in fact evidence of the economic hardships which were being faced by the community. In this context pylons and the power generation they represented were seen as a way of making the countryside once again economically productive.[35]

In part to placate protestors to the initial installation of pylons in the 1920s, the Central Electricity Board made much of their design credentials, repeatedly linking them with the prominent architect Reginald Blomfield. However, the pylon structure was based on a design by the American Milliken Brothers with modifications by Blomfield.[36] In a letter to the *Times* Blomfield felt it necessary to set the record straight, stating that his main input was on the colour of the pylons, for which he recommended green – a choice which he presumably thought would add some element of camouflage, toning down the contrast between the stark modernist forms and the surrounding landscape.[37] In the Campaign to Protect Rural England archive, a correspondence file from 1948 contains a number of paint samples, some of which were contributed by the landscape architect Peter Shepherd. Letters show that Shepherd spent some time carrying the samples around the countryside and trying them out against various settings, concluding that a very dark grey colour provided the best camouflage.[38] It appears that there were some instances around the country of pylons being painted green and opinion seemed to vary. It was mentioned that after a few years pylons painted grey looked shabby after a few years and that they best solution was to leave their galvanised surface visible.

However, the fact that we feel that pylons and wire are out of place in the countryside and need to be camouflaged brings to the surface ingrained assumptions about the countryside, namely that it is not a place of technological development and that it is shaped by nature rather than man-made interventions. Alternatively, the presence of these starkly modern structures could instead be viewed as giving a new perspective on what the countryside is, a complex arena of flow and overlay, an active site of intertwining binaries of ancient and modern, development and preservation. Once again, the Binsted scrapbook (see Figure 8.2) shows the day-to-day negotiations of these forces in action:

> Binsted differs little from any other village today in its wide use of electricity. It has made possible the mechanisation of hop picking and hop-drying. There is no street lighting, but it is a pleasure to know that underground cables have been used in the vicinity of the Church, the beauty of whose surroundings is preserved.[39]

Here we can see that old agricultural processes are being modernised through electrification, while anxieties about the visible consequences of the village's electricity supply are communicated in the relief that the electric cable have been buried and will not mar the old part of the village by the church.

As we have seen, the process of rural electrification both mobilised and challenged long-held beliefs about what the countryside should be and how it should look. However, once connected, many rural places found themselves ahead of the curve in the adoption of one of the aspects made possible by electrification: frozen food.

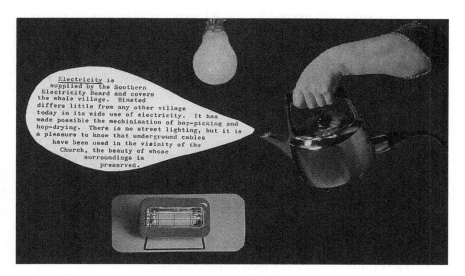

Figure 8.2 Detail from the Binsted WI scrapbook, 1965.

Source: Detail from Public Services page, Binsted Women's Institute Golden Jubilee Scrapbook, 1965, Hampshire Record Office, Binsted Women's Institute: 153M85/2.

146 *Rosemary Shirley*

Freezing time

There is a mania for frozen food evident in the scrapbooks, perhaps made more prominent by its unexpectedness. The WI is synonymous with the highest standards in home cooking, however frozen food is often mentioned as the marker of something new, modern, necessary and up to date. This is in contrast to today's attitudes to frozen products, which are often regarded as a lower class form of food, inferior to their fresh counterparts. In the scrapbooks, however, frozen food carries little of this stigma. On the page concerned with 'Shopping', the Binsted scrapbook notes that 'frozen and pre-cooked food has considerably widened the choice of food in the country districts.'[40] The scrapbook from the village of St. Johns in East Sussex tells of how a WI member has changed the fortunes of the shop, stating that profit has increased by 300 per cent; among the introductions to the shop which she seems very proud of is 'a large frozen food cabinet'.[41] Also from East Sussex, the Burwash scrapbook notes that the village has three grocers' shops, all of which sell frozen foods.[42]

The arrival of frozen food in rural places had a significant effect on the average WI member. It meant that the village shop could now stock a whole range of food that otherwise would be unavailable; it also meant that women did not have to make the trip into a larger village or town to buy fresh food so regularly. At this point in time most WI members would probably have had a refrigerator with a freezer compartment. Nationally 48 per cent of the population had a refrigerator in 1965.[43] That the effective use of the refrigerator was a subject of interest for the WI members is evident in an article that appeared in the organisation's magazine that year called 'You and Your Refrigerator'.[44] These developments are also evident in other publications of the time. In 1960 *Farmers Weekly* carried an article about production of food for freezing which included a photograph captioned 'Even the village shop has its frozen food cabinet – with both British and foreign packs.'[45] While *The Grocer* in the same year ran an interview with the chairman of Birds Eye in which he notes:

> One has to bear in mind that in this country there is still only one household in six that is equipped with a refrigerator and even then there is inadequate storage space for frozen foods. Notwithstanding this handicap there are now over 65,000 retail selling points and the sale of consumer and catering packs has reached £50 million . . . the housewife has come to accept frozen foods – they no longer are a mystery to her.[46]

As the WI were celebrating their golden anniversary in 1965, a similar organisation, the Electrical Association for Women (EAW), were marking their ruby or forty-year anniversary. There is some evidence of a crossover between the two organisations, for example the scrapbook made by the village of Llanilar in Wales includes in their 'Electricity' section a leaflet issued by the EAW called *Electricity for the Country Woman*. The EAW functioned in a comparable way to the WI, albeit a with a significantly lower membership: it was an organisation for women; it had a national committee based in London and regional groups, which held monthly or fortnightly meetings consisting of talks, demonstrations and outings; and it published its own magazine for members, *The Electrical Age*. Its aims as an organisation were to educate women about electricity use in the home and to encourage further education and research in the use of electrical energy in connection with matters of particular interest to women. Its central remit was education, developing examinations for girls in a form of domestic science termed 'Electrical Housecraft', and providing bursaries for women to study electrical engineering at university. It is clear to see from *The Electrical Age* magazine how its members, and women more generally, were also being educated as consumers of mass-produced electrical goods. The publication mainly consisted of articles discussing in detail how various products worked and what to consider when making a purchase. Women were not only being informed how to make educated purchasing decisions but they were also being trained as consumers. Design historian Penny Sparke cites a post-war government report which places women's role as consumers as being central to the economic and, in a way, moral development of the nation:

> Our standards of design, and therefore, our very continuance as a great commercial nation, will depend on our education of the consumer to the point where she rejects the functionally futile and aesthetically inept and demands what is fitting and beautiful. . . . Woman as purchaser holds the future standard of living of this country in her hands. . . . If she buys in ignorance then our national standards will degenerate.[47]

The role of women as consumers was not lost on the creators of the scrapbooks. One contributor to the Llanilar scrapbook writes:

> The British housewife of today is bombarded with various types of advertisement to try and persuade her to buy more of everything. Television is possibly the most popular way of catching the housewife's eye. . . . Magazine, newspapers, hoardings, all shout conflicting views on what sort of food, polish, or what-not to buy.[48]

In terms of refrigerators and freezers this educational campaign was in evidence around the time when the scrapbooks were created, with *The Electrical Age* running several articles on these products. In keeping with the EAW's aims these articles contain a lot of technical information about types of refrigerators, enabling the reader to know the difference between an absorption type or a compression type together with their various capacities in cubic feet – information that seems mind-bogglingly unnecessary to the twenty-first-century consumer. However, running through the articles it is

148   *Rosemary Shirley*

possible to see the twin themes of abundance and economy coming to the surface. The feeling of abundance is created through text which highlights the amount and variety of food which can be accessed as if by magic, 'they make available a great variety of food at a moment's notice,' 'fresh fruit and vegetables of all kinds . . . baked cakes and cake type puddings . . . casseroles, soups, stews, hot dishes, commercially frozen foods including ice cream'.[49] These mouth-watering lists are combined with images of open-doored, well-stocked fridges and freezers including bottles of champagne, joints of meat and creamy desserts with cherries on top. This type of seductive advertising has been analysed by Sandy Isenstadt, where, focusing on American examples, he characterises these displays as landscapes of plenty, arguing that advertisers sought to establish the link between consumer goods and increased leisure, and that leisure at this time in America, as in Britain, was most often associated with enjoying the landscape.[50] In these photographs the refrigerator interiors become those landscapes, consisting of goods brought together from all over the world. Opening the fridge door was the equivalent of throwing open a window onto a 'pastoral fantasy: abundance without labour'.[51] Here it is possible to see Harrison et al.'s formulation of 'flow' in action as landscape becomes compressed or folded into the interior of the refrigerator creating new or different ideas of space and geography. The UK company Lyons Maid produced adverts for frozen food which also used this idea of the freezer as being a window or portal to a different landscape. In 1966 an advert 'American Style Ice Cream' from *Woman's Realm* magazine was divided into three different window-like squares, each holding a bowl of ice cream in the foreground with an iconic American view – New York skyline, Golden Gate Bridge and Grand Canyon – in the background. This advert has the added valence of the glamour of foreign travel, all made possible by this new device in your kitchen. It is interesting that while the manufacturers of electrical consumer goods were using images or fantasies of the landscape and new and more fulfilling relationships with the outside world, the organisations who were tasked with providing the increased electrical capacity necessary to power these consumer goods were in constant negotiations around the impact that such installations were making on the landscape. While the metaphorical landscapes inside the kitchen were getting more verdant and plentiful, the landscape outside the kitchen door was becoming home to an increasing amount of pylons, poles and wires.

The second theme which would seem to be counter to abundance is economy. This is talked of in terms of how refrigerators and freezers can save time and save money. The EAW conducted a survey where eight households were given refrigerators for a period of time and asked to report back on their findings. The results recorded that

> time, money and energy were saved by using a refrigerator. Housewives could plan weekly or twice weekly shopping expeditions instead of

more frequent excursions, and this saved as much as 26 hours over a 6 week period. . . . On the other hand two housewives spent more time in the kitchen when they had a refrigerator; they tried a greater variety of recipes and enjoyed more entertaining.[52]

This demonstrates the perhaps familiar argument that so-called labour-saving devices did not really reduce workloads, but instead created different forms of labour or increased the standards to be met.[53] An example of this can also be seen in the EDA film *The Modern Electric Refrigerator*, which states that in order to make best use of the appliance it is necessary to defrost it every two weeks, an involved and time-consuming process. Another film, *Time to Freeze*, demonstrates the necessary skills and equipment needed by the housewife in order to package food before freezing, together with a 'useful' colour-coded notebook to record what goes in and what comes out.[54] Drawing on Ann Oakley's classic work *The Housewife*, Adrian Forty notes that in 1950, a survey of full-time housewives showed that they spent an average of seventy hours a week on housework, and another survey in 1970 showed an average of seventy-seven hours.[55]

However, the film *Frozen Summer* demonstrates a different way in which time could be saved or manipulated.[56] Echoing Isenstadt's ideas around refrigeration advertising and landscape, the films begins with the abundance of a summer garden, in bright Technicolor; it then cuts to a close-up of a bowl of delicious-looking raspberries, but as the camera pans out from the bowl we see a large window through which is a snowy rural scene. Here, rather than space that is being condensed, it is time, the seasons are brought to a standstill. Again this is multivalent, the narratives around this piece of technology encourage a closer relationship with nature – growing your own produce, eating fresh fruit and vegetables, yet at the same time, manipulate or distort that relationship. The final words of the film seem to sum up these themes of abundance and economy:

> At last with the help of her freezer, the housewife can be a true hostess, able to relax and enjoy her own entertaining. The delights of summer fruits are to be yours even on a cold winters evening when summer is just around the corner in your home freezer.[57]

The housewife can save enough time in order to be able to relax at leisure with her guests, perhaps enjoying the view of a snowy landscape through her window, while her freezer acts as a magic gateway to another time and place; simply opening the door will give a view onto a summer garden.

The chest freezer was slower to arrive in Britain than in America. The take-up of domestic freezer ownership and the popularity of frozen food rose rapidly in the USA during the 1930s, and by the mid-1940s the deep freeze was appearing as a feature of all the most desirable kitchens.[58] Britain was, however, some way behind in its widespread adoption of the deep

150   Rosemary Shirley

freeze. Shove and Southerton show that in pre-1970 Britain the freezer was thought of as essentially appealing as a novelty item, the latest technology to be transferred from industry to home.[59] As mentioned earlier, at the time that the scrapbooks were made, slightly less than half of the households in Britain owned refrigerators; this meant that many women would have only been buying frozen food and storing it for a short time in a refrigerator or small freezer compartment. However, there is some evidence to suggest that WI members may have been part of the home-freezing avant-garde and were early adopters of the chest freezer. A section from the Llanilar scrapbook on food states:

> An increasing number of farms are investing in the purchasing of a Deep Freeze. These items are found useful for preserving their home produces, Poultry, Vegetables, Fruit, Meat (Home Killed or otherwise), cakes and pastries are also made in bulk and stored in the deep freeze, – Little need by said of the value of this item in the house (though costly in outlay). Shopping expeditions are reduced, and visitors though unexpected can be supplied with a meal of home produce.[60]

From a section detailing developments on the local farms written by farmer's wives from Llanilar, one writer states that 'electricity is a great achievement too; a deep freeze was bought five years ago and that has been a great help for the housewife.'[61] From this we can estimate that this member of the WI had a chest freezer in 1959–1960, which significantly predates the general take-up in urban and suburban areas, which is generally thought of as happening in the 1970s and '80s.[62]

The connection between the preservation of food and the freezer places it directly into the territory of the WI, which had its origins in promoting the effective preservation of fresh produce both at its inception in 1915 and famously during the Second World War, when the WI were tasked with jam making.[63] Indeed the imagined consumers of these early freezers were a niche market of housewives/families with a lot of home produce, a predominantly rural market. A Helifrost deep freeze promotional leaflet from 1965 reads, 'This chest freezer is particularly suitable for the storage of seasonal bulk items, such as game, fish, surplus home grown vegetables and fruit.'[64] Helifrost also advertised in *Country Life* magazine in the same year, evidence that the rural middle classes were a key target. The strapline for this advertisement is 'There are no seasons in the year with Helifrost'; most of the space of this advert is taken up with a picture of the big white box, its contents barely visible, with all emphasis on the magic piece of technology and its power to manipulate time. It is worth noting how with the methods of intensive farming being developed and implemented during this time, the idea of beating nature into more efficient forms of productivity was prevalent in both the most economically viable farms, as well as the most well-equipped kitchens. This idea runs in stark contrast to the current middle class occupations with small-scale food production and seasonal eating.[65]

The Women's Institute goes electric   151

This new consumer technology was not only changing the way in which food was stored and consumed but also changing the landscape and economies of the English countryside, and not simply in terms of the presence of additional electrical infrastructure. During this period more and more land was being put into pea production for the frozen food market, especially in East Anglia. An article in *Farmers Weekly* states that in 1952, 6,000 tonnes of peas were being produced, whereas in 1959 this number had increased to 24,000 tonnes.[66] There are even references to frozen pea production and consumption in Ronald Blythe's portrait of an East Anglian village based on oral history accounts, *Akenfield*.[67] When the *Observer* magazine printed a feature on the WI scrapbooks, it is interesting that it was decided to represent the project on the front cover with a photograph of pea pods in a bowl, fresh from the garden waiting to be shelled.[68] In a world where even in very rural households garden peas were replaced by frozen peas, this image choice may represent the familiar concerns associated with the loss of a largely imaginary rural past, a need to preserve a world where peas are still part of a traditional country garden, rather than acres of East Anglian monoculture. However, it also communicates something of the complex flow and negotiations of old and new, preservation and development, which textures rural everyday life and is evident on the pages of the scrapbooks themselves. These documents do not illustrate a picture of the village as a place that was enduring change imposed from elsewhere, but rather as an important agent in implementing change. They complicate received ideas about the anxieties and effects of rural electrification, demonstrating the integration of both the physical impacts on the landscape and the changes in domestic technology into the lived experience of rural modernity.

Notes

1 Other celebratory activities included a garden party at Buckingham Palace, a new rose variety called WI Jubilee, and a poem written by Cecil Day Lewis.
2 J. Harrison. 'Report from the N.F.W.I., 43rd annual general meeting', *Home and Country*, July 1964, p. 227.
3 Harrison, 'Report from the N.F.W.I., 43rd Annual General Meeting', p. 227.
4 The scrapbooks I consulted are held at Hampshire Record Office, The Keep, Brighton and the National Library of Wales, Aberystwyth.
5 W. G. Hoskins, *The making of the English landscape*. London: Hodder and Stoughton, 1955.
6 G. E. Evans, *The pattern under the plough*. London: Faber and Faber, 1966, p. 24.
7 See D. Ades, *Photomontage*. London: Thames and Hudson, 1986.
8 Each scrapbook was produced by a team of at least six members.
9 L. Lippard, 'Hot Potatoes: Art and Politics in 1980', in Jon Bird et al. (eds), *The Block Reader in Visual Culture*. London and New York: Routledge, 1996, p. 16.
10 R. Parker, *The subversive stitch*. London: I. B. Tauris, 2010, p. 60.
11 These decorative wooden valances are called 'dags' according to S. Clifford and A. King, *England in particular: A celebration of the commonplace, the local, the vernacular and the distinctive*. London: Hodder and Stoughton, 2006, pp. 125–126.

152 Rosemary Shirley

12 D. Lowenthal, 'European landscapes as national symbols', in David Hooson (ed.), *Geography and national identity*. Oxford: Blackwell, 1994, pp. 15–38.

13 S. Harrison, S. Pile, and N. Thrift (eds), *Patterned ground: Entanglements of nature and culture*. London: Reaktion, 2004, p. 49.

14 P. Jennings, *The living village*. London: Hodder and Stoughton, 1968, p. 252.

15 J. Sykes, 'The Wirescape', *Home and Country*, July 1964, pp. 235.

16 C. Williams-Ellis, *England and the Octopus*. London: Bles, 1928.

17 Sykes, 'The Wirescape', p. 235.

18 An example of one of these routes is a now defunct railway line (except for a section which has been preserved) from Southampton to London nicknamed the Watercress Line, as it called at Alresford, a great producer of watercress which was transported fresh into London each day, see A. C. Butcher, *Mid-Hants railway in colour*. Shepperton: Ian Alan, 1996. For further discussion of this relationship see R. Williams, *The country and the city*. London: Hogarth Press, 1973, and C. Steel, *Hungry city: How food shapes our lives*. London: Vintage, 2009.

19 Electrical Development Agency, *Farming films*. London: EDA, 1963.

20 K. Pople, *Power comes to Widecombe*. Film. Devon: South Western Electricity Board, 1962.

21 M. Powell and E. Pressburger, *A Canterbury Tale*. Film. London: The Archers, 1944.

22 I am thinking particularly of D. Vertov, *Man with a movie camera*. Film. London: British Film Institute, 1996 (USSR, 1929).

23 'Wires Underground: 2', *The Architectural Review*, November 1964, p. 323.

24 Pople, *Power comes to Widecombe*.

25 Pople, *Power comes to Widecombe*.

26 Lionel Brett (4th Viscount Esher) was president of the Royal Institute of British Architects in 1965 and went on to become the rector and vice provost of the Royal College of Art.

27 I. Nairn, *Outrage*. London: The Architectural Press, p. 373.

28 L. Brett, 'Landscape in distress', *The Architectural Review*, July, 1965, p. 23.

29 'Electricity Distribution and Works', *CPRE Annual Report*, vol. 15 (4), 1949–1950.

30 L. Brett, 'Landscapes in distress'.

31 'Wires Underground', *The Architectural Review*, April 1963, p. 238.

32 'Wires Underground', *The Architectural Review*, p. 243.

33 I. Nairn, *Outrage*, p. 379.

34 D. Matless, *Landscape and Englishness*. London: Reaktion Books, 1998, p. 52.

35 Matless, *Landscape and Englishness*, p. 44.

36 F. Bristow (2009) *UK pylon designs*. http://www.gorge.org/pylons/structure.shtml.

37 Blomfield quoted in G. Weightman, *Children of the light: How electricity changed Britain forever*. London: Atlantic Books, 2011, p. 156.

38 CPRE Archive, Museum of English Rural Life, University of Reading, C/1/62/70.

39 *Binsted Village Scrapbook*, National Federation of Women's Institutes, 1965, Hampshire Records Office.

40 *Binsted Village Scrapbook*, 1965.

41 *Crowborough St. Johns Village Scrapbook*. National Federation of Women's Institutes, 1965.

42 *Burwash Village Scrapbook*, National Federation of Women's Institutes, 1965, East Sussex Record Office, The Keep.

43 Weightman, *Children of the light*, p. 190.

44 'You and your refrigerator', *Home and Country*, June 1965, p. 234.

The Women's Institute goes electric   153

45 'Food for freezing', *Farmers Weekly*, 25 March 1960, pp. 60–61.
46 'Chill and glow', *The Grocer*, 23 January 1960, p. 33.
47 1948 Newson Report, quoted in P. Sparke, *An introduction to design and culture: 1900 to the present*. London: Routledge, 2013, p. 103.
48 Llanilar Village Scrapbook, National Federation of Women's Institutes, 1965, National Library of Wales.
49 'Trends', *The Electrical Age*, Summer 1966, p. 660.
50 S. Isenstadt, 'Visions of plenty: Refrigerators in America around 1950', *Journal of Design History*, vol. 11 (4), 1998, pp. 311–321.
51 Isenstadt, 'Visions of plenty', pp. 313–314.
52 'The value of a refrigerator', *The Electrical Age*, March 1967, p. 1005.
53 See R. S. Cowan, *More work for mother: The ironies of household technologies from the open hearth to the microwave*. London: Free Association, 1989.
54 D. Cons, *The modern electric refrigerator*. London: Electrical Development Agency, c.1955; *Time to freeze*. London: Electricity Council, 1979. Electricity Council Archive, Museum of Science and Industry, Manchester.
55 A. Forty, *Objects of desire: Design and society 1760–1980*. London: Thames and Hudson, 1986, p. 210.
56 B. Copplestone, *Frozen summer*. London: The Electricity Council, Film, 1970, Electricity Council Archive, Museum of Science and Industry, Manchester.
57 Copplestone, *Frozen Summer*.
58 C. Hardyment, *From mangle to microwave: The mechanisation of household work*. Cambridge: Polity Press, 1988, p. 144.
59 E. Shove and D. Southerton, 'Defrosting the freezer: From Novelty to convenience, a narrative of normalization', *Journal of Material Culture*, vol. 5 (3), 2000, pp. 305.
60 *Llanilar Village Scrapbook*, 1965.
61 *Llanilar Village Scrapbook*, 1965.
62 Shove and Southerton, 'Defrosting the freezer', pp. 306–310.
63 J. Summers, *Jambusters: The story of the Women's Institute in the second world war*. London: Simon and Schuster, 2013.
64 Helifrost, *Home freezing: A new life of carefree catering for your family*. Leaflet, 5 August 1965. Museum of English Rural Life, University of Reading.
65 The BBC Food and Farming awards in 2014 honoured small scale food producers using what were described as "artisan" and "traditional" methods, and farmers who were organic and free-range. BBC *Food and Farming Awards 2014*. http://www.bbc.co.uk/programmes/b03nycpj/features/awards-categories.
66 *Farmer's Weekly*, 25 March 1960, pp. 60–61.
67 R. Blythe, *Akenfield*. Harmondsworth: Penguin. [1969] 2005, pp. 101, 107.
68 *Observer Magazine*, 21 August 1966, contained a feature on the WI scrapbooks, reproducing a number of pages from the scrapbook made by the WI in Radwinter, Essex, who were one of the regional winners of the competition.

Part III

Comparisons over space and time

9 Rural electrification in Sweden

A comparison

Carin Martiin[1]

Introduction

The Swedish history of rural electrification tells of an initially dark landscape where scattered patches of light increased gradually in number and scale across the elongated country.[2] It was a diverse process that was neither a matter of central initiatives nor of spread from centre to periphery. Major parts of the history took place between the early and middle parts of the twentieth century, when most rural households were supplied with electricity, although the supplies were often insufficient and unreliable. This period is also the centre of attention in this chapter, which chiefly focuses on the early 1920s to 1950 and consequently omits any discussion of the following decades, when improvements were made to provide sufficient and reliable access to the new energy source.

The main source of electricity was hydro power, for which the natural resources of Sweden offered excellent opportunities. The landscape was thus of key importance – its topography, watercourses, waterfalls and their seasonal rhythms, location and distances, and potentials for exploitation and expansion.[3] The most impressive sources of hydro power were found in the north where huge volumes of water flow from the Scandinavian mountains down to the Gulf of Bothnia and the Baltic Sea. Large numbers of small but exploitable watercourses are found over almost all the countryside. Among the many different historical actors that had access to these water resources were the Swedish state, specialised electricity companies, people running traditional grain mills and saw mills, farmers and local communities. Once the hydro power plants were built, their owners could be managers of distribution systems as well. What is more, the electrification of the countryside engaged local organisations, county agricultural societies, a national organisation for electrification of the countryside (*Riksföreningen för landsbygdens elektrifiering*), and also the banks, whose trust could be decisive for the ability to realise ideas and plans.

The final parts of the power lines engaged hired workers and more or less voluntarily working farmers who felled trees for the poles and cleared narrow power line corridors through the forest. At the very end of the lines were children, women and men in rural households whose life was certainly influenced by electrification, if not immediately revolutionised. Quite the contrary: in contrast with common assumptions this study suggests that the fact that a household was connected to the grid should not be understood to mean that all functions that could theoretically be electrified were also electrified in reality. A more relevant view of the rural electrification of Sweden is that of relatively slow processes of change where modern electric equipment was used alongside manual work.

Access to electricity could influence life in different ways. First, it was a comfortable source of light that improved the standard of living, extended the length of the working day, and improved safety when working in cowsheds, barns and in the farm yard. Second, electric power could replace human or animal muscle power. Third, electric motors could enable more effective ways to work, for example with help of a small and movable electric motor instead of a pair of oxen. Fourth, the new energy source could pave the way for new or half-new functions such as a freezer, through which food storing and food preparation entered new paths.

This chapter does not describe the electrification of the Swedish countryside as an immediate success. It was not a matter of flicking a switch and bathing each corner of the farmyard in light; neither did the noise of an electric motor suddenly change everybody's lives.[4] Its history is instead presented as a mixture of inventiveness and cautiousness, combinations of old and new technologies, and of regional, socio-economic and interpersonal differences in benefiting from the new energy source.

The early history of electrification

A smallholder-dominated countryside

In spite of a harsh climate and short day length, almost the entire Swedish countryside was cultivated by the time rural Sweden was electrified. From south to north and east to west, plains and forested regions were farmed and comparably well populated, with exception for the sparsely populated arctic Scandinavian mountains high up in the northwest. By 1920 about 3.9 million people or 65 per cent of the total population lived in the countryside, and in 1950 about 3.1 million or 44 per cent.[5] Farming was dominated by smallholdings, with only about 6 per cent of the farms having more than 30 hectares of arable land.[6] Rural electrification was obviously a matter of interest for large shares of the Swedish population. The countryside was also inhabited by people who made their living through other businesses apart from agriculture, such as sawmills, paper mills, brickworks, glassworks, machinery production and repairing, or railways. All these categories were involved in rural electrification, in their jobs and/or at home.

Geographically scattered hydro power stations around the country

As already suggested, the electrification of Sweden was a matter of gradual expansion in many different places, rather than a centre-periphery process. The fact that the centre of Stockholm had electric light in the late nineteenth century did not mean that the surrounding rural parishes were electrified earlier than more remote areas. Central regions in the plains, lacking watercourses, could actually be electrified later than seemingly remote areas.[7] Neither was expansion directly related to population density, which is discussed later. Instead, among the influential factors were the landscape and its watercourses in combination with initiative takers, financers and other kinds of local engagement. Many of the early power plants were previously existing water-powered mills and saws that could easily be converted to generate power for other purposes, too.

Early attempts at rural electrification were made in the late nineteenth century, for example at the Falsterbohus estate (in the very south of Sweden, just opposite Denmark), which is reported to have had electric light in the manor, the dairy and the stables by the 1880s.[8] As regards more ordinary dwellings, a farmer in Delsbo parish in the southern part of the vast northern inland, more than 300 kilometres north of Stockholm, is said to have already installed electric light in 1887, at about the same time as there was light in the inner parts of Stockholm.[9] Another remarkable initiative was carried out in the in the same region in the early 1890s, when four farmers in the farm village of Stocksbo, Färila parish, combined their sawmill with a small hydro power station and managed to get electric light in their houses. The lines were soon extended and more farms connected, creating a small patch of light in this comparatively remote region, rich in forest land, watercourses and individual initiative-takers.[10]

Public engagement in electrification: ideas and considerations in the early 1920s

It was not until the 1910s that the electrification of the countryside was thoroughly discussed in the Swedish *Riksdag*. Ways to encourage rural electrification through information were discussed in 1915, and two years later the '1917 electrification committee' was appointed, asked to survey the current situation and suggest ways to promote further electrification of Sweden. Three main questions were to be answered: (1) how should as much as possible of the Swedish countryside be electrified; (2) should this be subsidised by the state; and (3) how should an advisory service on rural electrification be organised.[11] The committee of 1917 presented its general conclusions in 1923, with separate regional reports following soon afterwards.[12] It may be of interest for the readers of this book to note that the 1923 report included a brief report from study visits abroad, to Canada

160 Carin Martiin

and England. The account is short and not very informative but highlights the visitors' impression of huge public engagement in the electrification of England.[13]

In 1917 the *Riksdag* had agreed when the chairman of the agriculture committee argued that the state should support the electrification of districts that would otherwise probably not be electrified.[14] In 1923, however, the general economic situation in Sweden was less positive which made the electrification committee question the feasibility of what had previously been considered as economically relevant and to conclude that the electrification of the countryside could not be accomplished at any cost. They added, however, that economic considerations included other factors besides the financially quantifiable, such as social values and working hours in farm families.[15]

The electrification committee recommended an increase in information, both on 'external electrification', meaning the production and distribution of electricity, and on 'internal electrification', meaning electrification at farm level.[16] As regards the latter, a national association for rural electrification (*Riksföreningen för landsbygdens elektrifiering*) had suggested 'electric model farms', or specific farms equipped with all kinds of imaginable electric equipment: for milking, cooling of milk, hot water, grooming, threshing, water pumps, firewood cutting, cooking, vacuum cleaning and ironing. The electrification committee preferred, however, demonstrations at ordinary farms of varying size and location, which were seen as cheaper, more functional, and easier to keep up to date.[17] It has not been possible to extend this study to model farms, but it is worth noting that an electric model farm was built at the famous Stockholm Exhibition in 1930.[18]

Electrification in the early 1920s

A number of small-scale hydro power stations had been built already before the 1920s. In Jönköping County, for example, the 1910s saw the building of 274 small or very small power stations in the many watercourses around the county. Before that eighteen power stations had been built during the first decade of the century and six in the 1890s, chiefly at regionally leading factories such as Norrahammar.[19] The frequent building of new hydro power stations in the late 1910s coincided with the First World War, in which Sweden was not directly involved. Difficulties in importing energy sources such as paraffin and coal certainly contributed to increased engagement in domestic energy production, but it seems unlikely that the import problem was the only driving force for the expansion of hydro power. The technology was already known and experienced, and some projects may have been planned before the war, encouraged by the prosperous times of the early 1910s. Moreover, many farmers benefited from good prices on meat and other farm products during the war, which might have stimulated initiatives and investments in rural electrification.

Rural electrification in Sweden 161

The aforementioned '1917 electrification committee' was thus set in motion when a number of private initiatives were already at hand, developed from the 1880s onwards. What then was the situation when the committee presented their report in 1923? How much of the landscape could at that time be lit with electricity during dark winter evenings? There is no precise answer in number of households, but the committee reported that almost 40 per cent of the arable area was electrified in the early 1920s. Measuring in terms of so-called electrified arable land is confusing and mirrors a society where land was a general point of reference, for social status, impact and, apparently, for the spread of a new technology. The figure shows neither the number of electrified households nor the number of farms.[20] If the electrified farms had more land than the average, the degree of electrification was misleadingly high in relation to the number of households, and vice versa. A number of regional reports were also published in the early 1920s and these provide more detailed information and a better understanding of the situation by then. Two of these reports, published in1924, serve as basis for the following glimpses from the two geographically adjacent counties, Jönköping and Kalmar.[21]

A comparison between two counties in the province of Småland

Both Jönköping and Kalmar counties belong to the province of Småland. Jönköping County is found just south of the long lake Vättern, while Kalmar County is situated between Jönköping County and the east coast along the Baltic Sea, opposite to the islands Öland and Gotland, of which the former is part of Kalmar County (also see Figures 9.1 and 9.2).

The natural landscapes are relatively similar with a mosaic of forests, pastures and arable land, and numerous relatively small watercourses that flow from the South-Swedish Highlands around the lake Vättern and gradually find their way down to the Baltic Sea. Farming and small-scale local businesses dominated in both counties, together with some big industries, such as Husqvarna in Jönköping County. The industrial sector was somewhat bigger in Kalmar County, which was mirrored in their ownership of several power plants. Hydro power dominated greatly, although not completely. According to the 1924 reports Jönköping had 341 power stations, of which 330 were hydro power plants while the remaining ones were driven by steam or diesel. Kalmar had 166 stations, of which about ten were driven by energy sources other than hydro power.

In contrast with many other parts of Sweden, no state-owned hydro power stations were found in the two counties, where the power plants were instead owned by electricity corporations, towns, factories, privately or cooperatively owned small mills or sawmills, small local producer communities or individual farmers. Some small consumer cooperatives were found in Kalmar County, but these were primarily aiming at cooperative administration of contracts rather than energy production. The dominance

162 *Carin Martiin*

of private firms makes both counties differ from many other counties around Sweden, where local communities and farmer cooperatives were important actors in the late 1910s.[22]

The distribution of electricity was complex in both counties, explained by the combination of hundreds of small and spread out power stations, many and different kinds of owners and, not least, lack of organisation. A mixture of DC (direct current) and AC (alternating current) lines made things even more complicated due to the inability to connect the two systems and thus create a more efficient distribution network. Moreover the DC lines were frequently exposed to voltage drop, which disfavoured especially those living at the end of the line. The problem was found in both counties but appears to have been bigger in Kalmar County, where early initiatives and solutions had gradually created a disorganised structure where the distribution lines sometimes overlapped but sometimes were too distant and left farms and households out of reach. In contrast to this disorganised structure, in the north-eastern part of Jönköping County the distribution system was organised by a specialised electricity company which managed the entire process from power plants to delivery into the farm yard.

In line with prevailing patterns the county-wide reports from the early 1920s reported the degree of electrification in terms of arable land. By then Jönköping County had reached a share of 44 per cent electrified with light, slightly above the national average of 40 per cent.[23] The use of electric motors was lower, about 15 per cent of the arable land.[24] The 1924 report on Kalmar County presents even more approximate figures and suggests that the degree of electrification was 20 per cent on the mainland, and 15 per cent when including the unelectrified island of Öland.[25]

In their forecasts and recommendations, the authors of the 1924 reports considered that Jönköping County was less problematic than Kalmar. Both counties were urged to replace the DC lines with AC, and Kalmar was recommended to encourage more consumer cooperatives and, as a bigger task, to improve the capacity and reliability of the grids. Better organisation and standardisation of the grids would make it possible to connect the lines with regional mains which, in the case of Kalmar, was considered as a better way forward than to improve the many small hydro power stations.[26] Two decades later Jönköping was still on a par with the national average whereas the drawbacks in Kalmar County seem to have remained. The situation in the two counties in 1945 and 1950 is illustrated by Figures 9.1 and 9.2 (shown and briefly discussed in the next section).

Rural electrification in the mid-twentieth century

The mid-twentieth century saw another wave of the authorities' engagement in rural electrification. A general statistical survey was presented in 1944; another study of selected farms was carried out in 1945–1946; and three SOU reports were published in 1947, 1951 and 1953.[27] By this time the process of urban electrification was virtually completed, which meant that

Rural electrification in Sweden 163

the continued electrification of Sweden was now a matter of rural electrification. Moreover, rural electrification had come to be part of the welfare state ambitions for the countryside. The mid- and late 1940s was a time period with clearly pronounced ambitions to develop the Swedish welfare state, which among many other things included aims to rationalise farm work and improve the standard of living in farm households.[28] Access to electric power certainly played an important role in realising this, and the authorities were keen to learn how the state could become engaged in producing a more planned and systematic electrification than had hitherto been the case. It was high time for the welfare state to eliminate anomalies and to safeguard the supply of electric power in the countryside.[29] Huge steps forward were taken within a few years, illustrated by the maps in Figures 9.1 and 9.2. The authorities' efforts may not be the only explanation for the rapid change, but it is suggested that their organisation and economic support were important contributing factors.

Closing gaps between town and country

By the mid-1940s the total Swedish electricity consumption was about four times higher than in the 1920s. The electrified area had increased from 40 per cent in the 1920s to about 76 per cent of the total.[30] The rate of electrification was now primarily measured through the number of households, which gives a much better understanding of the situation. In 1944 only 8,000 town households lacked the possibility to turn on the lights, whereas this was the reality for 122,000 of 745,000 rural households in total.[31] Whereas about 84 per cent of all households in the countryside had access to electric light by the mid-1940s, the figure was only 79 per cent of the 480,000 or so households that were situated at farm holdings – the sum of farmer households and separate households for farm labour, elderly parents and others. The percentage was even lower, only about 70 per cent, when counting electrified farms instead of households, simply because some farms had more than one household.[32] As shown in Table 9.1, the national average of 70.5 per cent differed slightly between the three major geographical

Table 9.1 Number of farm holdings in each of the three major regions of Sweden and per cent with electric light by the middle of the 1940s.

Geographical main region	Number of farm holdings, all categories of arable land	Per cent with electric light
Götaland	204,119	68.8
Svealand	105,333	71.8
Norrland	109,821	72.6
Total	419,000	70.5

Source: Statistical Yearbook of Sweden 1947, p. 91, Table 80.

164   *Carin Martiin*

Swedish regions, Götaland in the south, Svealand in the middle and Norrland in the north.

Table 9.1 shows that the three main regions had large numbers of farms, although there were about twice as many in Götaland as in Svealand and in Norrland. Moreover, the table indicates that the degree of rural electrification was highest in Norrland, the comparably remote main region that stretches from north of Stockholm to north of the Arctic Circle. The region is extremely rich in watercourses and hydro power stations and was where the aforementioned very early farmer-initiated electrification took place. The lowest figure for the southern region of Götaland is probably explained by very low rates on the island of Gotland and in the previously discussed Kalmar County, as demonstrated by Figure 9.1, which also highlights the dramatic improvements between 1945 and 1950.

According to Figure 9.1 the coastland of Norrland was well electrified in 1945 and completely electrified in 1950, while the situation was quite different in the sparsely populated inland. The dark shading for the island of Gotland, with only 47 per cent electrification in 1945, is explained by its remote location in the Baltic Sea and its lack of watercourses.[33] The white portion in the far north-west, however, represents the sparsely populated arctic mountains, to which an electricity supply arrived late, or not at all, to the relatively newly settled farmers or the reindeer herding Sami people. With this exception, each region on the map improved by at least one level of shading from 1945 to 1950. Kalmar County, which as noted earlier had a low level of electrification in the 1920s and '30s, moved in these five years from the 60–70 per cent band to the 80–90 per cent band.

By 1950 the degree of electrified rural households had increased from about 84 per cent to about 93 per cent and the number of non-electrified rural households had more than halved, down to about 46,000 households. It should however be observed that the impressive decline conceals the fact that some non-electrified houses had become summer houses, or had been abandoned in the late 1940s, and that this reduced the number of countryside households on which the percentage was based.[34]

Remaining differences within the countryside

The increased general average of rural electrification within a five-year period certainly meant that electric light flowed out through many kitchen windows in the countryside. Still, differences remained, however, within regions, between adjacent parishes, and between households. Figure 9.2 reveals huge differences between parishes in the same region, differences that are not visible in Figure 9.1.

The situation on the island of Gotland provides a good example of this local variation. Whereas Figure 9.1 shows that on average 70–80 per cent of the rural households on Gotland had access to electric light in 1950, Figure 9.2 reveals a lot of darkness in the northern, southern and even eastern parts of the island. On the other hand the old Hanseatic town of Visby

Rural electrification in Sweden 165

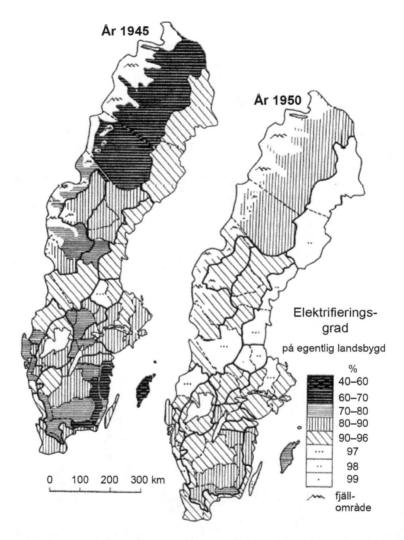

Figure 9.1 Degree of electrification of the Swedish countryside in 1945 and 1950. Dark shading indicates a low degree of electrification, further explained on the right in the figure.

Source: SOU 1951:14, p. 11. Published with kind permission from the Swedish government's editorial board.

and the next largest municipality Hemse were electrified to 80–90 per cent. The photograph in Figure 9.3 is from one of the late electrified parts of Gotland and shows the modest height of a slightly leaning electric pole alongside the gravel road in the middle of the parish centre.

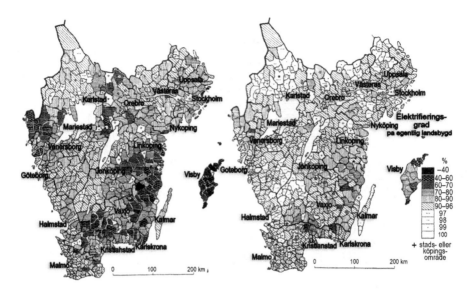

Figure 9.2 Degree of rural electrification in the two main regions of Götaland and Svealand, shown at parish level.

Source: SOU 1951:14, pp. 26 and 27. Published with kind permission from the Swedish government's editorial board.

Figure 9.3 Electrified, at last. Electric pole in a village on the island of Gotland by 1950.

Photo: Sven Martiin. In the author's possession.

Rural electrification in Sweden 167

Similar observations of a nuanced mosaic of lighter and darker shades of grey can be made in Jönköping and Kalmar Counties on the mainland immediately west of Gotland. In 1945 Jönköping County was electrified to 80–90 per cent and in 1950 to 93 per cent, which in simplified terms shows that the degree of electrification still kept pace with the national average, which was 93 per cent by 1950. As before, Kalmar County was still behind with only 70 per cent electrified in 1945 but rapidly improved to 87 per cent five years later.[35]

An even more detailed study reveals differences not only between parishes but also between households in the same parish. As a part of the comprehensive investigations of rural electrification by the mid-century, each rural household without electric light was counted, one by one, as part of what were, by 1950, systematic efforts to complete the electrification of the Swedish countryside. According to this survey thirty-one *landskommuner* (rural districts, often similar to the parish) of total almost 2,500 were still not yet electrified to the 70 per cent level in 1950. Two of these extremely under-electrified areas were found in Jönköping County, where only 61 per cent of the households in Askeryd and Vrigstad had access to electric light, let alone other kinds of electric equipment. Four were situated in Kalmar County (Djursdala, Hjorted, Locknevi and Mörlunda), where on average 66 to 70 per cent of the households were electrified, although on average 170 households in each of these areas were not.[36] Significant differences occurred also in the generally wealthy countryside in the province of Skåne in the very south, where some parishes were reported as 100 per cent electrified in 1950; others were far behind, for example 29 per cent, or thirty-nine households, in Everlöv parish.[37]

Differences like these, at a more or less individual level, must have affected people personally. It was probably less attractive to be employed on a farm that lacked electricity, to rent such a farm, or to marry and move to a home without electric light. Moreover, it is easy to imagine that children from homes without electric light may have been embarrassed, and would have had more problems in doing their homework than classmates in electrified households.[38]

Rural electrification and population density

Population density was not unimportant in determining the rate of rural electrification, but it was not the only factor. In the early days of the project local plants could supply remote areas, but the fact that streetlights were seen in the neighbouring town does not seem to have guaranteed early electrification of the surrounding countryside. The question about eventual correlation between degree of rural electrification and population density was discussed in the report of 1947 without showing any direct link. The three areas with the highest degree of electrification by the mid-1940s – 94–95 per cent in the coastland of Västernorrland County, the province Gästrikland, and the eastern part of the Dalarna County – had population densities of 18, 18 and 20 people per square kilometre respectively. This was similar to the least electrified areas – the northern and southern forested parts of Kalmar

County, and the southern coastland of the Östergötland County – where the population density was 14, 18 and 17 people per square kilometre, respectively. In comparison, Malmöhus County in the very south was electrified to 92 per cent and inhabited by as many as 70 people per square kilometre.[39] These examples do not suggest that the population density did not matter, but demonstrate that it was far from the primary decisive factor.

So far the electrification of rural Sweden has focused on so-called external electrification, the production and distribution chain from energy source to consumer. Our attention will now turn to the so-called internal electrification, which deals with all matters of electricity consumption at farm and household level.

The electrification of Swedish farming

The borderline between external and internal issues was often set by the pole from which the power was delivered into the farm yard and/or house, illustrated by Figure 9.4.

Generally speaking, the costs of internal electrification were the responsibility of the farm, although the economic arrangements differed depending on the actors involved, such as the state, a private electricity company, or a farmer-managed cooperative. The installation of electricity called for careful consideration in the farm household; it was not so much about whether to get included or not, which was probably more or less obligatory in the eyes of the local society, but to what extent.

Electricity was certainly not free. It needed substantial initial investment in electric equipment and its installation, plus the fact that the farm and

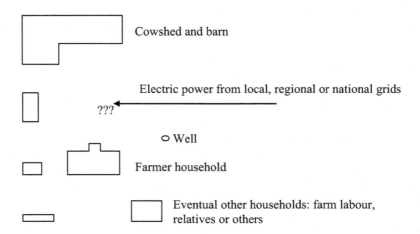

Figure 9.4 Farmyard, buildings and the electric line into the farm, where internal electrification took over.

household budget from now on had to include regularly arriving electricity bills. Among the factors that influenced the costs were the overall design of the installation, the number of electrified houses, and in many cases also the number of power points – plus, of course, the daily consumption of the power source. The details differed however between the various kinds of distributors across the country.[40] To pay for energy was nothing new, nor was paraffin free, but the 'electricity package' was of another dimension and character with its combination of high initial costs and continuing charges. This was probably difficult for many smallholders, whose economy was largely dependent on payment in kind and efforts to minimise cash expenditures.

Both the early and subsequent decades of rural electrification appear to have been complicated by insufficient capacity, which caused instability and frequent power outages.[41] This unreliability could be due to a lack of water supply to small hydro power plants, and the use of DC instead of AC, which was especially a limiting factor for those living by the end of the transmission line. Farms that only had a supply of 6 amperes (A) as opposed to 10 amperes often found that this provided insufficient capacity. There could also be problems arising from competition within the farm in relation to the capacity. If the local system supplied AC, not DC, and if the farm economy was good, it sometimes made sense to pay for more than the minimum supply, for example taking a 10-ampere (A) supply instead of 6 A, or even 16 A instead of 10A. This opened the way for new investments and increased mechanisation of the farm, and could make it possible to borrow engines requiring a high-capacity supply, such as the neighbour's wood cutter, from others.[42]

The problems with insufficient supply called for planning, so that tasks requiring electricity did not overlap in time. Hence, life and work could to some extent be ruled by the supply of electricity. Ironing or cooking, for example, might have to wait until the engines for threshing or hay transport to the hayloft went silent. Male work could thus be prioritised over female tasks. The hay harvest during a rainy summer could more or less occupy the electricity capacity in the afternoons and require the housewife to cook and wash the dishes late at night for week after week until the hay was safely stored under the roof. However, despite these consequences of the new technology, it is hard to believe that anyone on the farm would think of favouring anything but the hay harvest that was decisive for the existence of the farm and the farm household.

Questions about how to electrify the farm were probably frequently debated during the days of rural electrification, in farm yards and around in the parish, at the mill and outside the church on Sundays. What about the size of the system in terms of current? Was it worth the cost to plan for more than light? And how about the stability and reliability of the new technology, would it be able to replace other methods or be more of a complement? As regards planning, installation, and fire safety, a few handbooks

170 Carin Martiin

were published to support farmers and advisers.[43] Inside the farm kitchen the household members may have argued for and against various alternatives, such as running water in the cowshed in favour of the kitchen, or vice versa. When these decisions had been taken and the installations made, the daily routines were set. They affected the extent to which the new energy source could be used; where and for what kinds of electric equipment; and consequently, indirectly, also by whom. Electrification of the farm holding could favour or disfavour different kinds of work, tasks that were generally managed by men or women, as Tables 9.2, 9.3, and 9.4 demonstrate.

Outdoor electrification of the farm

Most of the previously presented figures on rural electrification have referred to access to electric light. Already the official reports from the early 1920s reveal that the authorities were eager to see the new energy source being used for motor power too, to modernise farming in general and to facilitate labour-intensive operations in particular, such as threshing and pumping water. It was, however, some time before rural electrification was as much a matter of electric power as a matter of light. The interval in between could be long, even decades, especially on farms that had been able to install electric light early in the century.

The authorities' views on improved rural electrification were mirrored in a number of investigations in the 1940s. A general survey of farming in 1944, '1944 års jordbruksräkning' (based on the 419,000 registered Swedish farm units in 1944), showed that about 70 per cent of all farms had electric light in 1944 and that 42 per cent used electricity also for motor power.[44] Electric motor power was obviously still not in general use by the mid-1940s. More details on the use of electric motors were achieved through another investigation, the so-called Elkraftutredningen, that studied outdoor and indoor use of electric equipment at 419 farm units of different size around the country. Some of the results are shown in Table 9.2 which gives an overview of

Table 9.2 Use of electricity for various kinds of farm work, based on the investigation of 419 farm holdings of different size and located all around the country (in per cent).

	With electricity	*By hand*	*Other ways*
Threshing	61	34	5
Cutting wood	60	34	6
Cutting straw for the animals	40	54	6
Water to the farm animals	19	65	16
Milking	18	82	–

Source: SOU 1953:13, p. 58.

Rural electrification in Sweden   171

the use of electricity in farm work by the middle of the 1940s.[45] As shown, some typical male jobs were now done with the help of electricity, such as threshing and cutting firewood (61 and 60 per cent, respectively). Milking and watering of the animals were still generally done manually, however, which in the Swedish case often meant manual female work.[46]

Among the more detailed results from the study it was found that the number of power points (often paid for according to numbers), ranged from nine to thirty-four in the farmer households, but averaged only five in separate farm labourers' households. Barns and stables at the smallest farm holdings had on average three power points, whereas the larger farms had about thirty. No electric water heaters were used on the 44 per cent of the studied farms that had less than 10 hectares of arable land. Electric fences were rare on smallholdings but found on about half of the farms with more than 100 hectares of arable land.[47]

The electrification of the Swedish farm household

The electrification of the Swedish countryside was generally a matter of providing light up to the mid-1940s. Electric lamps created opportunities for many activities during the long Scandinavian winter evenings and, among other things, made it possible to engage in individual activities such as hobbies, or to follow correspondence courses that could make it possible to reach higher education. At the county and parish levels, the abilities to do this still differed in the mid-1940s. Table 9.3 reveals differences according to farm size, and shows that only about half of the smallest holdings had access to light by this time, in contrast to about 80 per cent of the relatively few big Swedish farms.

Table 9.3 Access to electricity at Swedish farm holdings in 1944, categorised according to arable area (per cent of all Swedish farm holdings).

Farm size, hectares of arable land	No. of farm holdings	Per cent with electric		
		Light	Cooking	Water heater
0–0.26	3,970	48	4	
0.26–1	32,100	56	3	0.2
1–2	53,304	64	4	0.3
2–5	113,687	67	4	0.3
5–10	104,225	74	4	0.4
10–20	67,301	78	7	1
20–30	20,454	81	11	3
30–50	13,278	83	15	8
50–100	6,925	81	18	22
100	3,908	74	20	34
Total	419,000 ca	71	5	2

Source: Statistical Yearbook of Sweden 1947, Table 80.

172   *Carin Martiin*

The electric cooking stove was still rare in 1944, as Table 9.3 shows, especially on the smallest holdings, but to a surprising degree also on large farms where cooking for employees could be an important part of the business. In the few kitchens in which it existed the electric stove had most probably been installed without removing the wood stove, which was frequently utilised alongside the new modern equipment. Table 9.3 also shows that water heaters appear to have been used at large farms only, where they may have been welcomed as a comfortable and affordable way to get hot water in the summer time when the wood stove was not in use for heating.

A further survey of 419 farms in 1945 and 1946 included not only the farmers' households but also 374 associated farm labourers' households. Some of the results are shown in Table 9.4, which lists the top seven domestic appliances in the Swedish countryside by the middle of the twentieth century.[48] The table shows all the farmers' households but labourers' households only on the big farms, simply because of the very few labourers' households on smaller farms.

Table 9.4 highlights the radio as the most common item in the top seven. A radio appears to have been found in almost all rural households by the mid-1940s, a frequency that might have increased during the wartime years. In the second position was, more surprisingly, an electric iron, which was found at almost all big farms and in two-thirds of the smallholdings and in about every second farm labourer's household. The popularity of electric irons rather than stoves and refrigerators may perhaps have been due to their lower price, their suggestion of modernity, and their accessibility via salesmen and mail-order catalogues. Similar reasons may also explain the

Table 9.4 Electric equipment in farmers' households by the mid-1940s (per cent of the households surveyed).[49]

	Farmer households							Farm labourer households	
Farm size, ha arable land	2.1–5.0	5.1–10.0	10.1–20.0	20.1–30.0	30.1–50.0	50.1–100.0	100.1–	50.1–100.0	100.1–
No. of studied household units	68	115	87	49	30	39	31	102	246
Radio, %	91	96	96	94	97	100	97	90	88
Iron, %	60	69	78	84	97	90	94	40	47
Cleaner, %	4	13	31	37	53	79	90	–	1
Hob, %	35	24	32	22	50	38	35	15	7
Heater, %	10	2?	10	16	10	36	48	–	–
Electric stove, %	1	1	3	12	3?	23	35	–	6
Refrigerator, %	–	1	1	6	7	23	65	–	1

Source: SOU 1953:13, pp. 56 and 57.

high position of the vacuum cleaner, although this was primarily found at larger farms.

As regards the electric stove, Table 9.4 gives the same picture as Table 9.3, but the impression is modified by Table 9.4 that shows simple hobs as alternatives to the electric stove. Hobs were found in one-fourth or one-third of the small households, albeit seldom in farm labourers' households. A hob could be used for hot water and simple cooking, and served as an effective alternative to the expensive electric stove that may have required scaling up of the entire electricity system at the farm, or may have been impossible because of insufficient local electricity supplies. Technical constraints were however not the only reason. The wood stove (Figure 9.5) was the heart of the house and was appreciated for its many functions – cooking, hot water and heating. Moreover the electric stove was a new technology that was not always demanded by women who had learned how to use a wood stove and who were not motivated to learn new ways of cooking and baking.

According to Table 9.4 refrigerators were found almost only on the largest farms, which may be surprising. Among possible explanations it is suggested that refrigerators of that time were small and unable to replace the traditional methods of storing in larders and cellars. In addition, methods of storing and conservation were well developed during by the mid-twentieth century. As an alternative or complement, some rural households may have had access to a cooperatively built and organised cold-store, in later years often with possibilities to store frozen food, such as berries and meat from moose and deer.

Parts of the study of the 419 farms were followed up again in 1950, quite sensibly in view of the fact that the previous study took place during or just after the end of war in the surrounding world. As Sweden was in good shape substantial changes could have been expected to take place very soon. This was true as regards the overall use of electric stoves, which increased from 8 to 30 per cent of households within five years, although on small farms with between two and five hectares of arable land, their use remained low, with only five per cent of households having one.[50]

The electrification of the Swedish countryside – a concluding discussion

The electrification of rural Sweden was a scattered process that was managed by many different actors and spread out in both geography and time. The fragmented structure sometimes contributed to early electrification of remote villages where local initiatives could act independently, but the initial laissez-faire attitude among the authorities caused problems in the long run. Among the drawbacks were dysfunctional combinations of DC and AC systems, and messy structures with long gaps between the grids in some areas but overlaps in others. This made it complicated to extend and improve the structure during the later stages of rural electrification. It was considered

Figure 9.5 The electric stove was no immediate success. This kitchen is equipped with a modern sink, modern ceramic tiles and modern pots in aluminium with handles of Bakelite and the wood stove is probably not considered as unmodern by the neatly dressed woman in this farmhouse kitchen. This wood stove is of ancient date in comparison with the new modern wood stoves in light enamel that were marketed in the late 1940s when the photo was taken.

Photo: Sven Martiin. In the author's possession.

Rural electrification in Sweden   175

as a major problem by the authorities when the state became increasingly involved and, in line with the mentality of the mid-twentieth century, called for more and better planning.

Major parts of the electrification of the Swedish countryside took place between the 1910s and 1950, when 93 per cent of the almost 700,000 rural households had at least access to electric light. The remaining 7 per cent reveal that dark patches were still found here and there. The first decades of rural electrification can be seen as an initial quantitative stage when the new power source was made available, while the systems were made more reliable and the carrying capacity improved during the 1940s and '50s.

This chapter does not describe rural electrification as an immediate success, an event that suddenly made the Swedish countryside bathe in light from one day to another, but as a story of gradual change with progress and setbacks. As we reach the years around 1950 there was light in almost all farmhouse kitchens all around the country and many homes were equipped with radios, irons, refrigerators and hobs. Outside the house electric motors were increasingly in use, but the sound of the vacuum pump for the milking machines had not yet come to characterise early mornings and late afternoons. However, lamps flashed sometimes, hobs got warm slowly, the radio could be hit by too-high voltage, and the electric motor could be unwilling to start. Moreover power outages were common, especially during times when the system was heavily loaded, or exposed to thunder and lightning, heavy snow or to strong winds that made trees fall over the lines.

The period of rural electrification coincided with large-scale societal and technical changes in terms of urbanisation, industrialisation, enlarged public responsibilities and improved standards of living, changes that are often thought of in terms of 'the peoples' home' and, later, 'the Swedish welfare state'. This chapter has concentrated on its impact on farmers, farms, and farming, but it is worth remembering that other rural businesses, such as dairies, were also affected, and that further research is needed about its impact on them. Access to electricity all around the country was considered of greatest importance for the aims and political ambitions about welfare and equality in both town and country by the mid-twentieth century. The fact that early stages of the post-war version of the welfare state coincided with the late stages of rural electrification may have been a blessing for the countryside that may not have been equipped with a wide-reaching and fine-meshed net of functioning electric wires had the decisions been made whilst the more radical stages of rural exodus were on the political agenda.

Notes

1 This article has been made possible thanks to economic support from the Swedish foundation *Brandförsäkringsverket* and Magn. Bergvalls Foundation, SEB, to which the author is most grateful.
2 The Swedish research in the field is very limited and mostly in Swedish, which among other things means that the references are primarily in Swedish. The most important texts are probably those by Jan Garnert, who applies an ethnological

176 *Carin Martiin*

perspective on light and darkness in his PhD thesis from 1993, *Anden i lampan.* Stockholm: Carlssons. Another thesis was published already in 1940, written by Filip Hjulström, whose economic-geographical study pays most attention to electric plants and distribution of electric power, *Sveriges elektrifiering.* Uppsala: Lundequistska. Neither Garnert nor Hjulström focused exclusively on the countryside, which is however highlighted in a more popular book, *Bondeminnen,* Stockholm: The Nordic Museum (1995), where Anders Perlinge presents valuable material collected through study circles on farmers' memories of rural electrification and other changes in farming and rural life. Moreover brief overviews on rural electrification are found in Morell, *Jordbruket i industrisamhället.* Stockholm: Natur och Kultur/LTs, 2001, pp. 290–291, Flygare-Isacson, *Jordbruket i välfärdssamhället.* Stockholm: Natur och Kultur/LTs, 2003, pp. 181–183 and 196. In English Morell has a short text in Jansson (ed.), *Agriculture and forestry in Sweden since 1900.* Stockholm: Norstedts and The Royal Swedish Academy of Agriculture and Forestry, 2011, p. 47. This study has made use of these and other authors but is to a great extent based on official governmental reports on the electrification of Sweden, the so-called SOU reports. The abbreviation SOU is frequently mentioned in the references and stands for *Statens Offentliga Utredningar,* in English translation: Official Reports of the Swedish Government.

3 The Swedish history of hydro power is far from uncontroversial from environmental, social and regional points of view. Large-scale exploitation of the big watercourses in the north resulted in far-reaching encroachment on the landscape and displacement of people whose homes were flooded by dams. The exploitation generated widespread protests, both locally and nationally, although primarily after the time period that is studied in this article.

4 This view contrasts with the somewhat more enthusiastic descriptions of rural electrification by Garnert, *Anden i lampan.*

5 *Historical Statistics of Sweden I, Population,* 1969, p. 66, Table 14.

6 *Historical Statistics II, Agriculture and Forestry,* 1959, p. 27, Table D 14. The figures do not include leased land, but some farm units may have cultivated some additional land. As far as owner-occupied arable land was concerned, farm sizes were stable throughout the first half of the twentieth century.

7 Perlinge, *Bondeminnen,* p. 137; Garnert, *Anden i lampan,* pp. 162 and 167.

8 Hjulström, *Sveriges elektrifiering,* p. 45.

9 Garnert, *Anden i lampan,* p. 162 (Delsbo) and pp. 135–136 (Stockholm).

10 Hjulström, *Sveriges elektrifiering,* p. 44.

11 *Kort redogörelse för elektrifieringskommitténs verksamhet, SOU 1923:72,* p. 13.

12 *SOU 1923:72.*

13 *SOU 1923:72,* pp. 30–31.

14 *SOU 1923:72,* p. 12.

15 *SOU 1923:72,* p. 17.

16 *SOU 1923:72,* p. 14.

17 *SOU 1923:72,* p. 19f.

18 Kåhrström (ed.), *När landet kom till staden.* Stockholm: The Royal Swedish Academy of Agriculture and Forestry, 2013, p. 370.

19 *Planmässig elektrifiering av landsbygden i Jönköpings län, SOU 1924:44,* Appendix 1, pp. 20–49.

20 *SOU 1923:72,* p. 22.

21 *Planmässig elektrifiering av landsbygden i Jönköpings län, SOU 1924:44; Planmässig elektrifiering av landsbygden i Kalmar län, SOU 1924:49.*

22 *Elkraftutredningens redogörelse nr 1, SOU 1947:3,* p. 11.

Rural electrification in Sweden 177

23 *SOU 1924:44*, p. 8 and *SOU 1923:72*, p. 22.
24 *SOU 1924:44*, p. 8.
25 *SOU 1924:49*, p. 8.
26 *SOU 1924:49*, p. 12.
27 The so-called 'Elkraftutredningen av år 1943' ('The electric power investigation of 1943'). The reports were: *SOU 1947:3, Elkraftutredningens redogörelse nr 1*; *SOU 1951:14, Landsbygdselektrifieringens utbredning år 1950*; and *1953:13, Landsbygdens elkraftförsörjning.*
28 Decided through the agricultural programme of 1947 and clearly formulated in the underlying investigation *Riktlinjer för den framtida jordbrukspolitiken, SOU 1946:42*, for example at p. 15f.
29 *SOU 1947:3*, p. 9.
30 *Statistical Yearbook of Sweden*, 1947, p. 129, Table 108; *SOU 1923:72*, p. 22 and *SOU 1947:3*, p. 77.
31 *SOU 1951:14*, p. 7. The figures refer to an investigation of all Swedish households in 1945 (*1945 års allmänna bostadsräkning*).
32 *SOU 1951:14*, p. 10 and *Statistical Yearbook of Sweden*, 1947, p. 91, Table 80.
33 *SOU 1951:14*, p. 12.
34 *SOU 1951:14*, p. 9. Summer houses and abandoned farm holdings were both related to the contemporary urbanisation and rural exodus.
35 *SOU 1951:14*, p. 13.
36 *SOU 1951:14*, p. 38f.
37 *SOU 1951:14*, p. 42.
38 Homework difficulties, example from Perlinge, *Bondeminnen*, p. 138.
39 *SOU 1947:3*, p. 78.
40 *SOU 1953:13*, p. 50.
41 Perlinge, *Bondeminnen*, pp. 132 and 138.
42 Example from Perlinge, *Bondeminnen*, p. 144.
43 For example Jungholm, *En brandsäker lantgårdselektrifiering*. Linköping, 1923.
44 *SOU 1947:3*, p. 79.
45 The study was accomplished 1945 and 1946.
46 The low degree of electrification of animal husbandry may be surprising in the light of the importance of dairy farming. About 95% of all farm holdings had dairy cows in 1947 (*Statistical Yearbook of Agriculture*, 1949, p. 35).
47 *SOU 1953:13*, pp. 56 and 58.
48 The results in Table 9.4, based on a fairly small sample survey, differ somewhat from those in Table 9.3.
49 Two numbers in Table 9.4 deviate from the trends, and may be due to the investigator's miscalculations, printing errors, or to extreme circumstances at some of the surveyed farms. These numbers have been accompanied by a question mark.
50 *SOU 1953:13*, p. 66.

10 People, place and power
Rural electrification in Canada, 1890–1950

Ruth W. Sandwell

Introduction

Household electrification came late to rural Canada. In the census year of 1951, when almost all urban homes in Canada had electricity, a third of rural households were still without electric lighting, and three out of four were cooking over a wood-and-coal range. In the 1950s and 1960s, most of the country's ten provincial governments subsidised and otherwise supported rural electrification for the first time, and by the 1970s almost all rural households had electricity and running water.[1] This chapter focuses on the first half of the century, when the growing disparity between the energy choices available to rural and urban people generated urgent discussions about the much-touted benefits of the electrified home and farm. In Canada as elsewhere, electrification took on an almost emblematic or iconic status as a harbinger of modernity. If the growing gap between urban and rural electrification seemed to confirm deep-seated urban beliefs and concerns about rural backwardness and deprivation, it also provided a space where rural people expressed their views about the limitations of, as well as their frustrations with, the electrical grid and indeed modern life generally. In their comments and in their behaviours, it is possible to see a rural identity distinct from the urban culture gaining ascendancy in the first decades of the twentieth century. This chapter uses the history of rural electrification in Canada as a lens to explore some of the profound changes associated with the shift from the organic 'traditional' (wind, water and wood) to mineral modern (fossil fuels and electricity) energy regimes for rural Canadians in a country long associated with the some of the highest global rates of energy consumption per capita.[2]

The chapter begins with a quick look at the important geographic, social and economic contexts of rural electrification in Canada. After sketching out the distinctive nature of Canada's predominantly rural population in the first half of the twentieth century, it goes on to explore the twentieth century's changing energy landscape, with a close look at the rather curious social, economic, environmental and political problems attendant on getting central station electricity into rural, often remote, households. It will argue

Rural electrification in Canada   179

that, notwithstanding some real advantages that electricity brought to rural households, and notwithstanding vigorous rural electrification campaigns launched by corporations, governments, community groups and educational institutions, the transformative potential of electricity continued to be seriously limited by its diffuse and differential absorption into Canadian rural households throughout the entire first half of this century.

A short historical geography of rural Canada

A short lesson in historical geography is in order. Canada is the second largest country in the world, with a landmass of 3,854,083 square miles, or almost 10 million km^2 (9,984,670 km^2 or about 2.5 billion acres), making it just over seventy-six times larger than England (130,395 km^2 or about 32 million acres), and forty times bigger than the UK (243,610 km^2 or about 60 million acres). About 3% of Canada is arable; the largest landform in this northern country is the granite Canadian Shield. Most Canadian land is characterised by poor, thin, waterlogged and frozen soil, and its climate by frigid temperatures, long winters and a short growing season. Large and largely defined by rock and a sub-arctic (cold) environment much of the year, Canada is estimated to have about 20% of the world's supply of fresh water, which covers 10% of its entire surface.[3]

Largely because of its geography and climate, the country has always been sparsely populated. Canada's population density, at 3.3 inhabitants per square kilometre (8.5 per square mile) (compared to 244.7 per square kilometre in the UK), is among the lowest in the world. It was originally occupied by a variety of hunting and gathering people. By the end of Canada's great era of immigration in the late nineteenth and early twentieth centuries, almost 75% of Canadians settled, and continue to cluster, within 100 km of the country's southern border with the United States, and mostly in southern Ontario and Quebec.

In the first half of the twentieth century, Canada was still a nation of rural owner-occupiers. Demonstrating a pattern very different from England during the late nineteenth and twentieth centuries, the number of farm households in Canada kept increasing until 1941, and the number of acres being farmed increased steadily between 1871 and 1971. In 1931, more Canadians were still employed in agriculture – almost one out of every three men – than in any other single occupation; it was not until 1951 that the number working in manufacturing exceeded those in agriculture. Notwithstanding the fact that in 1921, a majority (51%) of the population was designated as 'urban' for the first time, it was not until 1941 that a small majority of the population was living in urban areas with more than 1,000 people, and not until 1961 that a small majority were living in urban areas with more than 5,000 people. Though farm populations began to decline after 1931, the rural population grew continuously in the century after 1871, more than doubling from 3 million to about 7.5 million in 1971. It fell for the first time

180 *Ruth W. Sandwell*

ever in 1976. Canada was predominantly a rural and small town country until well after the Second World War.[4]

Canadian rural households varied considerably across the country and over the 1900–1950 period surveyed here, but they shared some common features. With marginal lands and a short growing season often limiting the production and sale of agricultural commodities, and with food and wood fuel readily available, rural Canadians were not all farmers, or at least not all the time. Often living on isolated farmsteads, they depended on three pillars of support: the sale of commodities harvested or tended on their rural lands; a wide range of self-provisioning activities, including gardening, hunting and fishing on their own and nearby lands; and the sale of their off-farm labour on a seasonal and life-cycle basis (typically in the winter logging and other resource extraction industries or summer transportation industries). A household's exact place on the continuum between wage labour at one extreme and complete self-sufficiency at the other, ballasted with commodity sales in between, was varied and shifted due to a variety of factors, including the age of children and the composition of the household, the precise attributes of the local environment and the state of global and local markets for whatever commodities could be profitably produced. And there was always the weather. The political economy of rural Canadians was based on occupational pluralism, rooted in landownership, and sustained by a system of labour mostly organised according to kinship. Neither traditional nor modern, neither fully proletarian nor capitalist, a distinctive rural population sustained itself into the post–World War II period in Canada.[5]

From the late nineteenth century onward, wealth extracted from Canada's northern and western regions, most particularly mining, lumber, and pulp and paper, was beginning to transform Canada from a land defined by small-scale farms and scattered fishing and logging operations into a resource-rich nation. New forms of energy were facilitating not only the extracting and processing of resources, but the transporting of them vast distances across the continent and beyond. Manufacturing grew rapidly in response; coal-powered trains lowered transportation costs, and the number of factories increased dramatically. Indeed, 'Canada enjoyed a pace of growth in economic activity from 1870 which was among if not the highest in the world' as resource extraction expanded and became vastly more profitable.[6] Mines became safer and exponentially more productive due to electric lighting, ventilation, motors and pumps. Improved transportation by road, rail and (after the First World War) cargo aircraft joined fossil fuel–powered machines, such as trucks and bulldozers, which sped up the pace of extraction and transportation as the century progressed. Like mining, the pulp and paper, smelting and refining industries grew up around the vast amounts of electrical power that were being generated from Canada's water-abundant landscape in hundreds of hydroelectric dams across the country. Many of those working these projects and industries were the same landowning householders still trying to 'get by' in rural Canada in an era of lowering prices for farm produce and escalating costs of off-farm inputs.[7]

Canada's late nineteenth-century energy history was influenced by two important geological factors: the absence of coal in the industrial heartland and an abundance of water almost everywhere. A protracted coal miners' strike in the United States in 1897, and ensuing energy shortages, convinced the Ontario and Quebec governments and many private companies to make early massive investments in a publicly owned hydroelectric system in Niagara Falls (described as an exercise in 'state capitalism' by historian H.V. Nelles), and the private developments in Beauharnois and in the Lac St. Jean regions of southern Quebec, and later further north in Ontario, Quebec and Manitoba.[8] Between 1917, when the federal government began annually compiling national electrical energy statistics, and the 1960s, 90% or more of the country's electricity was being generated by water (Figure 10.1). As the Dominion Bureau of Statistics noted in its 1953 study, only 3.5% of electricity in Canada came from steam and internal combustion engines, compared to 73% in the United States. This, they noted, 'explains why American electricity cost about 70% more than in Canada, on average at 2.8 cents per kwh compared to 1.6 in Canada'.[9] While thermal power (generated mostly by coal, but some oil and later nuclear power) gained importance in the 1960s, as late as 2006 Canada was distinguished by the fact that it is the third-largest producer of hydroelectricity in the world, and one of the few countries in which hydro still provided a majority of its electricity (59%).[10]

Domestic electrification in Canada

Crucial for Canada's expanding resource and manufacturing centres, electricity was also making an impact on daily life for people in their homes. Statistics on domestic (i.e. household) electrification chart the rapid increase in the number of Canadian households with electricity between 1921 and 1951, from just over half a million to almost 3.5 million.

The percentage of households in Canada with electricity grew steadily from just under 50% in 1921 to almost 90% in 1951. These average Canadian Figures, however, cloak the great regional disparities that can be seen in both the absolute numbers of electrified households and in the widely varying percentages throughout the country (Figure 10.2). Although almost half of Canadian homes on average had electricity by 1921, Prince Edward Island, Nova Scotia, New Brunswick, Saskatchewan and Alberta had at least two-thirds of their population *without* electrical service. Even in 1951, when Ontario, Quebec and British Columbia were approaching 100% domestic electrification, more than a third of households in Manitoba and Alberta, and more than half in Saskatchewan, were still without electricity supplied by central power stations.

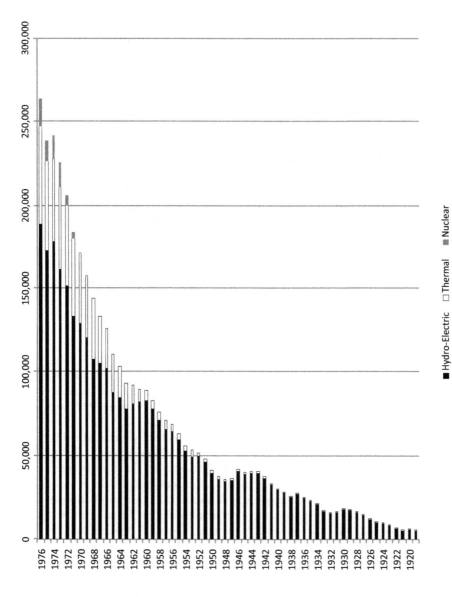

Figure 10.1 Electrical generation by prime mover, Canada, 1919–1976 (millions of kWh).
Source: Statistics Canada, Series Q85–91.

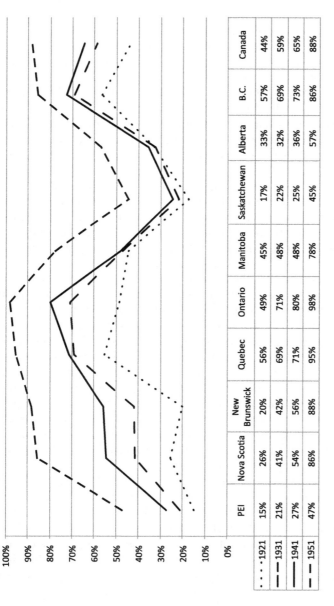

Figure 10.2 Percentage of households with central station electricity, Canada and the provinces, 1921–1951.

Sources: Canada: Dominion Bureau of Statistics, Census of Industry, Central Electric Stations in Canada, for 1922, 1931, 1941 and 1951; Census of Canada, 1951, Volume 3, *Dwellings and Households*, Table 1.

NB: The percentage of households is calculated by dividing the number of electric lighting customers by number of households, by province.

184 *Ruth W. Sandwell*

What accounts for the extreme variability in electrification across the country? The short answer is that the economies of scale involved in any electrical network, and hydroelectric networks in particular, were ill-adapted to Canada's population, which in most provinces remained predominantly rural and isolated well into the twentieth century. The problem was not simply a supply-sided one, however; there were significant difficulties in 'selling' the idea of electrification to rural people in the early years of the twentieth century that speak to the continued distance between rural and urban cultures and economies. The concentration of population and the existence of a large, near-monopoly power company were key supply related factors in the adoption of electricity by domestic customers.

The production of electricity from falling water was profoundly influenced not only by the reliability of the water supply, but by the economies of scale in building hydroelectric plants, dams and transmission lines, and the nature of electricity itself. Without a critical mass, production was uneconomical, and without constant movement of electricity through the lines – necessary because electricity cannot be affordably stored – transmission was impossible. In most Canadian cities, it was first street lighting, and later the urban network of electric trams or railways, appearing across the country in the 1880–1900 period, that provided the large consumers of electricity that made the first investments in hydroelectric generation possible.[11]

Historians have argued that the highly complex, integrated scientifically based and engineered network of hydroelectric generation and distribution mark it, like manufactured gas lighting and a system of national railways before it, as one of the earliest examples of the massive, highly engineered and scientifically complex second industrial revolution world at work.[12] For as historian Harold Platt has argued, Edison had fully understood when he developed the first incandescent light bulb that '[t]he light bulb [. . .] formed only one part of a symmetrical system that included prime movers, dynamos, regulators, measuring and safety devices, distribution wires and appliances, all working in instant harmony.'[13] The almost incomprehensibly vast and complex nature of hydroelectricity generation and transmission not only created problems for those designing and installing it but also, as we will see, for those using and paying for it.

Large consumers made the building of dams and the sale of electricity to domestic users economically feasible, even before the massive scaling-up of Canada's dam building projects in the post–World War II period. The flooding of millions of acres of northern rural lands in Canada's 'hydraulic hinterland' in that period, and its impact on rural, primarily Indigenous peoples and economies is an important aspect of rural electrification, and one that has been told elsewhere.[14] But from the earliest days, the importance of small household units to hydroelectric development should not be underestimated.[15] Electrical companies did not, by and large, need to make further substantial capital investments to provide electrical lighting for home use: with the capital costs of dams, turbines and transmission lines already covered, as more customers consumed more electricity, production costs per unit of electricity decreased dramatically, increasing the amount of money that the company could make. This was particularly the case with water power, where no additional fuel had to be burned to carry the domestic load. Domestic service, at least in urban areas, provided an important elastic market, one where returns could be increased simply by persuading more customers to purchase more electricity. Tacitly acknowledging that the transition to this new form of power was going to be driven, initially at least, by supply rather than demand, electrical companies took full advantage of this inexpensive potential for increasing consumption with extensive advertising campaigns and promotion programs.[16] Summarising the key importance of promotion, one Ontario Hydro newsletter exclaimed, 'the more KWH we sell without unduly increasing our demand (KW) the more cheaply we can sell them and the better our competitive position. INCREASED KWH USE IS A MAJOR FACTOR IN LOWER RATES.' As he concluded, 'it is the duty of every employee to do his or her part to encourage increased use by enthusiastically Selling Satisfaction with Hydro to everyone with whom he comes in contact.'[17]

The domestic market provided another important function: one of the vexing aspects of an electrical generation network is the prohibitively high cost of storing electricity:

> without storage, the amount of generating capacity required to supply any electricity use is determined by the maximum power requirements of that use, even if that maximum is used only for a brief period, a phenomenon known as 'peak-load problem'.[18]

Because the electrons must be kept flowing at a rate that meets the maximum demand for the energy that might be required, the energy provider 'has to pay the same amount for its demand in kw whether the peak holds for one hour or the entire 720 hours per month'.[19] The bigger the difference between the electricity provided and minute-by-minute use, the more electricity – and therefore revenue – is going to waste. The beauty of a large network system, as opposed to a system of small independent generators, therefore, lay in the fact that 'if different customers on a network have their maximum power requirements at different times, the unused capacity of one customer can meet the increased demand of another customer.'[20] Domestic electrical consumption was particularly useful in 'balancing the load' in off-peak hours, when industry did not require massive amounts of energy.[21]

The problem of rural supply

The complexities of electrical generation, particularly relating to the economies of scale and the need for electrons to flow or be wasted, made it very difficult to get service to low-density populations in most rural areas, at least

186 Ruth W. Sandwell

at a price that made it worthwhile to electrical companies. Compared to the proportion of all homes electrified by 1951, summarised in Figure 10.3, farm totals were extremely low. In 1941, British Columbia and Ontario had the highest rates of farm electrification at about 38%. By 1951, just over half of Canadian farms had power line service, compared to about four-fifths of the farms in the United States. While the report *Central Electric Stations 1951* went on to note that 'many other Canadian farms generate their own electricity by the use of engines, windmills, etc.,' it was widely recognised that even for the 5% of farms possessing their own generators, this did not consist of full-time, 'modern' service.[22]

Some rural populations lived in remote areas that were close to resource industries like pulp and paper mills or mines that used significant amounts of electricity supplied by their own plants. In these areas, companies were often willing to extend their electrical power from industrial uses to domestic customers, though often at special rates that reflected any extra costs that might be incurred.[23] Rural people living just outside municipalities could also tap into municipal supplies. In Ontario, for example, where the publicly owned Ontario Hydro Electric Power Commission prided itself on getting electricity to its politically significant rural households (Ontario had elected a pro-farmer government after the First World War), those 'agreeing

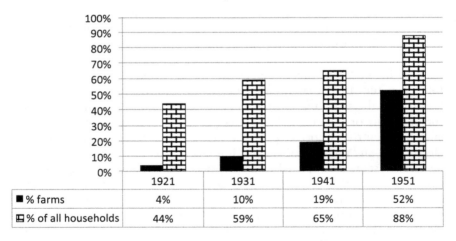

Figure 10.3 Percentage of Canadian farm dwellings and all Canadian households with central station electrical service, 1921–1951.

Sources: 1931 Census of Canada, Agriculture, Vol. 8, Table 26, p. lxvii, 'Farm facilities by province, 1921–1931'; 1941 Census of Canada, Housing, Vol. 9, Table 13, 'Lighting facilities in occupied dwellings, 1941'; Farmholdings in Canada Statistics Canada Series M12–22, http://www.statcan.gc.ca/pub/11-516-x/sectiona/4147436-eng.htm; 1951, Census of Canada, Vol. 3, *Housing and Families*, Table 36, 'Occupied dwellings by tenure, showing lighting, cooking and refrigeration facilities, for provinces, rural farm, rural non-farm and urban size groups, 1951'.

to finance construction of the necessary connecting lines' or willing to pay 'a consumption surcharge commonly set at the urban rate plus 10 per cent'[24] could obtain electricity with relative ease. The British Columbia provincial commission on rural electrification argued in 1945 that location relative to a large consumer was indeed the key to rural electrical service. As they explained, whether or not rural homes received electricity

> depends in large measure upon their location in respect to urban centres. If the latter have adequate and efficient service it is usually possible to extend the distribution systems to the rural areas. If, however, the towns are too small to permit the development of an efficient urban utility, neither the townspeople nor their rural neighbours will have available electrical service in accordance with modern standards.[25]

Away from a towns or factories, rural households and farms had little chance of electrical service before the 1950s. Hydro companies across the country struggled to sign up the minimum number of customers; generally five households per mile of line were required to make a rural extension economically feasible for the company and affordable for the rural consumers. The contrast between rural and urban areas was a source of increasing concern to governments, utility companies and social reformers. Though the proportion of farm families with electricity more than doubled from 4% in 1921 to 10% in 1931 and 19% in 1941 (Figure 10.3), detailed questions on the 1941 census discovered that while 97% of urban Canadians had electric lighting and 91% had inside running water, the figures for rural households were 20% and 12% respectively[26] (see Figure 10.4). These statistics were far from encouraging for either the hydro companies, hoping to build the load and improve their profits, or for those rural consumers hoping to 'get the juice'.

Disappointed by low rates of rural electrification, hydro companies were also frustrated by very low rates of usage for the customers who did sign up. Indeed, low levels of usage, and not just for rural customers, were a significant cause of concern for electrical companies across the country in the first half of the century. As Figure 10.5 documents, the average monthly consumption rates of electricity were tiny by today's standards; the vast majority of homes, urban and rural, across the country were only using enough electricity to provide minimal lighting up until 1941. Even by 1951, only the households of Ontario and Manitoba (the latter of which had the highest consumption rates due to a combination of its cold temperatures and its scheme of flat rate electric hot water heaters) were consuming enough electricity for lighting, refrigeration and cooking. Half of all Canadians were still cooking with wood in 1941.[27] These national figures are particularly striking from the perspective of early twenty-first-century consumption, where average per capita consumption in Canada is the second highest in the world, just over 18,000 kWh per year, or 1,500 kWh per month per

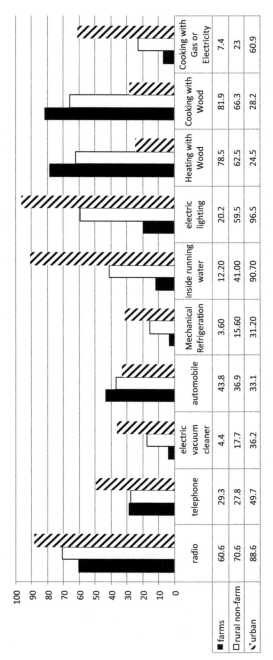

Figure 10.4 Percentage of farm, rural non-farm and urban households with specified conveniences, Canada, 1941.

Source: Census of Canada, 1941, Volume 9, *Housing*, Table 18.

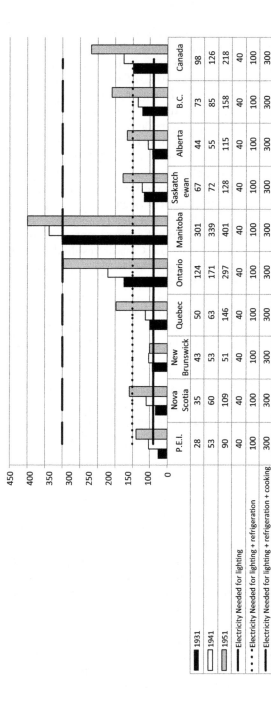

Figure 10.5 Average monthly consumption of electricity (kWh) by province, Canada, 1931, 1941, 1951.

Source: R. W. Sandwell, 'Mapping Fuel Use in Canada: Exploring the Social History of Canadians' Great Fuel Transformation', in Jennifer Bonnell and Marcel Fortin, *Historical GIS in Canada*. Calgary: University of Calgary Press, 2014, pp. 239–268.

190   *Ruth W. Sandwell*

individual, or (at an average of 2.6 people per household in 2001) almost 4,000 kWh per household per month.[28]

Electricity usage in rural areas was even lower. In 1951, one of the first years in which comparative farm/non-farm data on electrical consumption rates are available, the average farm across the country that had electricity at all was using between 50% and 80% of the national average.[29] There were a number of reasons for this. Rural areas were typically served by a disparate collection of small rural utilities. In British Columbia alone, there were 111 utilities selling electricity outside of the area serviced by BC Electric, 81 of which served fewer than 500 customers.[30] Although these stations, most of which had capacities less than 1,000 KWA, were 'insignificant in comparison with the large fuel plants and the hydro-electric plants', they were important in as much as they 'gave service to approximately 57,000 customers [in Canada in 1926] in small towns and villages which would otherwise have been without the benefits of electric service'.[31] But as the Central Electrical Stations of Canada annual report went on to note, the small output of small rural stations throughout Canada resulted from the fact that 'small plants sell almost entirely to lighting customers, requiring service for a comparatively short period of time each day.'[32] Small plants meant in practice that increased levels of service, such as that needed for small or large appliances, simply were often not available. It often meant that electricity was only provided for a short amount of time each day, ensuring that consumption rates remained low. As the rural electrification Progress Report summarised in 1945,

> in 90 percent of the [rural] distribution areas, the use of electricity is limited to lighting only. In fact, the plant equipment in many cases apparently has been installed for lighting only; the utility is operated for lighting only, and the operation cannot be regarded as a modern electric utility service.[33]

Precisely because of the minimal consumption levels, service from these plants was expensive. Whereas consumers in Vancouver in 1944 were paying about $2.30 to consume the average 85 kWh per month, consumers in Castlegar were paying $4.05, in Vernon $5.88, in Field $9.00, and in Burns's Lake a record $15.00 per month for the same amount of electricity.[34] As the rural electrification commission summed up, the 'cost of electrical service. . . . is relatively high [though] the quality of service is relatively poor.'[35] Because of the economies of scale, their view was that rural electrification could never be self-supporting:

> Nowhere has rural electrification been accomplished as a separate and distinct business[. . . .] Private companies and publicaly [sic] owned regional utilities have been able to furnish electricity in rural areas because their organization have been developed first to supply urban

areas. Having established a sufficient volume of business, they have been able to extend their areas of service to rural communities wherever the new consumers can provide the increment cost of the service. [. . .] rural electrification is not a distinct brand of the utility business; it is an outgrowth of the central station industry – the widening of the areas to which certain average costs are applied.[36]

Campaigning for rural power

If numbers of rural customers and their rates of consumption remained low into the 1940s and '50s, it was not for lack of trying on the part of electrical utility companies. Companies tried a wide variety of strategies in the 1910–1950 period to persuade rural dwellers to electrify their homes and barns, from magazine and newspaper advertising to the more innovative institution of the Power Circus and 'Rural Travel Shop', traveling trailers carrying the latest electrical appliances and giving demonstrations at open-air shows.[37] Most of the large electrical utility companies began distributing pro-electrification pamphlets from the 1920s onward, to convince rural dwellers of the benefits of electrification that would, incidentally, also increase the load, the customer base and company profits. The British Columbia Hydro Rural Commission's aptly titled *Progress* journal advertised its work and more generally, the advantages of electricity to the rural population. With articles like 'Why a Refrigerator?', 'Boosting Egg Production' and 'Does Mother Do the Pumping on the Farm?,' BC Electric's *Farm Service News* had brought good electrical tidings into the homes of Fraser Valley farm families since 1933, and *Progress* followed its lead in convincing rural dwellers of the convenience, savings and happiness they would find by using electrical appliances. Such education/propaganda campaigns across the country suggests that company officials, at least, believed that they could influence people's relation to electricity not by simply decreasing the price of electricity, but by increasing its appeal as a modern, clean and labour-saving form of power.

Other strategies to boost the number and consumption by rural consumers included cheap loans, offers of (temporarily) free power, promotional offers on appliances, and their free installation, 'all intended to expand the Rural System's customer base and power load'.[38] Companies also experimented with methods of charging for electrical consumption that allowed them to meet their bottom line while tempting rural consumers into purchasing more than the bare minimum of service to which many agreeing to 'get the juice' naturally gravitated. These met with limited success. Districts charged different rates for different levels of minimum service, ranging from 15 to 1,000 kWh per month, and consumers were encouraged to purchase more electricity by the declining rate per kWh with each level of increased consumption. In many areas, consumers were charged per light bulb or appliance, or by the square footage of the house.[39] Ontario Hydro

192   *Ruth W. Sandwell*

changed its rural rates structure every few years between 1909 and 1970 in the attempt to build its rural service, often having more than eight different classifications for rural customers at one time.[40] While some schemes attracted more customers, many rural customers were confused and irritated by the complexities:

> Speaking of rates, no one ever saw a kilowatt-hour, yet the public has paid for billions of them. When a merchant sells you a sack of potatoes he talks about the potatoes, and not the sack; when he sells you a gallon of whisky [sic] he talks about the whisky, not the gallon. We have talked too long about rates and kilowatt-hours, rather than the cost and value of service.[41]

But it was not only hydro and appliance companies who urged the increased consumption of rural electrification. Indeed, an ever-increasing array of organisations, from appliance retailers (usually part of the electrical company's operations) and provincial agricultural colleges to women's institutes and new university home economics departments urging rural electrification. There is not time here to explore the rural reform movements of the 1910–1940 period, or the rural problems, protests and promise that played a role in discussions of rural electrification. But within a larger, and growing discussion about the importance of 'the modern rural' in Canada and the growing disparity between rural and urban standards of living, electrification was increasingly seen more widely as the panacea not only for all ills of rural society, but for Canadian society generally.[42] Promotional campaigns reached deep into the countryside, promoting electricity as the overarching solution to the problems that Canada was encountering with crime, poverty and vice associated with increasing urban industrialisation. While many farm families were from the 1930s onwards identifying falling prices and increasing production costs as their most significant problems, many reformers believed that electrification could more easily provide the means to make rural life more appealing. This, in turn, would stem the alarming outflow of rural young people off the farms and into the cities, and preserve the kind of peace, order and good government that rural Canada seemed to represent.

Rural households: the problem of demand

In spite of aggressive marketing and educational campaigns from many directions, the number of customers grew slowly and rates of consumption remained stubbornly low before 1950. As electrical companies were well aware, part of the problem with demand, particularly in the early years, spilled over from the problems of supply: low usage meant that electricity was expensive and often perceived to be dangerous, and its value was

Rural electrification in Canada 193

unproven at best.[43] Before 1950, many power advocates had become frustrated by the seeming impossibility of stimulating increased demand. As the authors of the Report on Rural Electrification concluded in 1944, the more prosperous farmers in Canada, those involved in kinds of urban-hinterland agriculture where electricity is 'particularly helpful – dairying, poultry farming – were already within the reach of central energy systems, or were supplied by individual plants'. With regards to other rural populations, 'the consensus of those involved in various ways in the electric industry is that there has been, up to the present, no concerted demand for electric service from those who are not now served'. As they went on to explain,

> A general interest in rural electrification has been kept alive by public ownership advocates and has been recently stimulated by rehabilitation committees. It is stated that in many cases where a request is made for rural service, an active campaign of salesmanship is necessary to secure enough contract to justify the construction of the line.[44]

As W. L. Houk, Ontario Hydro's vice chairman, told the Ontario Agricultural Council in 1939, 'the only growth on the Rural System would be "in volume" [. . .] due to increased usage of power by existing customers rather than in new customers.[45]

But even opportunities for 'building load' seemed limited, as most rural customers seemed only interested in using electricity for lighting: as the B.C. report on rural electrification explained it,

> The fishermen farmers of the Maritimes, the habitants of Quebec, the grain-growers of the Prairies, and the cattlemen of British Columbia, generally those living in the sparsely settled areas, have little use for electric current other than for household lighting.[46]

Cost was certainly an issue that curbed demand. High initial installation and ongoing usage costs discouraged many rural people, particularly those whose incomes had fallen substantially with the Depression. Many rural people

> have not in the past had the means to wire their homes and purchase appliances. The cost of their present methods of lighting are so small that even a low monthly cash outlay for electric current would be a big factor in the family budget.[47]

Even the most basic electrical service was expensive in rural households where every penny counted. Most houses were not wired with the electrical outlets – termed 'convenience outlets' – needed to plug in the appliances that would boost electricity consumption. The only plugs available in most houses were created by screwing a plug outlet into one of the light bulb sockets in the ceiling. Always inconvenient and sometimes dangerous, this method of obtaining electricity was not conducive to increased demand for electrical consumption. Upgrading the service to include heavy-load items such as electric stoves and even small electric appliances usually meant the installation of new and prohibitively expensive wiring.

But if rural people worried about the costs of installing and using electrical power, they also had considerable difficulties understanding just what they were being charged for, and how. As one writer phrased it, people watched substations go up 'like ancient temples; they are places of mystery understood only by those who design build and operate them',[48] and the system of charging for electricity remained as obscure as the processes of generation and transmission.

Electrical companies throughout North America and Britain were acutely aware of the reluctance on the part of many electrical consumers to spend their money on electricity, which was not only a new kind of commodity, but it was delivered in a way that, for most people, was also new.[49] And it was invisible. People, rural and urban, harboured deep suspicions about the new network system, and particularly with regard to pricing.[50]

Many consumers clearly could not understand the nature of the electrical grid, particularly why they should consume more electricity in the interests of reducing the per-unit cost. When electricity was metered at a regular rate, canny consumers tended to be careful to use as little as power as possible, due to the high rates that low usage created. Because of the expense of reading meters in rural areas, many rural utilities relied on flat rates for a minimum amount of power. In most cases, this also put a ceiling on usage, because customers would, to the extreme irritation of the producers, refuse to exceed their maximum flat rate consumption, that was generally for a level of service that provided lighting only.[51]

In response to constant and widespread complaints about billing and rates, the Canadian government began in 1917 to compile an annual index of different rates across the country. As the Department of Trade and Commerce Branch of the Dominion Bureau of Statistics, charged with describing and explaining on an annual basis what everyone across the country was paying and why they were paying such different rates for their electricity, put it, 'the cost of electricity is one of the most controversial topics in Canada.' As he went on to explain, 'there is no "cost of electricity" in the same sense as cost of flour, sugar, milk and such like which enter into the budget of the housewife where the cost of ten pounds is approximately ten times the cost of one pound'. Acknowledging that to many consumers, it may all be 'Greek' he then went on to 'simplify the discussion to the factors entering into the cost of electricity' with a well-meaning, but almost incomprehensible series of definitions, including watt, watt-hour, horsepower year, connected load, load factor and power factor.[52] The published Index sought to further allay concerns

Rural electrification in Canada   195

about price-gouging by articulating the 'great many factors entering into the price of electricity' including:

> costs of power houses, machinery, power dams, storage dams, flooded lands, water rights, transmission lines, right-of-way, sub-stations, distribution lines, etc. Operating expenses including losses of power through transformers, transmission lines and distribution lines, fuel costs, labour, maintenance, depreciation through both wear and obsolescence, interest charges, taxes, and the nature of the market or load factor which governs the extent to which the equipment is utilized. The effect of each of these factors on the price charged for electricity for residence lighting varies with different plants and locations, and without an extensive analysis, it is impossible to even approximate values to the factors.[53]

Struggling to understand the claim that neither industry nor the government could account for the price of electricity, hundreds of customers every year requested government-sponsored meter-testing, as they simply did not believe that they were being charged correctly.[54] Rural customers without meters complained about what seemed incomprehensibly high rates for little service. The files of the domestic lighting departments across the country were filled with requests like this one from puzzled and angry customers simply unable to figure out just what they are being charged for:

> January 29, 1909
> Dear Mr. Goward
> My complaint is about the absolutely unreasonable bills we get for electric light. It is really beyond all reason. I want to know if you can't possibly remedy the matter, for I am quite positive we do not burn half the light we are charged for . . . Now Mr. Goward, honestly don't you think that $4.20 for a months light in a house where after dinner there is one reading lamp burning until ten or eleven o'clock is rather steep? . . . I am very sorry to have to complain, but there must be something wrong somewhere. With kind regards, believe me sincerely, Marie L Wilby.[55]

In addition to cost, and the opaque nature of its cost, another factor limiting demand was the fact that the system just did not work very well, particularly in the early years. Even in the cities, power could be intermittent due to power failures, which were due to frequent equipment failure brought about by droughts, storms and scheduled maintenance.[56] These problems were more frequent in rural areas. Brown-outs were common. As one rural dweller complained in 1932,

> The electric cooking stove is not supplied with the requisite amount of juice for satisfactory cooking. . . . The lights go down in my house if

I turn on my cook stove, also my neighbours state their lights go down on this occasion[. . . .] It takes approximately 20 minutes to boil a kettle.[57]

Even when the service was an extension of an urban one, it was subject to frequent interruptions and poor quality. On July 14, 1930, for example, B.C. Electric received a complaint from resident of Aldershot, B.C., complaining that he 'cannot get enough power to run our pump properly and sometimes even the radio will bring in local stations only faintly'. Receiving yet another complaint about low voltage, the operating engineer wrote to the irate customer to explain:

> This district is served by a 40,000 volt line only and for that reason is liable to interruptions for repairs as well as breakdown and the service in consequence is not as reliable in communities served by a duplicate transmission line. I feel sure that the service compares favourably with rural service furnished by the Commission in other districts.[58]

Complaints from rural residents extended to more than the inconvenience of poor lighting. As Mrs Robertson complained to BC Electric Co. in 1932 from her home in rural Sooke,

> Out of the 164 pheasants hatched out of the incubator, BC Electric killed 124 by chilling and cutting off the current from time to time during the most critical time of their existence. This means a dead loss to us of $76.20, the cost of the chicks at that age.

As she plaintively went on to explain,

> I had hoped this year to have added quite a lot to a very small income to help with my two little children and the many other overhead expenses in keeping a good home together. But you have ruined all my hopes! I shall never use the brooders again as you will not guarantee electricity at all times.

She summed up her letter by aptly stating, 'But I think it is very unfair to coerce us to buy electrical appliances before you can guarantee electrical current at all times.'[59]

If the service was expensive and often worked poorly, a final reason why demand for electricity remained so muted until the Second World War was that, to use Graeme Gooday's term, most rural people had not yet 'domesticated' electricity in the farm or rural home; electricity had not been integrated into the patterns of rural lives, where people already had established ways of doing things that worked well.[60] Under these circumstances, as Ronald Tobey has argued in his study of electrification in Chicago, 'the power of advertising to influence consumers' habits was tightly constrained by traditional family and gender roles.'[61] The massive public education campaign finally 'worked' in the post–World War II period, when rising incomes, increasing use of other new forms of energy, and falling rural populations eventually led to dramatic changes in rural life that better accommodated electricity. But before that time, Canada's largest hydroelectric developer, the Hydro-Electric Power Corporation of Ontario, shared with other early electrical companies 'the unenviable position of attempting to market a service the potential of which it did not fully comprehend'. Some rural people might have conceded by the early years of the twentieth century that 'hydroelectricity would eventually revolutionize the home and workplace, but its adaptability to specific tasks and situations remained, if not totally unknown, largely untested.'[62]

Part of the problem lay in the conflict between age-old patterns of farm and rural life and the demands and preferences of the electrical grid. Certainly electric lighting, with its flame-free qualities, was particularly welcome in the large hay-filled Canadian barns that sheltered cattle and pigs for weeks at a time from the worst depredations of winter, but this generally did not consume enough electricity to make it economically feasible. Indeed, electricity could not be cost-effectively applied to much of the rural household's outdoor labour, particularly that involving field and forest work. While rural dwellers recognised the benefits of a load-building stationary electric motor – 'it could be used in three different locations to operate a three-unit milking machine, a grinder, cutting-box, fanning-mill, turnip-pulper grindstone saws, and a washing machine'[63] – electric motors did not fit well into the overall patterns of rural work. Farmers were accustomed to intense forms of labour for short bursts of time, for example grain threshing or woodcutting, enacted according to seasonal rhythms. By contrast, the most efficient use of electrical power was work that evened out the difference between maximum and minimum power usage (the 'load factor') on a regular daily and weekly basis. In using electric power for farm work, 'both Hydro and the customer were paying year-round for a service that was used to optimum advantage for only a few days.' While Ontario Hydro blamed farmers for clinging to 'old methods' of work that were not suited to the modern world (aka the needs of the electrical grid), farmers remained sceptical and generally resistant.[64]

Inside the home, many rural women (who in Canada as elsewhere were particular targets of rural electrification edu-advertising campaigns) simply did not see the advantages of the kinds of electrical appliances that were needed to boost the load, or at least not at the prices they were obliged to pay. Happy enough to have electric light if it could be available for a low price, most balked at purchasing technologies that were unfamiliar and often seemed wasteful, redundant and ill-adapted to patterns of rural life.[65] The coal-and-wood stove is a case in point. By the later decades of the nineteenth century, open-hearth cooking had been replaced by cast iron wood and coal stoves in most rural, and many urban, households. These versatile stoves, credited as being 'the most drastic of all steps taken to reduce the housewife's drudgery' in the nineteenth-century rural home,[66] were kept fired up all day and most of the night, and provided a variety of functions. In 1941, four out of five farm households were still heating and cooking with wood (Figure 10.4).[67] Wood cook stoves doubled as the main source of heat for the kitchen and often the rest of the house, often through ventilating holes in ceilings where an upper floor existed, or through a series of large-diameter pipes running through the house. From the 1880s onward, hot water tanks or 'reservoirs' were often attached at the side or an end, providing hot water that could be ladled out and used to wash dishes; the large volume of hot water for washing clothes and for the weekly bath continued to be heated in a large copper pot on the top of the stove. By the end of the nineteenth century, stoves often included a warming shelf and could include a built-in waffle maker and teapot warmers, as well as providing a place to dry laundry and snow-covered clothing. They also provided the means for heating the 'sad irons' used to iron sheets and clothing. Some women even claimed that the considerable labour involved in keeping the stove burning provided an important element in disciplining growing boys, who were almost always responsible for keeping full the kindling and wood box for the kitchen stove: 'no wood, no fire, no food'.[68]

Given these varied functions – cooking, heating, ironing, disciplining, and washing – and the considerable economic advantages of use of locally harvested, and generally inexpensive or free wood fuel, it is no wonder so many women foreswore the expense of installing the new heavy duty wiring and of running an electric stove. This was a considerable limiting force in rural electrification across the country: for as B.C. Electric marketing manager Halls explained to his staff in 1915, 'the electric range offers the best opportunity to enable us to increase our revenues, as from past experience the average KWH sales per consumer have been more rapidly improved by this major appliance than any other.' In weighing the benefits of providing fee installation for electric stoves, and figuring in the profits from selling and running the electric kitchen heaters and the water heaters that people would need once they dispensed with their coal and wood stoves, he estimated that the increased load alone would improve the company's bottom line substantially.[69]

Conclusion

As the vigorous insistence of the 'triumphalist discourse' itself suggests, indifference to electricity, and not simply an inability to purchase it, continued to thwart sales of electrical service and products in rural Canada throughout the entire first half of the twentieth century. In spite of the discourse that linked modernity and progress to electrification, electricity did not transform Canadian rural society into a culture of modern consumers in

Rural electrification in Canada   199

the first half of the twentieth century. By the 1950s and '60s, most provincial governments decided that rural electrification was a priority, and established various strategies and schemes, public and private, to insure that most rural households finally received central station electrical service.[70] Canada never did have a national program equivalent to the Tennessee Valley Authority or Britain's rural electrification campaign. The success of rural electrification by various provincial governments coincided with the mass exodus of rural populations for the city. More research is needed into the exact timing of these two trends – urbanisation and rural electrification – in Canada's post–World War II period, but by the early 1970s the vast majority of rural Canada was electrified through central generating stations.

More research is needed as well into the varied alternative cultures and economies that preceded and overlapped with the 'modern' and homogeneous world in which we now live, and which persisted in rural Canada until the mid-twentieth century. But in the behavior of Canada's rural population we can see the outlines of the two features that have distinguished Canada's energy regime from that in other countries: the very high per capita use of energy and the continuation of the 'traditional' nature of that energy, particularly wood, for many decades after fossil fuels took precedence in the United States, and most particularly in England.[71] Some of the patterns of daily life sketched out here help to explain why.

Notes

1 Marie-Josée Dorion, 'L'électrification du monde rural québecois', *Revue d'historie de l'Amerique Francaise* vol. 54, 2000, pp. 3–37; Lionel Bradley King, *The electrification of Nova Scotia, 1884–1973: Technological modernization as a response to regional disparity.* PhD thesis, University of Toronto, 1999, pp. 287–288; Frank Dolphin and John Dolphin, *Country power: The electrical revolution in rural Alberta.* Edmonton: Plains, 1993; Keith R. Fleming, *Power at cost: Ontario hydro and rural electrification, 1911–1958.* Kingston and Montreal: McGill-Queen's University Press, 1992, pp. 221–247; James L. Kenny and Andrew Secord, 'Public power for industry: A re-examination of the New Brunswick case, 1940–1960', *Acadiensis*, vol. 30 (2), 2001, pp. 84–108; Alexander Netherton, *From rentiership to continental modernization: Shifting policy paradigms of state intervention in hydro in Manitoba, 1922–1977.* PhD thesis, Carleton University, 1993, pp. 111–223.

2 Christopher Jones, *Routes of power: Energy and modern America.* Cambridge, MA: Harvard University Press, 2014, provides a detailed examination of these terms in his introduction. Canada's unusual energy status is discussed in Richard W. Unger and John Thistle, *Energy consumption in Canada in the 19th and 20th centuries.* Consiglio Nazionale delle Ricerche – Instituto di Studi sulle Societa del Mediterraneo, 2013, esp. p. 13.

3 Environment Canada, http://www.ec.gc.ca/eau-water/default.asp?lang=En&n=1C100657–1#ws46B1DCCC. Accessed 20 May 2014. Canada has only 7% of the world's 'renewable' water.

4 This anomaly can be explained by the fact that before 1951, the designation 'urban' bore no relationship to community size or population density; a community was designated 'urban' if it was incorporated, regardless of size, and

everywhere else was designated rural. R. W. Sandwell, 'Notes towards a history of rural Canada, 1870–1940', in John R. Parkins and Maureen G. Reed (eds), *Social transformation in rural Canada: New insights into community, cultures, and collective action*. Vancouver: UBC Press, 2013, pp. 21–42.

5 Ibid., and R. W. Sandwell, *Canada's rural majority, 1870–1940*. Toronto: University of Toronto Press, 2016.

6 Unger and Thistle, *Energy consumption in Canada*, p. 83.

7 Sandwell, 'Notes towards a history of rural Canada'.

8 As Nelles has argued,

> The rhetoric of free enterprise notwithstanding, business could not get along without the active co-operation of the state [. . .] as an understanding accomplice. The values that guided government intervention in Ontario during the first half of this century have been basically those of its business clients.

> H. V. Nelles, *The politics of development: Forests, mines and hydro-electric power in Ontario, 1849–1941*. Toronto: Macmillan of Canada, 1974, pp. 491–492.

9 Government of Canada, Dept. of Trade and Commerce, Dominion Bureau of Statistics, *Census of Industry Central Electric Light Stations in Canada, 1921–1951,* pp. 8–9. In 1911, the Commission of Conservation published the first national study of electrification, *Water-powers of Canada*. Ottawa: Mortimer, 1911.

10 Statistics Canada, *Electric Power Generation, Transmission and Distribution*, Catalogue No. 57–202-X; Canada is the third-largest hydro-electric producer after China and Brazil. William J. Hausman, Peter Hertner, Mira Wilkins, *Global electrification: Multinational enterprise and international finance in the history of light and power, 1878–2007*. Cambridge: Cambridge University Press, 2008.

11 Ronald Tobey, *Technology as freedom: The new deal and the electrical modernization of the American home*. Berkeley: University of California Press, 1996, chapter 1.

12 See Leslie Tomory, *Progressive enlightenment: The origins of the gaslight industry, 1780–1820*. Cambridge, MA: MIT Press, 2011, and 'Building the first gas network: 1812–1820', *Technology and Culture*, vol. 52, January 2011, pp. 75–102 for a delightful and detailed account of the administrative, technical and 'people' (i.e. customer) problems created by 'scaling up' from an artisan-styled industry to a network.

13 Harold L. Platt, *The electric city: Energy and the growth of the Chicago area, 1880–1930*. Chicago: University of Chicago Press, 1991, p. 17.

14 For a history of dam building and its devastating impact on Indigenous peoples in the Canadian north, see James B. Waldram, *As long as the rivers run: Hydroelectric development and native communities in Western Canada*. Winnipeg: University of Manitoba Press, 1988, and David Massell, *Amassing power: J. B. Duke and the Saguenay River 1897–1927*. Montreal and Kingston: McGill-Queen's University Press, 2000, and his *Quebec Hydropolitics: The Peribonka concessions of the second world war*. Montreal and Kingston: McGill-Queen's University Press, 2011. For the impact of these megaprojects projects on rural people more generally, see Joy Parr, *Sensing changes: Technologies, environments, and the everyday, 1953–2003*. Vancouver: UBC Press, 2010.

15 The importance of these large-scale industries can be seen in the statistics of the Central Electrical Stations in Canada. In 1942, domestic consumption of electricity constituted only 7% of all electricity consumed, a figure that had risen to 10% by 1951. 'Domestic Service, 1942', Census of Industry, 1942 (Ottawa, 1944), p. 12.

Rural electrification in Canada 201

16 Jones, *Routes of power*, p. 9. Graeme Gooday, *Domesticating electricity: Technology, uncertainty and gender, 1880–1914*. London: Pickering and Chatto, 2008, and Anne Clendinning, *Demons of domesticity: Women in the English gas industry, 1889–1939*. Farnham: Ashgate, 2004 for examples of the huge role played by advertising and promotion in ushering in the new energy regime. For an examination of Canada's massive energy re-education campaign, see R. W. Sandwell, 'Re-educating Ontario women for the modern energy regime, 1900–1940', *Ontario History*, Spring 2015.

17 Ontario Hydro Archives, catalogue number 92.032. The Hydro Electric Power Commission of Ontario, *Good will monologues, by L. D. Pengelly* [n.d. 1959?], p. 45. Emphasis in the original.

18 Hausman et al., *Global electrification*, p. 13.

19 Hydro Electric Power Commission of Ontario, *Good will monologues*, p. 43.

20 Hausman et al., *Global electrification*, p. 13.

21 As the marketing manager at B.C. Electric wrote in 1915,

> I believe that the better [than electric stoves] load endeavour to get is one consisting of the various small appliances, such as the toaster, percolator, disc stove, etc, all of which may be operated from the present lighting wires and meter at practically no extra cost to the Company and at a minimum of expense to the consumer, and the use of which appliances will be mostly off peak.

January 15, 1915 to A. T. Goward from A. H. Halls, Add Mss 4, vol. 194–133 A, British Columbia Electric Railway Fonds, BC Archives.

22 Government of Canada, *Central electrical stations, 1951*. Ottawa, 1953, p. 11. Of the 629,785 occupied farms, only 29,995 (4.76%) had electricity from a home generated source. Census of Canada, 1951, Volume 3, *Housing and Families*, Table 36. Home generators were known to be noisy, expensive and subject to frequent breakdown.

23 For an examination of the impact of mining on the development of electricity in south eastern British Columbia, see Jeremy Mouat, *The business of power: Hydro-electricity in southeastern British Columbia, 1897–1997*. Victoria: Sono Nis Press, 1997.

24 Keith Fleming, *Power at cost: Ontario hydro and rural electrification, 1911–58*. Montreal and Kingston: McGill-Queen's University Press, 1992, p. 25; Mouat, *The business of power*.

25 *Progress Report* of the Rural Electrification Committee as of January, 1945 (Victoria, B.C. 1945) p. 11.

26 Census of Canada, 1941, Volume 9, *Housing*, Tables 13 and 14.

27 Census of Canada, 1941, Volume 9, *Housing*, Table 12.

28 In 2001, average individual consumption of electrification in Canada was 18,000 kWh per year. Hausman, *Global electrification*, p. 5.

29 Farm Service (p) Domestic Service (p) Government of Canada, *Central Station Electricity, 1951*. Ottawa, 1953.

30 Report of the Rural Electrification Committee, 1945, p. 25.

31 *Central Electric Stations of Canada, 1926*, p. 12.

32 *Central Electric Stations of Canada, 1926*, p. 12.

33 *Progress Report*, p. 81.

34 *Progress Report*, pp. 40–43. The average consumption for B.C. was 85 kWh per month in 1941, and the figures stated here are for 75 kWh per month, which is the closest gradation of consumption for which figures are available.

35 *Progress Report* p. 9.

36 *Progress Report*, p. 20.

37 Fleming, *Power at cost*, p. 169.

38 Ibid.

202 *Ruth W. Sandwell*

39 Canada Bureau of Statistics Public Finance and Transportation Division, Index Numbers of Cost of Electricity for Domestic Service and Tables of Monthly Bills 1930 (57–203). Published by authority of the Hon. James Malcolm, MP, Minister of Trade and Commerce (Ottawa, 1931), 2–3.

40 Appendix C, Rate Classifications for Rural Customers, 1909–70; Fleming, *Power at cost*, pp. 264–265.

41 Public Utilities Commission, Kingston, Ontario: A Brief History of the Electric Department Prepared for the Commission by Frederic F. Thompson, Royal Military College, Kingston and Kingston PUC Archives, quoted as being from 1935 but statement not attributed, p. 43.

42 See for example, Nancy Christie and Michael Gauvreau, *A full-orbed Christianity: The Protestant churches and social welfare in Canada, 1900–1940*. Montreal and Kingston: McGill-Queen's University Press, 1996; James Murton, *Creating a modern countryside: Liberalism and land resettlement in British Columbia*. Vancouver: UBC Press, 2007; R. W. Sandwell, 'Read, listen, discuss, act: Adult education, rural citizenship and the Canadian National Farm Radio Forum', *Historical Studies in Education*, vol. 24 (1), Spring 2012, pp. 170–194; Nelles, *The politics of development*, p. 404; Fleming, *Power at cost*, p. 29.

43 See Gooday, *Domesticating electricity* for discussion of electricity's real and perceived dangers. My oral histories contain many references to fear, including one memory of lines sparking wildly where it was attached to the pole due to 'too much power'. Sandwell Heat Light and Work Oral History Project, A.M., file 4.0, 2010.

44 *Progress Report*, p. 7.

45 Fleming, *Power at cost*, p. 176.

46 *Progress Report*, p. 71.

47 Ibid.

48 Thompson, 'A brief history of the electric department' p. 55.

49 As Leslie Tomory argues, gas lighting, though unavailable in most rural areas, was the first modern power network and on which Edison deliberately modeled his electrical network. Tomory, 'Building the first gas network', p. 75.

50 Tobey, *Technology as freedom*, pp. 21–36; Bill Luckin, *Questions of power: Electricity and environment in interwar Britain*. Manchester: Manchester University Press, 1990, pp. 57–67.

51 Tobey, *Technology as freedom*, pp. 12–15; Luckin, *Questions of power*, pp. 57–67.

52 *Index Numbers of Cost of Electricity for Domestic Service and Tables of Monthly Bills* 1930, p. 1.

53 *Index Numbers of Cost of Electricity for Domestic Service and Tables of Monthly Bills 1913, 1924–26, 1930*. Published by authority of the Hon. James Malcolm, MP, Minister of Trade and Commerce Ottawa, 1927, pp. 3–4.

54 See for example British Columbia Electric Railway Fonds, Add Mss 4, vol. 140–15, Victoria, Local Manager: Correspondence, memoranda, etc. lighting consumers accounts, disconnections and connections, Nov 1908–Dec 1910 BC Archives; Correspondence regarding Complaints Hamilton Cataract Power, Light and Traction Co., RG1-1/1–4; File 3.22, Box 3, 1928–1930 Ontario Hydro Archives.

55 Wilby to Goward, January 29, 1909, British Columbia Electric Railway Company Fonds, Add Mss 4, vol. 140–15, Victoria, Local Manager: Correspondence, memoranda, etc. lighting consumers accounts, disconnections and connections, Nov 1908–Dec 1910, BC Archives.

56 Tobey, *Technology as power*, chapter 1. For more Canadian examples, see B.C. Electric and Ontario Hydro lighting customer accounts files already cited.

Rural electrification in Canada 203

57 British Columbia Electric Railway 1932–1933 Company, Add Mss 4, vol. 241–539, Victoria, Vice-President: correspondence, memoranda, etc. – power complaint; (MG Woodmass, View Royal, RMD 1, 12 April 1932).

58 Correspondence regarding Complaints, Hamilton Cataract Power, Light and Traction Co., RG1–1/1–4; file 3.22 Box 3 [labelled 15–3] RG1–1/1–4, correspondence from W.C. Thomson, 28 August 1928, 14 July 1930, Ontario Hydro Archives.

59 British Columbia Electric Railway Fonds, Add Mss 4, vol. 241–539, Mrs. Robertson, 5 September 1932, BC Archives.

60 Gooday, *Domesticating electricity.*

61 Tobey, *Technology as freedom*, p. 242. The discernment of rural dwellers in choosing which technologies to adopt and which to reject is explored in Ronald R. Kline, *Consumers in the country: Technology and social change in rural America.* Baltimore, MD: Johns Hopkins Press, 2000.

62 Fleming, *Power at cost*, p. 30.

63 Fleming, *Power at cost*, p. 32.

64 Fleming, *Power at cost*, p. 31. As Meyer has argued, similar problems attended the adoption of early steam powered farm machinery and explain the appeal of gasoline motors. Carrie E. Meyer, 'The farm debut of the gasoline engine', *Agricultural History*, vol. 87 (3), Summer 2013, pp. 287–313.

65 Bea Millar, interview with author, May 20, 1998. Joy Parr, 'Shopping for a good stove: A parable about gender, design and the market', in Joy Parr (ed.), *A diversity of women: Ontario, 1945–1980.* Toronto: University of Toronto Press, 1995, pp. 75–96. This point was made repeatedly in my oral history interviews with rural women.

66 Loris Russell, *Handy things to have around the house: Old-time domestic appliances of Canada and the United States.* Toronto: McGraw Hill Ryerson, 1979, p. 29.

67 Just under 50% of all Canadian homes were heating with wood in 1941, 25% of urban homes, 63% of rural non-farm homes, and 79% of farm homes. 'Principal Heating Fuel in Occupied Dwellings, Canada, 1941,' Census of Canada, 1941, Volume 9, *Housing*, Table 11. These numbers fell in 1951 to 28% of all homes, 11% of urban, 51% of rural non-farms, and 62% of farms. Census of Canada, 1951, *Housing and Families*, Table 24.

68 Sandwell Heat Light and Work Oral History Project, file 2.3, 2010.

69 A.H. Halls to A.T. Goward, 15 January 1915, British Columbia Electric Railway Fonds, Add Mss 4, vol. 194–133 A, BC Archives.

70 See note 1, and as well Matthew Evenden and Jonathan Peyton, 'Hydro-electricity', in R.W. Sandwell (ed.), *Powering up Canada: A short history of energy from 1600.* Montreal and Kingston: McGill-Queen's University Press, forthcoming; Neil Freeman, *The politics of power: Rural electrification in Alberta, 1920–1989.* MA thesis, Department of History, McGill University, Montreal, 1989; Lois Carol Volk, *The social effects of rural electrification in Saskatchewan*, Ottawa, National Library. MA thesis, University of Regina, 1980; Yves Tremblay, *Histoire sociale et technique de l'electrification au Bas-Saint Laurent, 1888–1963.* Ottawa, National Library, PhD thesis, Université Laval, 1993; Keith Fleming, *Ontario hydro and rural electrification in Old Ontario, 1911–1958: Policies and issues.* PhD thesis, University of Western Ontario, 1988; Marilyn Barber, 'Help for farm homes: The campaign to end housework drudgery in rural Saskatchewan in the 1920s', *Scientia Canadensis*, vol. 9, June 1985, pp. 3–26. Dorotea Gucciardo, *The Powered generation: Canadians, electricity, and everyday life.* PhD dissertation, University of Western Ontario, History, 2011; Bruce Stadfeld, *Electric space: Social and natural transformations*

204   *Ruth W. Sandwell*

in British Columbia's hydro-electricity industry to World War II. PhD thesis, University of Manitoba, 2002.
71   'England was already heavily reliant on fossil fuels by 1800 and it took Canada until about the 1970s before it caught up with English practice.' Unger and Thistle, *Energy Consumption in Canada*, p. 53.

11 Rural broadband

A twenty-first-century comparison with electrification

Martyn Warren

Introduction

This chapter charts the progress of broadband adoption in England, with particular attention to the 'mutating divide'.[1] Parallels with the twentieth-century adoption of electricity are drawn with particular respect to supply-side influences. Strong similarities can be seen in the two processes, including the emergence of oligopolistic suppliers, and governments torn between a wish to promote a beneficial innovation and a hope that private enterprise would ensure its equitable distribution. As governments edge closer and closer to regarding broadband internet as a public good, while stopping short of declaring a universal service obligation, the question remains whether rural users will ever achieve the kind of parity with city-dwellers that they enjoy with mains electricity.

The hypothesis

> Like railroads and highways, broadband accelerates the velocity of commerce, reducing the costs of distance. Like electricity, it creates a platform for America's creativity to lead in developing better ways to solve old problems. Like telephony and broadcasting, it expands our ability to communicate, inform and entertain. Broadband is the great infrastructure challenge of the early 21st century. But as with electricity and telephony, ubiquitous connections are means, not ends. It is what those connections enable that matters.[2]

Means, not ends, but nonetheless essential, and connectivity is the key factor that links the story of electricity supply and broadband internet. Are there, then, lessons to be drawn from a comparison of the two? Let's start with a general hypothesis:

> The process of adoption of broadband internet in rural England is similar to that of mains electricity supply in the twentieth century.

206 Martyn Warren

A scan of the preceding chapters might result in the following crude summary of the features of diffusion of mains electricity:

- Dependence on connection of rural locations with urban;
- Dependence on capital-hungry infrastructure, creating conditions for:
- Exercise of monopoly power:
  - Initial dependence on private and municipal corporations whose profit orientation inhibited interest in supplying to sparse populations;
  - Those corporations requiring guarantees of demand at 'acceptable' prices before agreeing to supply;
  - Failure to use cooperative structures to counter the market dominance of urban-oriented supply companies;
  - Eventual substitution of local monopolies by a nationalised monopoly with greater obligation to meeting social objectives.
- Government intervention reluctant:
  - Initially aimed at improving distribution without significant financial contribution from central government;
  - Subsequently more direct (and expensive), strongly influenced by pressure groups and members of parliament from rural constituencies.
- Limits to supply in sparsely populated areas (e.g. low voltage of supply, dependence on direct current) reduced by technological advance.
- Initial demand arising from domestic rather than industrial/commercial requirements.

What *is* broadband?

First it is important to define terms.

Specification

'Broadband' is a term used to denote a variety of technologies designed to enable delivery of high-speed internet services. In the early years of its existence, it was primarily defined by its difference from 'dial-up', that is connecting a computer to the internet via a conventional telephone connection. Thus broadband was:

- Fast: the initial standard download speed was 0.5 megabits per second (Mbps), which was approximately ten times the speed of dial-up modem when both were working effectively;
- Able to carry large files without long waiting times or crashing systems;
- 'Always there': charging policies meant a zero marginal cost of use, so that there was no financial penalty in leaving the connection open permanently, unlike a telephone line;

Rural broadband   207

- Capable of allowing real-time interaction over the web: audio, video, games and so forth;
- A credible vehicle for sophisticated e-commerce, e-government and so forth, in particular allowing businesses and individuals to create a web presence which could respond rapidly to suppliers, customers and others.

Since its emergence in the late 1990s, broadband has undergone a process of continual transformation, both in the speeds that can be expected and in its uses (see discussion on the rate of broadband adoption to 2013, later in this chapter).

Delivery methods

The predominant delivery vehicle for broadband is asymmetric digital subscriber line (ADSL). Download speeds are higher than upload (for instance 2 Mbps download, 128 Kbps upload), hence 'asymmetric'. It uses existing landline telephone infrastructure, but needs investment in adaptation of telephone exchanges. Its efficacy is affected by length of cable between exchange and premises (of the end user), and the quality of the cable (old copper and especially aluminium cables are notoriously fallible, and in plentiful supply in rural areas). In 2008 British Telecom (BT) began rolling out ADSL2+ as part of an upgrade of its core services, a technology that doubles the number of downstream channels, and thus increases the capacity.[3] In urban areas media companies established their own cable infrastructure, initially as a vehicle for digital television services, but subsequently acquiring significant importance in conveying fast broadband internet services. In recent years the laying of optical fibre – with far greater capacity and durability than copper – has become the focus of initiatives to provide so-called next-generation broadband (see later), either to the premises (FTTP) or to a street cabinet from which feeds can be taken to individual premises (FTTC). Other delivery vehicles include satellite, mobile wireless (e.g. via smartphones and tablets), and wide-area fixed wireless (e.g. Wimax), but in England, at least, they have so far competed only at the margin with cable-based technologies. The most likely alternative in the near future is mobile wireless services using HSPA (high-speed packet access) – that is 3G (third-generation), 4G and eventually 5G – though it remains to be seen whether they can keep up with the increases in bandwidth offered by cable.

What it brings

When the internet first moved from the scientific into the public domain, and acquired the user-friendly overlay of the World Wide Web (WWW), its primary uses were for email and browsing for information. As the technology advanced, and particularly with the advent of broadband and its greater capacity and speed, so the services supplied via the WWW increased in number and sophistication. Information provision developed into active marketing, direct retailing, distance learning and public service provision; communicating with friends and relatives developed into building online social networks and business collaborations. Using email to express political opinion led to pressurising politicians and officials, e-petitioning, protest and direct action, and to reaction from politicians in the form of websites, blogs, and Twitter campaigns. And entertainment grew to be the single most intensive use of the internet as it moved from text and low-resolution video through to highly complex interactive video games and streaming of high-definition television programmes and films. Thus by 2014 a large part of the population of England had become highly dependent on broadband internet for its daily work, rest and play (see Figure 11.1).

Those who can get it, that is. For to be able to benefit fully from these services, one needs to be able to access not just basic broadband (currently defined as 2 Mbps download), but next-generation or 'superfast' broadband (currently defined by Ofcom and the EU as more than 30 Mbps download

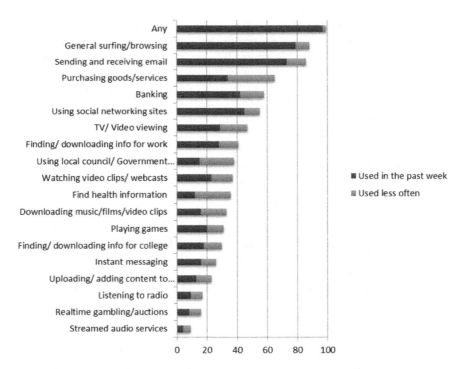

Figure 11.1 Individual use of the internet anywhere, United Kingdom, 2013.

Base: Adults aged 16+ with a broadband connection at home (n = 2,666 UK). Question: Which, if any, of these do you use the internet for?

Source: Ofcom, *The Communications Market Report: United Kingdom.* Ofcom, UK, 2013; http://stakeholders.ofcom.org.uk/market-data-research/market-data/communications-market-reports/cmr13/?a=0. Accessed 11 June 2014. Quarter 1, 2013, fig. 4.34.

speed), usually reliant on fibre-optic cable.[4] The experience of electricity supply suggests that private-sector providers will focus investment in such an expensive infrastructure in densely populated areas, and that governments will twist and turn to avoid commitments to subsidising provision in low-density (predominantly rural) areas. This would represent a double blow for country-dwellers, as the remote access to services and entertainment offered by the internet is likely to have more utility for those in sparsely populated, remote areas than in urban areas.[5] Without the internet, a city-dweller can walk to the record store, the job centre, the council offices, the cinema. The country-dweller would have to drive, or catch a bus (if there is one) to the nearest town, where he/she would probably find that the cinema and the record store have closed due to competition from Amazon, and all public offices have moved to the city to be replaced by e-government websites.

Broadband supply in England – a chronology

The early days of ADSL

During the early 2000s 'broadband' appeared as an affordable commercial offering, primarily in the form of ADSL, relying on the conversion or 'enablement' of telephone exchanges by the owner of the exchanges, BT. BT had originated in the Post Office in 1980, becoming privatised in 1984. Unsurprisingly, BT focused primarily on areas of dense population in the initial stages of the roll-out of broadband. When it did turn its attention to smaller centres of population, BT set target numbers of subscribers to be formally registered before it would enable exchanges, resulting in a slow roll-out to medium-sized towns, and little hope of coverage in the near future for those living in villages and lone dwellings. Technological limits on distance of subscribers from enabled exchanges (at that time 3.5 km) made the likelihood of rural broadband an even more remote prospect.[6] The concept of a 'digital divide' – exclusion of certain sectors of society from use of the internet by factors outside their control – was already current, linked to such social factors as poverty, education, ethnic origin and age.[7] The advent of broadband brought another factor to the fore – that of geographical location.

Politicians take notice

By 2002, broadband provision for rural areas was being increasingly debated.[8] The UK government recognised the need for broadband in rural communities, while resisting suggestions that it should intervene in the market. E-Commerce Minister Stephen Timms said on one hand:

> There are still too many people – in rural and remote parts of the country – who can't access an affordable and reliable broadband service. And what's worse, in some cases – due to technological and market constraints – they have no realistic prospect of getting affordable

210 *Martyn Warren*

broadband in the near future. This is unacceptable, it does threaten the prospects for broadband to be a boon both to our economy and to our society, and it presents a major challenge to policy-makers and to industry alike.[9]

And on the other:

> Past experience underpins our view that inappropriate use of taxpayers' money can distort the market and – in the long term – delay widespread availability of the most up to date services. Competition is a much more effective driver . . . in our thinking about rollout in rural areas we must not be too quick just to throw money at the issue.[10]

The government's preferred approach was first to initiate a £30m investment programme into an experimental roll-out of broadband networks 'to parts of the country where they wouldn't otherwise be commercially viable', to test innovative responses to the problem and to produce case studies of 'best practice'. Second, a programme of 'aggregation of demand' aimed to facilitate public procurement of broadband, focusing on local government, doctors' surgeries and schools, in an attempt to create critical mass in internet use.

Meanwhile BT spoke on behalf of the telecommunications corporations.

> 'Tony Harris, president of business internet services at ISP BT Openworld, disagrees that there is significant latent demand in rural areas for broadband, and argues that firms should instead focus on areas where the technology is available but not being taken up.'[11]

Faced with a perceived intransigence in public and private sectors, some rural communities sought their own solutions, for instance using wireless technology to distribute access to a communally leased broadband feed.[12] At the same time, various interest groups championed the cause of 'broadbanding' rural Britain, including groups such as Broadband4Britain, Rural Broadband Interest Group, the Country Land and Business Association (CLA) and other more local, often village-based organisations. Their message was summed up by Sir Ewen Cameron, Chairman of the Countryside Agency:

> Whilst overall two thirds of the UK population can access affordable broadband, in market towns the figure is 26%, in rural villages 7% and in remote rural areas 1%. Only 3% of rural businesses have DSL broadband connection compared with 11% of urban ones. This can present an expensive obstacle to new rural businesses, including farm businesses that need access to new technology and markets. Perhaps this is one reason why rural businesses seem to be a little less optimistic than their

Rural broadband   211

urban counterparts. Rural communities, who could most benefit from remote access to services such as banking, could be missing out. And rural young people cannot get the same access to the latest entertainment, education and training, delivered through broadband.[13]

For many, BT was the villain of the piece, seeming to drag its heels over the enablement of rural exchanges. In 2004 it unexpectedly abandoned its registration targets and accelerated its programme of roll-out to small towns, although it still appeared that it would be many years before a majority of the population in villages and scattered dwellings were connected.[14] Local loop unbundling (LLU) meant that third-party suppliers were able to use the 'last mile' (the link between exchange and customers' premises) to deliver broadband services. A side effect was the demise of many community broadband schemes, now rendered redundant and/or or undercut by the competition.

In 2004 Ofcom set up a Strategic Review of Telecommunications, reporting finally in 2005.[15] Perhaps the most important element of this for broadband provision was the establishment in 2006 of Openreach, a new business unit operating independently of BT, managing the provision and maintenance of services in the last mile, with the aim of ensuring that all telecommunications providers enjoyed the same operational conditions as BT.

By 2006 the Commission for Rural Communities (CRC) was reporting that internet usage in 'less sparse' rural areas was similar to that in urban areas, given the increased availability in those areas of ADSL broadband, while lamenting that in sparsely populated areas 'usage remains notably lower.'[16] At the same time, the phenomenon of a 'mutating digital divide' was beginning to make its presence felt.[17] Where a technology is adopted more slowly by one sector of society than another, it is reasonable to assume a 'catch-up' effect such that the divide eventually disappears. But, as Katzman had long ago pointed out, the world is not a closed system, and any innovation is likely to be overtaken by a new innovation before its adoption has reached 100%.[18] In Information and communications technology (ICT) innovation the frequency and speed of the process exacerbates the impact, resulting in a seemingly never-ending game of catch-up as one innovation is overtaken by others in quick succession. So while the CRC could report heightened availability of broadband to less-sparse rural areas, most households in those areas were able to obtain only the basic 0.5 Mbps service, while most urban dwellers had no trouble in obtaining bandwidths of 2 Mbps, and those in metropolitan areas could have access to 8 Mbps.[19] In 2006 the CRC welcomed a forecast that over 50% of UK households would be able to access high bandwidths, but continued: 'It is almost certain that most rural communities will be excluded from this capability. This will leave them (and potentially much of the urban fringe) at great disadvantage compared to urban households.'[20]

212   Martyn Warren

The emergence of a universal commitment

During this time the stance of government was essentially 'hands-off' while expressing concern, intervening mainly to correct 'market failure' and to aggregate demand through a vigorous policy of moving government processes online. This was consistent with EU policy, as expressed in its *E-Europe Action Plan 2005* and *i2010 – A European Information Society for Growth and Employment*, which effectively left the issue of broadband provision to member states, though the latter were allowed to use structural funds and financial incentives for that purpose: for instance the 'actnow' project in Cornwall using Objective 1 structural funds.[21] A sea change was signalled by the Labour government's commissioning in late 2008 of *Digital Britain*, arising from growing awareness of the economic potential of new media. This report, published in June 2009, presented a three-year plan to boost digital participation, including inter alia a fund to invest in 'next generation' broadband, liberalisation of the 3G mobile spectrum and support for public service content partnerships. Crucially, it also established the principle of a Universal Service Commitment (USC), while apparently confronting the 'mutating divide' issue:

> More than one in 10 households today cannot enjoy a 2Mbps connection. We will correct this by providing universal service by 2012. It has a measure of future-proofing so that, as the market deploys next-generation broadband, we do not immediately face another problem of exclusion.[22]

The Universal Service Commitment would be delivered by a mixture of ADSL, fibre to the street cabinet, wireless and possibly satellite. Two hundred million pounds would be made available for the plan from direct public funding (partly from an underspend in the Digital [TV] Switchover Help Scheme), together with contributions from public and private sectors. In December 2009 the government published its *Digital Britain Implementation Plan* for the roll-out of these measures.[23]

Digital Britain represented a major shift in policy: an acceptance of responsibility for broadband infrastructure distribution which would prove a real headache for the government – or rather its Conservative/Liberal-Democrat successor – which adopted the essence of the plan after its election in 2010. In 2011 the Culture Secretary announced that 90% of premises in every local authority in the UK should have access to broadband of 24 Mbps by 2015, and the remainder should have a minimum of 2 Mbps. Five hundred and thirty million pounds would be made available, to be matched by £730m from local authorities (£1.2bn in all), with the aim of giving the UK 'the best superfast broadband network in Europe'.[24] Implementation of the scheme was held up by, amongst other things, delays in obtaining approval from the EU (the fact that BT won all the contracts had raised concerns that EU competition rules had been broken), and in July 2013 a National Audit Office report revealed that only nine of forty-four rural areas would achieve broadband targets by 2015, and four might still be unconnected by the end of 2017.[25] Targets were revised to 95% of premises having superfast broadband by the end of 2017 (thus postponed until after the next general election in 2015). In the meantime the natives grew increasingly restless, with discontent strongly expressed by pressure groups, rural media, and parliamentary committees.[26]

In September 2013 the House of Commons Public Accounts Committee (PAC) accused the government of mismanaging the process, and BT of exploiting its quasi-monopoly position to win all the contracts. The chair of the Committee, Margaret Hodge, stated that 'the taxpayer has been ripped off,' while BT riposted that the Committee had ignored its point-by-point rebuttal of the accusations, and that 'we have been . . . willing to invest when others have not. It is therefore mystifying that we are being criticised for accepting onerous terms in exchange for public subsidy – terms which drove others away.'[27] The chair of the Environment, Food and Rural Affairs Committee, Anne McIntosh, entered the fray in October 2013, echoing the PAC's call for BT to publish roll-out plans to enable those communities that would not be covered by the scheme to make alternative plans.[28] This would also help to avoid community groups being undercut (shades of 2004–2005) when local authorities signed blanket contracts with BT, as had happened already in, for instance, Oxfordshire and Dorset.[29]

Nonetheless, by mid-December 2013 the government was able to announce the hook-up of 5,000 homes in rural counties to superfast broadband, with another 200,000 promised by the end of the month. Rory Cellan Jones of the BBC was more than a little sceptical, pointing out:

> That, by my reckoning, is 1% of UK households, and as the rural broadband programme is supposed to serve the 30% which will not be reached by the market, there is obviously quite a way to go . . . whenever I raise the issue, I get a flood of messages from people across the UK angry that they are still missing out on any kind of decent broadband connection.

A good example would be response number 348 to his comments:

> We live with Fibre within 1 mile, 3 towns within 5 miles all FTTC, yet have to put up with best 1mbps. We are not even on the roadmap the Broadband is appalling. This country should be ashamed my friend has a home in Turkey in the mountains miles from no where and yet he gets 7mbps. Fibre is a pipe dream.[30]

214 *Martyn Warren*

In February 2014 the PAC called for a halt to new payments to BT until it could demonstrate that it was passing on economies of scale achieved by winning each of the previous contracts (the government declined to intervene in local procurement processes) and in April of the same year criticised BT's broadband roll-out maps for lacking essential detail.[31]

The result: broadband adoption up to 2013

The growth of broadband penetration in the UK is illustrated by Table 11.1, which clearly shows the rapid pace of broadband adoption from 6% to 75% of adults in the Ofcom technology sample between 2003 and 2013, with a doubling of uptake between 2004 and 2005 following BT's accelerated programme of exchange enablement. It also suggests a plateau in adoption of fixed broadband concurrent with a rapid increase in the access of internet by mobile device between 2009 and 2013 (likely to increase still further given the popularity of smartphones, tablets and wearable devices).[32]

Ofcom data suggest that average UK broadband speed in the second quarter of 2013 was 14.7 Mbps, with 73% of total UK households being able to access superfast broadband. Those same data show a clear disparity between rural and urban areas, though, with 21% rural households compared to 86% urban households having superfast broadband available, and an average rural speed of 9.9 Mbps compared to 26.4 Mbps in the

Table 11.1 Household internet take-up, UK, 2001–2013 (% adults).

Quarter 1:	2001	2002	2003	2004	2005	2006	2007	2008	2009	2010	2011	2012	2013
Internet[i]	34	46	45	53	60	60	64	67	73	75	78	79	80
Total broadband[ii]			6	16	31	41	52	58	68	71	74	76	75
Fixed broadband[ii]									65	65	67	72	72
Internet on mobile[ii]									20	22	28	39	49

Notes:
[i] Question: Do you or does anyone in your household have access to the internet / WWW at home (via any device, e.g. PC, mobile phone etc.)?
[ii] Question: Which of these methods does your household use to connect to the internet at home?
[iii] "Internet on mobile" is the % of adults who use a mobile phone for any of the following activities: instant messaging, downloading apps or programs, email, internet access, downloading video, video streaming, visiting social networking sites.
[iv] From Q1 2009 the 'internet' figure includes those who access the internet on mobile phones.

Source: Ofcom technology tracker, Q1 2011 and Q1 2013. Base: All adults aged 16+ (n = 3,474 [2011]; n = 3750 [2013]).

2011 data: http://stakeholders.ofcom.org.uk/market-data-research/market-data/communications-market-reports/cmr11/uk/?a=0. Accessed 4 June 2014.

2013 data: http://stakeholders.ofcom.org.uk/binaries/research/cmr/cmr13/UK_4.pdf. Accessed 4 June 2014.

Rural broadband   215

towns.[33] This is amplified by Table 11.2, showing ranges of speeds rather than averages.

Inevitably these general data conceal significant variation between and within areas, as illustrated by examples within the chronology above. Ofcom uses its panel data (see Table 11.3) to provide a neat illustration

Table 11.2 Average download speeds (in Mbps) for fixed broadband connections in urban, suburban and rural areas: May 2011 to November 2013.

	May 2011	May 2012	May 2013	Nov 2013
Urban				
Lower limit	12.7	20.3	25	30.4
Upper limit	14.4	22.8	27.8	33.5
Suburban				
Lower limit	7.7	11.6	16.3	19.6
Upper limit	9.8	14.7	19.4	23.9
Rural				
Lower limit	3.3	4.8	7.7	9.6
Upper limit	4.9	6.9	12	13

Note: The sizes of the rural samples from which these averages were taken are not large enough for the change to be deemed statistically significant. As such, the figures should be treated as indicative only.

Source: Ofcom (2014) *UK fixed-line broadband performance, November 2013 – The performance of fixed-line broadband delivered to UK residential consumers.* http://stakeholders. ofcom.org.uk/market-data-research/other/telecoms-research/broadband-speeds/broadband-speeds-nov2013/. Accessed 4 June 2014.

Table 11.3 Average download speeds (in Mbps) experienced by panellists in rural areas: May 2010 to November 2013.

		May 2010	Nov/Dec 2010	May 2011	Nov 2011	May 2012	Nov 2012	May 2013	Nov 2013
Panellist H	ADSL1	2.2	2.3	1.7	1.2	0.9	1.3	1.4	0.9
Panellist I	ADSL1								
	ADSL2	10	10	12.7	13.2	12.3	13.5	13.8	13.5
Panellist J	ADSL1	0.9	0.8						
	ADSL2								
	FTTC			14.3	16.1	18.3	21.8		17.8
Panellist K	ADSL1								
	ADSL2	8.4	8.8	6.3	9.2				
	FTTC					16.9	16.9	20.7	22.4

Source: Ofcom (2014) *UK fixed-line broadband performance, November 2013 – The performance of fixed-line broadband delivered to UK residential consumers.* http://stakeholders. ofcom.org.uk/market-data-research/other/telecoms-research/broadband-speeds/broadband-speeds-nov2013/. Accessed 4 June 2014.

216 *Martyn Warren*

of the impact of improvement in broadband technology (or the lack of it), comparing the experience of Panellist H, using first-generation ADSL, with more fortunate individuals able to access ADSL2 and/or 'superfast' optical fibre to the street cabinet (FTTC).

Conclusions

The story of broadband is thus one of a technology dependent on connectivity, which in turn has to rely on costly fixed infrastructure. Development has been rapid, resulting from interaction between innovation in supply and demand from consumers. The supply is dominated by one corporation which started life as a nationalised, public landline monopoly but, shortly before the introduction of ADSL, became a privatised corporation in an ostensibly free market – but with advantages (e.g. ownership of landline infrastructure) that gave it a quasi-monopolistic position in that market.

EU and UK competition legislation makes exploiting a monopoly or oligopoly position much more difficult than in the formative days of electricity supply, and there is competition, notably from cable providers (specifically Virgin), media companies (e.g. Sky) and mobile telephony companies (although the many small, local schemes that were initiated have never grown collectively to provide a serious challenge).

Nevertheless BT does still dominate the market, particularly in rural areas. To some extent one could say the privatised BT is an accidental monopolist, having inherited the landline infrastructure from its former incarnation, and with it both opportunities and responsibilities. It is quite possible that, freed from those responsibilities, it would be happy to focus on densely populated, highly competitive areas and to forsake its somewhat onerous market domination in the unprofitable rural areas. That has certainly been the approach of other commercial providers, understandably concentrating on provision to areas of dense population in order to maximise returns on their capital outlay, leaving rural populations to play catch-up with respect to access to high-speed services. Government hung back for as long as it could, hoping to be able just to intervene to correct isolated instances of 'market failure', but eventually, recognising the cost of inaction to economic growth (and to the votes of white middle class rural voters who consider broadband access to be a fundamental human right), edged more and more into the fray, eventually making a commitment to universal service provision, and supplying funding for infrastructure enabling superfast broadband provision to the vast majority of households.

On the demand side, email and personal browsing drove much of the early interest in the internet.[34] Even now the pressure for high-speed services is fuelled by demand for streaming of high-definition video and interactive video games rather than industrial imperatives. But at each stage of innovation, industrial and professional users have adapted quickly to take advantage of the market-creating and cost-saving potential of the new developments.

Thus the story of broadband internet supply in England does indeed exhibit distinct similarities to the story of mains electricity supply in the twentieth century, as would be demonstrated by a point-by-point comparison with the list at the beginning of this chapter. It would be wrong to be more emphatic, though, since the complexity of the adoption process in each case defies simplistic conclusion, and the technologies have different natures, functions and dynamics. There is very little variation in the nature of the product supplied through an electricity main, for instance, compared to the ever-expanding panoply of services channelled through broadband internet – and its consequence in the shape of the 'mutating divide'. While poverty has been a negative factor in adoption of both technologies, the information-rich nature of the internet means that a range of other factors (e.g. age, ethnicity, educational attainment, language, disability) are implicated in its adoption. Long before the invention of the internet, Tichenor demonstrated that

> as the infusion of mass media into a social system increases, segments of the population with higher socio-economic status tend to acquire this information at a faster rate than the lower status segments, so that the gap in knowledge between these segments tends to increase rather than decrease.[35]

In other words, the (information) rich get richer and the poor get poorer, and the progressive development serves to widen the gap between the digital haves and the have-nots: a 'digital vicious cycle' ensures that social exclusion leads to digital exclusion which in turn reinforces and deepens social exclusion.[36]

Fascinating as the broadband story has been so far, the most interesting element may well still lie ahead of us. UK government commitments are 'future-proofed' to some extent, in an attempt to counter the mutating divide. How long will that commitment last? How long will it be before a new technology, less reliant on expensive local infrastructure, allows rural populations to leapfrog and make debates about optical fibre distribution redundant? What will that new technology be: 4G or 5G mobile, new-generation wide-area wireless, low-tech satellite, Google balloons, unused capacity in powerlines? Watch this space. Just don't try watching Netflix yet if you happen to live in the English countryside . . .

Notes

1 This concept is postulated in M. F. Warren, 'The digital vicious cycle: Links between social disadvantage and digital exclusion in rural areas', *Telecommunications Policy*, vol. 31 (6–7), 2007, pp. 374–388.

218   *Martyn Warren*

2 Federal Communications Commission (USA) – National Broadband Plan 2010, quoted in K. Mossberger, C. J. Tollbert and W. Franko, *Digital cities: The internet and the geography of opportunity.* New York: Oxford University Press, 2013.

3 Wikipedia, *G.992.5.* Wikipedia; http://en.wikipedia.org/wiki/G.992.5. Accessed 11 June 2014.

4 Ofcom, *Superfast broadband available to three-in-four homes.* Ofcom 2013. http://media.ofcom.org.uk/2013/10/24/superfast-broadband-available-to-three-in-four-homes/. Accessed 11 June 2014.

5 O. Furuseth, 'Service provision and social deprivation', in B. Ilbery (ed.), *The geography of rural change.* Harlow: Pearson, 1998, pp. 233–256. See p. 236.

6 S. Skerrat and M. F. Warren, *Buckfastleigh broadband community network: Final report.* Plymouth: University of Plymouth, 2004, p. 58.

7 See, for example, NTIA, *Falling through the net II: New data on the digital divide.* National Telecommunications and Information Administration 1998. http://www.ntia.doc.gov/ntiahome/net2/. Accessed March 2001.

8 B. Hindman, 'The rural-urban digital divide', *Journalism and Mass Communication Quarterly*, vol. 77 (3), 2000, pp. 549–560; European Commission, *The development of broadband access platforms in Europe: Technologies, services, markets. Full report.* Brussels: European Commission, Information Society DG, 2001, p. 163; Anon, 'CLA campaigns to "broadband rural Britain"', in *Country Life* 2002; BBC News. *Pressure on for rural broadband.* BBC 2002; S. Millar, 'Rural area have-nots lose out on the net'. *Guardian* 2002.

9 S. Timms, *Broadband in the regions. Speech given at the broadband Britain conference, London, June 2002. Released 27–06–02.* East of England Telematics Development Trust 2002.

10 Timms, *Broadband in the regions.*

11 R. Agnew, *Broad concerns: Broadband Britain still hangs in the balance*, in *Sector Report: Broadband Britain*, U.f.B. Net Imperative, Editor. 2002. pp. 4–8.

12 Anon, *Kington connected community.* The Planning Exchange 2001. http://www.planex.co.uk/value/kington1.htm. Accessed 18 March 2002; BBC News, *Wireless web tested in hills.* BBC 2002. http://news.bbc.co.uk/hi/english/uk/wales/newsid_2071000/2071601.stm. Accessed 3 July 2002; T. Richardson, *Cambridgeshire snuggles up to NTL. Register* 2002. http://www.theregister.co.uk/2002/09/24/cambridgeshire_snuggles_up_to_ntl/. Accessed 12 June 2014; T. Richardson, *North Yorks to get wireless broadband network. Register* 2002. http://www.theregister.co.uk/2002/10/09/north_yorks_to_get_wireless/. Accessed 12 June 2014; J. Leyden, *Rural wireless broadband goes national. Register* 2003. http://www.theregister.co.uk/2003/05/15/rural_wireless_broadband_goes_national/. Accessed 12 June 2014; J. Leyden, *Revolution needed for rural broadband success, Register* 2003. http://www.theregister.co.uk/2003/07/09/revolution_needed_for_rural_broadband/. Accessed 12 June 2014; T. Richardson, *Northants villages set up own BB network. Register* 2003. http://www.theregister.co.uk/2003/09/24/northants_villages_set_up_own/. Accessed 12 June 2014.

13 Countryside Agency, *The state of the countryside 2003.* Wetherby: Countryside Agency, 2003. http://www.countryside.gov.uk. Accessed May 2003.

14 T. Richardson, BT moves to 'universal availability' of broadband. *Register* 2004. http://www.theregister.co.uk/2004/04/27/bt_broadband_exchange/. Accessed 5 May 2005.

15 Ofcom, *Strategic Review of Telecommunications: 2005 update.* 2005. http://stakeholders.ofcom.org.uk/consultations/telecoms_p2/statement/.

16 Commission for Rural Communities, *The state of the countryside 2006.* Cheltenham: Commission for Rural Communities, 2006, p. 166. http://www.rural communities.gov.uk/files/SoTC06_Complete.pdf.

Rural broadband 219

17 Warren, 'The digital vicious cycle'.
18 N. Katzman, 'The impact of communication technology: Promises and prospects', *Journal of Communication*, vol. 24, 1974, pp. 47–58.
19 BBC News, *UK broadband gets speed injection*. BBC 2004. http://news.bbc.co.uk/go/pr/fr/-/1/hi/technology/4016031.stm. Accessed 16 November 2004.
20 P. Sumner and M. Yardley, *Predicting UK future residential broadband bandwidth requirements*. Cambridge: Analysis for Broadband Stakeholder Group, 2006, p. 97. http://www.broadbanduk.org/reports/BSG%20reports/0605_Band widthRequirements_Analysysreportfor_BSG.pdf. Accessed May 2006; Varley, J., *Predicting UK future residential bandwidth requirements (open letter)*, B.S. Group, Editor, London: Commission for Rural Communities, 2006. http://www.ruralcommunities.gov.uk/publications/predictingukfutureresidentialband widthrequirements. Accessed 4 January 2007.
21 Commission of the European Communities, *The eEurope 2005 action plan: An information society for everyone* [COM(2002) 263 final]. 2002. http://europa.eu/legislation_summaries/information_society/strategies/l24226_en.htm. Accessed 12 June 2014; Commission of the European Communities, *i2010 – A European Information Society for growth and employment*. 2005, Commission of the European Communities: Brussels. http://europa.eu.int/information_society/eeurope/i2010/docs/communications/com_229_i2010_310505_fv_en.doc. Accessed 1 June 2005; One. *Cornwall invests to attract new knowledge-based business*. One – The Objective One Partnership for Cornwall and the Isles of Scilly 2004. http://www.objectiveone.com/client/media/media-350.htm. Accessed 12 June 2014; M. F. Warren, *Business adoption of Broadband Internet in the South West of England*, in European Federation for Information Technology in Agriculture, Joint International Agricultural Conference, 6–8 July 2009, Wageningen, The Netherlands. http://www.efita.net/. Accessed 12 June 2014.
22 BIS, *Digital Britain: Final Report, June 2009*. 2009. p. 240. https://www.gov.uk/government/uploads/system/uploads/attachment_data/file/228844/7650.pdf.
23 BIS, *Digital Britain Implementation Plan. December 2009*. p. 10. http://web archive.nationalarchives.gov.uk/+/http:/www.culture.gov.uk/images/publications/DB_Implementationplan_Dec09.pdf.
24 BBC News, *UK rural broadband rollout criticised by auditors*. 2013. http://www.bbc.co.uk/news/technology-23173157. Accessed: 12 June 2014.
25 National Audit Office (2013). *Department for Culture, Media & Sport: The rural broadband programme*. London: NAO. http://www.nao.org.uk/wp-content/uploads/2013/07/10177–001-Rural-Broadband_HC-535.pdf. Accessed 24 November 2014.
26 See, for instance, FWI, *Rural broadband. Farmers Weekly Interactive* 2012. http://www.fwi.co.uk/business-archive/rural-broadband-campaign/. Accessed 12 June 2014.
27 BBC News, *Rural broadband rollout: Taxpayers being 'ripped off', say MPs*. 2013. http://www.bbc.co.uk/news/technology-24227096. Accessed 12 June 2014.
28 Farming Online, *Defra secretary faces questioning in Parliament*. 2013. http://www.farming.co.uk/news/article/9112. Accessed 12 June 2014.
29 BBC News, *Plug pulled on rural broadband projects in favour of BT*. 2013. http://www.bbc.co.uk/news/technology-24919148. Accessed 12 June 2014; BBC News. *Rural broadband: How the money will be spent*. 2013. http://www.bbc.co.uk/news/technology-26338920. Accessed 12 June 2014.
30 BBC News, *Superfast broadband – Are we getting there?* 2013. http://www.bbc.co.uk/news/technology-25430032. Accessed 12 June 2014.
31 BBC News, *Delay BT broadband cash bid, MPs urge*. 2014. http://www.bbc.co.uk/news/technology-26366893. Accessed 12 June 2014; BBC News. *Rural*

220   Martyn Warren

broadband maps criticised for lacking detail. 2014. http://www.bbc.co.uk/news/technology-26819483. Accessed 12 June 2014.

32 R. Myslewski, Analysts: Bright future for smartphones, tablets, wearables. *Register* 2014. http://www.theregister.co.uk/2014/04/11/analysts_bright_future_for_smartphones_tablets_wearables/. Accessed 12 June 2014.

33 Thinkbroadband, *Broadband Factsheet Q1 2014.* http://www.thinkbroadband.com/factsheet/. Accessed 12 June 2014.

34 See, for instance M. F. Warren, *E-farming or e-folly? Adoption of internet technology by farmers in England.* Newton Abbot: University of Plymouth, 2000. p. 77; M. F. Warren, 'Farmers online: Drivers and impediments in adoption of internet in UK agricultural businesses', *Journal of Small Business Enterprise Development*, vol. 11 (3), 2004.

35 P. G. Tichenor, G. Donohue, and C. Olien, 'Mass media flow and differential growth in knowledge', *Public Opinion Quarterly*, vol. 34, 1970, pp. 159–170, quoted in P. Kingsley and T. Anderson, 'Facing life without the internet. Internet Research', *Electronic Networking Applications and Policy*, vol. 8 (4), 1998, p. 307.

36 Warren, 'The digital vicious cycle'.

12 Conclusion
Electricity, rurality and modernity

Paul Brassley, Jeremy Burchardt and Karen Sayer

The electrification of the countryside was a long-drawn-out process with four interwoven but distinct components: the uptake and use of generators and other forms of self-supply; rural electrification; farmhouse and cottage electrification; and farm electrification. The first of these components, although an important and under-researched subject, falls largely outside the scope of this book. The second, rural electrification, was to a large extent accomplished before the Second World War, at least if it is measured in terms of making electricity available for installation to consumers living in villages of 500 or more inhabitants. The electrification of most farmhouses and cottages had to wait until after the war, but once a mains supply became available to these more isolated dwellings it was adopted relatively quickly for lighting, although other uses only evolved over time. The use of electricity on the farm itself, not only for lighting but also for heating and power, often took much longer to develop.

Rural electrification posed different challenges, required different solutions and had different consequences to the electrification of urban areas. It was also a complex and in some ways unexpected process. For example it was sometimes more rapid in what are often regarded as peripheral states such as Sweden, where by 1944 only one in six rural households lacked electricity, than in supposedly more advanced economies such as England, in which as many as two in three rural households are thought to have had no electricity supply in 1939. These spatial contrasts were, if anything, even more marked, and at least as surprising, within than between countries. In Sweden, a higher proportion of farm holdings had an electricity supply in the remote province of Norrland, much of which is north of the Arctic Circle, than in the central province of Svealand (chapter 9). There is, therefore, an important international, national and regional historical geography of rural electrification, into which several of the chapters of this book make forays, but which deserves much further exploration. It is also worth remembering that it is an unfinished story. Even today, it may be easier to get a three-phase supply, which some machinery requires, in towns than in the countryside.

222 *Paul Brassley et al.*

Supply

The central problem besetting efforts to provide electricity to rural areas was the high cost of supply – the fixed capital problem described in the introduction. This was inherent in the physical properties of electricity generation and transmission on the one hand and the spatial characteristics of the countryside on the other, and was therefore not amenable to change. Electricity is most efficiently generated on a large scale (although further research is required to gauge how far the relationship between size and generating costs has changed over time) and can in practice only be transmitted over long distances by means of a physical link (i.e. wires). Where population is less dense, as by definition it is in rural areas, the length of wire required to connect each user will be correspondingly greater than in an urban setting. In Canada, for example, as Ruth Sandwell explains (chapter 10), it was generally reckoned that electrification was only profitable for electricity distributors at a price affordable to consumers if there were at least five households per mile of line. Where these costs were passed on directly to rural users, the price of electricity was far higher than in urban areas. In Vancouver in 1944, for example, a typical monthly bill was $2.30 for 85 kilowatt-hours (kWh), whereas in the rural settlements of Castlegear, Vernon, Field and Burns's Lake the cost of the same amount of electricity ranged from $4.05 up to $15.00. Unsurprisingly, then, in most countries the electrification of rural areas lagged a long way behind that of towns and cities. In England, for example, 89% of urban but only 42% of rural areas had been connected to the national grid by 1928. Karl Ditt suggests that the countryside was ten years behind the towns with respect to electrification in England in the period up to 1945 (chapter 2).

As far as centrally generated mains supplies were concerned, the rural electrification problem, as we have already argued, was essentially one of transmission cost. To provide an electricity supply required not only generating stations but also pylons, transformers to convert the long-distance high voltage supply into the lower voltage appropriate to the individual consumer, and local supply lines, poles and insulators. The pylons and poles themselves generated numerous way leave negotiations. In 1950 it was calculated that a yard of high-tension cable cost £2.10s., in comparison with the £1.10s. required to construct a yard of 'A' road or the 12s. needed for a yard of mains water piping.[1] In 1924 W.C. Dampier Whetham made an elaborate estimate of the potential demand for electricity in the parishes for ten miles around Cambridge, excluding the town and its suburbs. This area contained some 277 square miles, with 165 people per square mile, whose probable demand he estimated at 2,100 units, costing £52 per square mile. He then added in the demand from farms, at 4,000 units per square mile, at the same price, and arrived at a total of £150 per square mile. In comparison, the Cambridge Electric Supply Company, which served the town, had revenues of £3,800 per square mile, and in addition, he noted, the costs

Conclusion   223

of transmission wires and transformers would be increased by the greater distances to be covered in the countryside. He pointed out, however, that the rural population was not evenly spread over the countryside, but, apart from the farms, concentrated in villages, and then went on to examine the costs of supplying chains of villages. For a capital cost of £15,000 he provided an example in which the estimated gross return would be of the order of £2,300 per year. Village power stations, he suggested, might be one way of avoiding the long distance distribution costs. Water power was best and cheapest, he argued, and he cited examples of water-powered local schemes near Bala in Wales, in Berwickshire and in Berkshire, together with stationary engine-powered schemes in Somerset and Hertfordshire. In future, he predicted, it was possible that windmills might be used.[2] But clearly, isolated farms were the main problem.

These cost considerations would seem to provide an adequate explanation of the reluctance of municipal electricity undertakings to extend their power lines beyond their borders, and in any case the 6.6 kilovolt (kV) potential that many of them used was too low to make supplies economic at any distance.[3] In 1927 the standards required for overhead supply lines were relaxed, so cutting costs by between 25% and 30%. The Central Electricity Board conducted research on rural electrification, and provided cheaper supplies through the national grid to some rural undertakings in Sussex, Lincolnshire, Cumberland and southern Scotland. But the inescapable fact that a mile of rural power line might serve ten consumers, while a similar mile in an urban area might serve 300, meant that rural supply costs remained significantly higher. Rural supplies were thus left to private companies, and by 1931 the Electricity Commissioners had granted supply franchises to most rural areas, either to new distribution companies formed expressly to supply rural areas, or to existing companies.[4]

While the high cost of supply appears to explain why it took so much longer to electrify rural than urban areas, accounting for the sometimes dramatic difference in how long it took mains electricity to reach one rural area compared to another is more complex. It would be easy to extrapolate from the urban-rural contrast and assume that the decisive issue was the density of population. This was certainly a factor, and on the whole the wires did take much longer to reach remote farmsteads than more populous rural areas. In the sparsely settled uplands of Radnor (Wales), for example, not a single farm was connected to the national grid as late as 1941, whereas in rural Glamorgan, with a population density nearly ten times greater, 30% of farms had mains electricity by the same date (chapter 4). However, other factors were involved, too. One obvious one was proximity to existing power lines. In England, villages and farms close to towns or to industrial undertakings with their own supply usually seem to have obtained a connection to the grid sooner than less favourably located settlements. However, neither population density nor proximity to urban centres appears to explain the timing of electrification in rural Sweden, as Carin

224   *Paul Brassley et al.*

Martiin shows (chapter 9). Here, a higher proportion of farm holdings had electric lighting in the least densely settled of the country's three provinces (Norrland) than in the other two provinces in late 1940s. This seems to have been because Sweden relied overwhelmingly on hydroelectricity rather than coal- or oil-fired power stations. In Jönköping county, for example, 330 out of 341 power stations were water-powered in 1924. These hydro-electric power stations tended to be very small – because there was no need to transport fuel to the site, there were not the same economies of scale as with thermal power stations (a situation that also prevailed in northern Scotland, as David Fleetwood describes in chapter 5). The decisive factor was the existence of a sufficient head of water, and it is this that explains the surprisingly good availability of electricity in Norrland, which is more mountainous than most of the rest of Sweden. Hydroelectricity was also comparatively cheap. In Canada, where, as in Sweden, hydroelectricity was almost completely dominant, electricity cost on average only 1.6 cents per kWh in 1953, compared to 2.8 cents per kWh in the USA, where 73% of electricity was generated by steam and internal combustion engines. This meant that it was easier to supply electricity to areas of scattered settlement at a price consumers could afford. A somewhat similar situation pertained in Denmark, where farmers set up a number of small-scale DC power stations between 1902 and 1920, using wind, steam and internal combustion engines as the power source. These paved the way for later high voltage AC stations, and, in some cases, for district heat and power schemes.[5] Where and how electricity was generated could, therefore, influence the extent and timing of rural electrification in some areas as much as population density and proximity to an existing supply.

While production and distribution costs set the broad parameters of rural electrification, institutional factors sometimes played a major role in determining how quickly the barriers to providing electricity to rural areas were overcome. In England and Wales, the Electric Lighting Act of 1882 established a framework that, as Ditt demonstrates in chapter 2, ultimately inhibited rural electrification severely. This may partly explain why England performed poorly in this respect compared, for example, to France, Germany, the Netherlands and Scandinavia (as late as 1941, only 30% of English farms had access to electricity, whereas five years earlier 80% of German, 65% of French and 50% of Swedish farms already did). Under the 1882 Act, companies wishing to sell electricity were required to obtain consent from local authorities, which acquired an effective local monopoly. Many urban local authorities set up their own electricity generation and supply undertakings, to the point where local authorities controlled about two-thirds of England's electricity generating capacity by the late 1920s. Local authorities typically had different aims from private companies. Rather than seeking to maximise profits, for example by expanding their customer base, promoting increased consumption or raising prices, they typically aimed to keep costs and prices as low as possible to benefit business and personal users within their municipal boundaries. Cheap electricity would give local businesses a cost advantage, allow them to expand and ultimately yield higher tax returns. Local authorities were also acutely conscious of the concerns of their ratepayers, who naturally preferred to pay as low a price for their electricity as possible. Such policies doubtless benefited urban consumers, especially in the great northern cities on or close to the coalfields, but stood in the way of rural electrification. As urban politicians were well aware, extending the wires into the countryside would substantially increase costs, and their own ratepayers and businesses would ultimately have to foot the bill. This applied even to rural areas within the municipal boundaries and a fortiori to those belonging to adjacent rural authorities.

Yet policies that were rational at a local scale did not necessarily make good sense nationally. There were strong grounds for regarding it as an important policy goal to extend electricity to as high a proportion of the population as possible. In both world wars the rapid expansion of munitions production often required electricity. In peacetime electricity raised living standards, especially for women because appliances such as electric irons and vacuum cleaners took much of the drudgery out of housework, and offered huge prospective productivity gains, for example through better lighting and extending working hours and through the almost limitless applications of the electric motor. Where, as in Britain, institutional obstacles were slowing the pace of electrification, there was clearly a case for nationalisation. The Labour Party adopted the nationalisation of electricity supply in 1924 but the political dominance of the Conservative Party between the wars (effectively in power for all but three of these years) meant that this was never likely to be implemented. However, the creation of the Central Electricity Board in 1926 did mark a significant shift. As its willingness to supply cheaper electricity to rural counties suggests, the Central Electricity Board was in favour of rural electrification, as were the Electricity Commissioners, thanks to the encouragement of Members of Parliament with rural constituencies. In 1929 the Commissioners appointed E. C. Dickinson to take charge of the rural electrification programme, and he and his colleagues produced several model schemes for areas around Bedford, Norwich, Kirkcudbright and Dumfries, none of which was especially successful, since their running costs exceeded the revenue received from consumers.[6] The common conclusion of writers in the 1930s and early 1940s was that rural electrification was unlikely to prove commercially successful in the sense that it would produce an adequate return – or, indeed, any return – on capital invested.[7] In Golding's view 'rural electrification [was] to some extent a social question,' and Luckin's extensive survey of the contemporary literature confirms this, emphasising the connections that were being made with rural revivalism and the preservation of rural England.[8] The 1936 McGowan Committee on electricity distribution considered that rural electrification would prevent the drift to the towns, and increase the efficiency of dairy and poultry farms. The McGowan report specifically

226   Paul Brassley et al.

avoided recommending any form of government subsidy, arguing instead that rural areas should be 'grouped' with urban areas, in effect arguing that existing consumers should subsidise new ones.[9] Both the Electrical Association for Women and the Women's Institutes were enthusiastic and effective supporters of rural electrification, and in 1939 the Electricity Council Commercial Section produced a film, *The Village That Found Itself*, which emphasised the role of housewives as a pro-electrification pressure group.[10] Speaking in 1943, one engineer voiced the opinion that farmers would find it difficult to attract a wife without an electricity supply in the farmhouse.[11]

In the long run, however, more important to the electrification of rural Britain than this chorus of professional and institutional advocacy was the success of the Central Electricity Board's national grid, connecting the most efficient power stations with each other and hence with consumers across the country. This had notable advantages. Electricity can only be stored in dry batteries and accumulators, so local producers were obliged to generate enough electricity to cope with peak local demand. This necessitated expensive spare capacity that remained unused most of the time. The national grid enabled this spare capacity to be reduced, because to a certain extent surges in demand occurred at different times in different areas, so aggregate national demand was less variable than local demand. The grid also meant that electricity generation could be concentrated on the biggest power stations, which were much more efficient. The result was that between 1926 and 1936, when the grid came into full commercial use, the capacity of spare generating plant was reduced by almost two-thirds and the average cost of generation fell from 0.42d. to 0.19d. per unit. This made electricity much more cost effective in the countryside, because the fixed capital cost could be offset against much lower operating costs, and 90% of rural areas had electricity supplies by 1936 (chapter 2).

However, electricity generation and distribution remained in the hands of urban local authorities and private companies, who proved unable or unwilling to extend transmission to more isolated settlements and dwellings, including most farms. The influential Committee on Land Utilisation in Rural Areas (the Scott Committee) estimated that only 25,000 to 30,000 of 365,972 agricultural holdings in England and Wales were served with electricity in 1938 (section 65) and laid down an important principle:

> The supply of electricity is an essential service which in due course should be available in the home of practically every citizen in town and country alike, at no higher price to the consumer in the country than in the town.

The committee expressed the rather vague hope that this could be achieved by 'appropriate reorganisation of the distribution side of the industry' (section 165), and seized on optimistic calculations made by some electrical engineers on the assumption that the marginal costs of extending supplies to less favourable areas would be the same as those of existing schemes. However, it was difficult to see how universal provision at a standard price could be effected without nationalisation, which was duly implemented by the post-war Labour government in 1947.[12] This at last made it feasible to subsidise the costs of rural electrification sufficiently to allow all but the most remote farms to be connected. In the South West Electricity Board's area, for example, only 18.5% of farms were connected to the national grid in 1948 but by 1967, after only twenty years of nationalisation, 92% of farms had mains electricity (chapter 6).

Institutional factors therefore played a crucial part in determining how quickly the inherent obstacles to rural electrification could be overcome. Nationalisation and other forms of state direction were one way forward, but there were others. Perhaps the most obvious missed opportunity in the British case was electricity distribution cooperatives. This could have enabled rural settlements, especially farms, to share the costs of poles and wiring and might have allowed many farms to connect to the grid at an earlier date. Farmers' cooperatives were a well-established feature of the rural landscape in many European countries, including France, Belgium, the Netherlands and Scandinavia, and in some areas took an active part in securing electricity supplies at a local level (in Denmark and Sweden, for example).[13] By contrast, rural historians have frequently drawn attention to the absence of agricultural cooperatives in England, despite the strenuous efforts of Horace Plunkett and the Agricultural Organisation Society to promote them. Explanations range from the deadening effect of the estate system on independent initiative by farmers to the strength of anti-socialism in rural England.[14] Whether rural electricity supply cooperatives would have been able to negotiate the adverse institutional environment established by the 1882 Electric Lighting Act is, of course, a matter of speculation.

Demand

While supply-side difficulties were undoubtedly the main obstacle to extending electricity to the countryside, the studies in this book demonstrate that demand (or, more often, the lack of it) played a much more important role in the history of rural electrification than has sometimes been recognised. To put it bluntly, during the first half of the twentieth century there was limited enthusiasm for electricity in rural areas. It was mainly valued for lighting. But lighting used little power, and, moreover, was predominantly needed in the evening – in other words it offered no prospect of the substantial, balanced consumption that electricity suppliers needed to cover their costs. Admittedly, there were a number of farm tasks that lent themselves readily to electric power but these tended to require intensive use over a short period of time, and hence just the kind of highly variable load factors the electricity companies disliked. A good example is the milking machine, potentially the

228   *Paul Brassley et al.*

most important application of electricity to agriculture, which was typically used for an hour or so twice a day.

There were, of course, significant differences in the demand for electricity depending on farming type. Dairy farmers valued electricity to power not only milking machines but also steam-sterilisers and milk coolers. As food hygiene standards rose and became increasingly subject to regulation, dairy farmers found themselves obliged to purchase stainless steel equipment, to steam-sterilise it and to store milk at a constant cool temperature, a situation that obtained in Britain from the establishment of the Milk Marketing Board in 1933. These requirements were difficult to meet without electricity. Intensive poultry and pig production were also to a large extent dependent on electricity for lighting and heating.[15] Crop farmers used it, where available, for corn drying, although it was only after the Second World War that this became prevalent, and in the late 1950s and early 1960s there was some interest in barn hay drying using large fans, sometimes accompanied by electric heaters, among dairy farmers, although the economics of the operation were rarely sufficiently clear-cut to ensure its widespread adoption.[16] Among the other important agricultural applications of electricity were water pumping, sawing, chaff cutting, root pulping and sheep shearing (see chapter 6). However, although there was no doubt that electricity had its uses, these were rather limited for most livestock rearing and fattening and by no means critical in the arable sector. It was only for large scale milk and egg producers and in the small but growing intensive broiler and pig sectors that electricity was rapidly becoming essential between the wars.

Many farmers were initially doubtful about the benefits of electricity. This was perfectly rational, since in the early days electricity supply was often affected by inadequate power output and lack of reliability. This had particularly serious implications for poultry farmers. In the long run, electricity was to prove crucial to intensive poultry rearing because it allowed optimal lighting and temperature conditions to be maintained for laying and incubating eggs and keeping chicks warm. However, even relatively short power cuts could be catastrophic in this sector, as Mrs Robertson of Sooke in British Columbia found in 1932, when she lost 124 of 164 pheasant chicks due to the failure of BC Electric Company to maintain electrical current (chapter 10). Even for less critical applications, unreliable supply was a significant disincentive to the use of electricity as a source of power on the farm, although the scale of the problem diminished as distribution networks were linked and transmission characteristics standardised, a process that began in Britain with the decision to create a national grid in 1926.

Another reason farmers were often unenthusiastic about electricity at first was that plenty of alternative sources of power were available on most farms. Horses were almost universal; steam engines were in quite widespread use, especially for ploughing; tractors were increasingly common, although in most countries they did less agricultural work than horses prior to the Second World War; and stationary petrol and diesel engines were used to a very large extent.[17] Even after the Second World War, in the brave new world of agricultural modernity, electricity was not absolutely necessary. The adoption of milking machines, separators, water heaters, cooling and lighting of milking parlours did not *require* electricity, but could be powered directly by petrol/diesel at least through to the end of the 1950s. Importantly, tractors and stationary engines could be, and often were, used to drive generators, allowing farmers to use electricity without necessitating an expensive connection to the mains. There was also a question of skill and knowledge. By the interwar years several generations of farmers and farm workers had become used to dealing with mechanical contrivances and keeping them going. It was often said that the average farm worker could work wonders with a bit of binder twine and an old nail. The Rural Industries enquiry carried out by the Development Commission in 1930 found that the greatest training demand was for classes concerned with motors and oxy-acetylene welding.[18] Mechanical equated to modern with rural youth. On the other hand there was much less accumulated and newly acquired skill with electricity, and it took time for it to emerge. Professional advice was not always helpful. After the Second World War, at a time when most farms only had access to DC supplies, at least one standard reference was mostly concerned with extolling the virtues of AC, and clearly non-professional electrical installations and repairs produced more safety concerns with electricity than with other sources of light and power.[19] There is also evidence of some queasiness about too much labour saving. It might be justifiable to replace labour lost as prisoners of war were repatriated, but what of the English labourer who might lose *his* job? Work study books stress that efficiency gains are to the benefit of all and must be negotiated and owned by both farmer and men.[20] Hence as late as the mid-1960s the question of whether mains electricity was the preferred power source could enter into technical discussions on farm production costs and the scale of farm operations.[21]

Even in a domestic setting, there were often good alternatives to electricity, such as paraffin-fuelled Tilley lamps and, from the 1930s, bottled gas, which could be used for lighting as well as heating and cooking. In Canada, for example, wood stoves were very popular in rural areas. As Sandwell points out, they were cheap to run, easy to maintain and surprisingly versatile – they could be used not only for cooking but also to heat the whole house (through pipes) and provide hot water (by means of an attached tank). Possessed of such familiar and functioning equipment, many consumers were unwilling to make it obsolete and incur the connection and capital costs of its electrical equivalent, especially when times were hard in the 1930s and '40s, or when the mains supply was unreliable and candles, torches, lamps and generators had to remain on standby. Electricity was often represented in a domestic context as a distinctively modern technology, but unfortunately for the electricity companies many rival technologies also enjoyed a 'modern' cachet. The British equivalent of the Canadian wood stove was

230   *Paul Brassley et al.*

the Aga or Rayburn, and contemporary advertising suggests that these were seen as the last word in modernity in the farmhouse kitchen. Even paraffin and oil lamps were comparatively new technology in the first half of the twentieth century and it is perhaps only in historical retrospect that they seem less modern than electric lighting (see chapter 7). Modern or not, they evidently gave adequate service in the eyes of many farmers, as in the case of the Devonshire farmer quoted by Brassley who continued to hand-milk his cows by paraffin lamp long after mains electricity had reached his farm in 1935 (chapter 6).

How far there was an element of cultural conservatism in this reluctance to embrace electricity is difficult to determine. Despite the stereotypical representation of farmers as conservative and custom-bound, mid-twentieth-century agriculture was on the cusp of a second and greater agricultural revolution, in which science and technology would take centre stage, and farming would become one of the most dynamic and innovative sectors of the economy. If farmers collectively had been doggedly resistant to change, this would hardly have been possible. It seems unlikely that wholesale conservatism was a major factor slowing the rate at which farmers adopted electricity. However, there may have been specific cultural attachments that impeded electrification among some elements of the farming community. In Sweden, for example, the traditional wood stove had an iconic status and the electric cooker made little headway (chapter 9). This was significant because on many farms there was little demand for electricity except for lighting. Had electric cookers been more popular in rural areas, household consumption would have been higher and electrification more cost effective for providers. Similarly, Moore-Colyer suggests that 'concern at the possibility of the disintegration of a centuries-old tradition' was one of the reasons Welsh hill farmers were reluctant to adopt a technology that they may have regarded as culturally alien (chapter 4).

Electricity suppliers and government agencies were aware of the ambivalence towards electricity in the countryside and deployed inventive strategies to promote consumption. In Canada, for example, electricity distribution companies paid for travelling demonstration trailers carrying the latest electrical appliances, published pamphlets and magazines extolling the benefits of electricity, offered cheap loans and free electricity to new customers for an initial period, and made promotional offers on new appliances, including free installation (chapter 10). Often the rural housewife was at the centre of such advertising campaigns, a shrewd strategy given that rural consumers usually seem to have valued electricity more in a domestic than farm business context, and in view also of the cultural nexus between the feminine, the domestic and the modern in the interwar years.[22] Farmers were also targeted, for example in Britain by the Electrical Development Association, which published handbooks explaining how electricity could be harnessed for water pumping, grain drying, in dairying and so forth (chapter 6).

Government departments and advisors also attempted to persuade farmers to obtain a mains electricity connection or to make more use of it if they already had one. In Britain, a specialist branch of the government's Electricity Council was dedicated to agriculture and horticulture, attempting to promote electricity use through a range of media including films, publications, exhibitions and conferences. Potentially the most significant way in which governments attempted to encourage rural electrification, however, was through subsidies. In the British case, however, these were offered to encourage infrastructural investment in general rather than electrification in particular. Interestingly, farmers often seem to have preferred to direct investment towards more traditional capital projects such as refurbishing or constructing farm buildings, fencing, drainage and soil improvements (for example through liming). Electrification was, for example, an allowable expenditure under the Hill Farming Act (1946) and Livestock Rearing Act (1951) but, in Wales at least, few farmers chose to use the available subsidies for this purpose. Only 4% of the grant income claimed by farmers in mid-Wales up to July 1955 was for electrification, in comparison to 28% for farm buildings (excluding farmhouses), 19% for grassland improvement (for example reseeding) and 15% for fencing (chapter 3). For this group of farmers, it would seem, promotional campaigns and even subsidies for electrification fell on deaf ears. However, the predominant enterprise on most Welsh hill farms was livestock breeding and rearing, which perhaps offered less scope for electrification than any other major agricultural sector. On the whole, once nationalisation had made rural electrification affordable in Britain, farmers were willing to connect and a wide range of new applications was developed, including improved feed mills and mixers, automatic feeders, step-lighting patterns for poultry, better electric fencing and a host of other devices. In this sense, demand for electricity seems to have followed supply, in that prior to electrification few farmers regarded it as among their highest priorities, but once they had obtained a connection, new ways of exploiting it were quite quickly identified. The process was undoubtedly assisted by generational change: while farmers born before the First World War grew up in an essentially pre-electric world, this was very much less the case for those born after the Second World War.

Consequences

Several of the chapters in this book consider the consequences of electrification for farmers (see in particular Part II). The broad outlines, including which types of farm enterprise were most affected and what the principal uses of electricity on the farm were, are reasonably clear and have been described, although once the necessary research has been undertaken, it is to be hoped that agricultural historians will be able to provide quantitative estimates of the effects of electrification on the volume and composition of agricultural output and (especially) productivity. As a preliminary

232   *Paul Brassley et al.*

observation, it may be suggested that despite its profound impact on dairying and poultry, electricity was probably a less transformative technology in agriculture than it was in industry. In this it was like the steam engine, which revolutionised industry in the nineteenth century but, although significant, did not change agriculture to the same degree. The problem with both was fundamentally their lack of mobility. Agriculture is an extensive industry and technologies that are immobile or spatially inflexible are less well adapted to it. The steam engine proved to have limited applications in agriculture because it suffered from a poor power-to-weight ratio that restricted it to hard surfaces, while electricity depends on a fixed infrastructure of wiring that can deliver power very efficiently to a static point (within a factory, for example) but is much less easily harnessed to freely moving point (e.g. an implement being pulled over a field) or supplied across an extensive area. The technologies that truly transformed agriculture in the twentieth century, such as the internal combustion engine, chemical fertilisers and pesticides, and improved plant and animal breeding, did not suffer from this constraint.

What of the wider effects of electrification on the countryside? Initially, the general retardation of electrification in rural areas was perhaps more important than its arrival at a few farms and villages. The wide gap that opened up between town and country with respect to electricity supplies, especially in countries like England and Wales where the time lag was substantial, served to emphasise the difference between urban and rural at a time when, in other respects such as transport, communications, education and citizenship, such differences were eroding. Since other services such as street lighting, mains water, sewerage and telephone lines tended to follow the same pattern as electricity, a perception that the countryside was dark, cold, dirty and uncomfortable gained traction, a perception endorsed but lamented by rural reformers such as Robertson Scott, editor of *The Countryman*, and mercilessly lampooned in satirical novels like Stella Gibbons's *Cold Comfort Farm*.[23] The latter work, published in 1932, was premised on the notion that the countryside represented the antithesis of the modern. This was a powerful and in many respects pernicious idea, contributing to the so-called rural exodus – the migration of agricultural workers and their families to larger settlements, and overseas – and intertwining with existing romanticised perceptions of the countryside as a beautiful unchanging landscape rather than a place where people lived and worked.

The sense that country people were excluded from full participation in the forwards march of the nation could foster resentment, which found political expression in some national contexts. Rural people and the organisations that represented them argued that electricity supply and, indeed, other services were so much worse in the countryside, and called for governments to take action. Urban politicians, like Sir Charles Wilson, Lord Mayor of Leeds, were often deeply unsympathetic to this argument, maintaining that the higher costs of living in the countryside should be met by the people

Conclusion   233

who chose to live there, rather than borne by urban consumers and taxpayers (chapter 1). These, of course, were not wholly new arguments. Debates about agricultural tariffs and relief from local taxation were major political issues in many European countries in the mid- and late nineteenth century. However, in the main these debates pitted the agricultural interest against non-agriculturalists. Even in the nineteenth century this did not map perfectly onto the rural-urban divide. In Britain, for example, there were many rural members of the Anti-Corn Law League.[24] What was perhaps new about the mainly twentieth-century question of rural service provision was that it was a consumer issue and tended to foster an awareness of the shared interest of rural people, farmers and non-farmers alike, as against their urban counterparts. This set a pattern for further conflicts, construed in terms of rural need on the one hand versus a discourse of 'featherbedding' on the other, for example in relation to the closure of 'uneconomic' rural railways, bus routes, post offices, schools and medical centres, or more recently the inadequacy of mobile phone reception and broadband availability in rural areas. At times of crisis, as during the 1990s when a severe squeeze on farm incomes coincided with a succession of livestock diseases (notably bovine spongiform encephalitis, or BSE), this rural consumer consciousness could contribute to a sharply polarised sense of rural identity in opposition to dominant urban identities, as with the Countryside Alliance in Britain.[25]

In the long run, though, the eventual provision of electricity to the countryside probably had more important consequences than the fact that, in many places, it had been so long delayed. The main emphasis should be on the social consequences, above all lighting. As Moore-Colyer and Fleetwood vividly describe (chapters 4 and 5), the arrival of electric light was a step change in the quality of life in the countryside. It could be quite transformative for the convenience, ease and indeed safety of work, especially in the livestock sector where many potentially hazardous tasks had necessarily to be undertaken during the hours of darkness. Above all, however, it gave the inhabitants of the countryside the freedom to use their evenings as they wished, especially the long, dark autumn and winter evenings, which the old paraffin and oil lamps had illuminated only dimly, inconveniently and expensively. The implications for family life and personal development were vast. Electric lighting facilitated conversation, shared family activities such as board games and perhaps above all reading. Without electric light, as Martiin points out, it would have been much more difficult for rural children to do their homework, impeding their education and reducing their prospects of social mobility. Dispelling the darkness of the countryside, especially in northerly countries like Sweden where daylight hours were brief to non-existent for weeks either side of the winter solstice, was one of the great extensions of human freedom in the twentieth century.

As Sayer and Shirley suggest (chapters 7 and 8), electrification had especially significant implications for women, although in the main these were not distinctive to the countryside. As in the towns, electricity offered to

234   *Paul Brassley et al.*

alleviate the drudgery of housework, and it seems that electric irons, vacuum cleaners, washing machines and cookers were adopted quickly once mains electricity was available, especially the first two. However, it remains unclear how far these appliances actually did save time – it is possible that they simply enabled higher standards of cleanliness and cookery to be achieved. The practical implications of electrification for rural women's lives deserves further scholarly attention. One aspect that was certainly significant is home freezing. Evidence suggests that rural women may have been in the avant-garde of the adoption of chest freezers. The food in their freezers consisted not only of purchased but also homemade foods. This dovetailed with long-standing traditions of food production, gathering, preservation and processing in rural areas, and enabled locally produced poultry, meat, fruit and vegetables to be stored in greater quantity and variety than had previously been possible.

The economic and demographic implications of rural electrification were also considerable. At first, it was often seen in the context of prevailing fears about rural depopulation. It was widely held that farmworkers, and especially their wives, were reluctant to live in remote cottages without adequate services.[26] Increasingly from the 1930s onwards radios became a vital part of rural life, in parallel to local newspapers and the farming press, which together operated as vehicles for information (market information, national and local news, employment opportunities, and the dissemination of new methodologies, research/innovation, etc.), but radios could be run from batteries and small lighting plants. In the end, the consequences depended much on the demand for electricity, and the key demand according to policymakers, commentators and the Women's Institute was domestic. Electrification, ideally, brought the rural home up to a standard equivalent to that of the town, and therefore stemmed rural depopulation and the loss of skilled labour from the land. This came as a package that included other services such as mains water, sewage and decent roads/bus services. Together they added up to 'modernity'. Whether or not this was the case, the 'rural exodus' continued apace even after electricity supplies had reached most rural areas. Electrification was certainly no panacea for depopulation, but it may have made a difference. Gasson, for example, found that farmworkers in the most remote parishes often moved not to the towns but to less isolated rural areas.[27] Such areas would have been more likely to have electricity supplies. Further research is necessary to establish to what extent spatial variations in electricity availability had an impact on rural depopulation.

Ironically, electrification was probably more significant in attracting ex-urbanites to live in rural areas than in preventing farmworkers from leaving. Improved transport, especially the car, is usually regarded as the most important enabling factor for counter-urbanisation but it is interesting that in the USA and Britain, where counter-urbanisation was first detected, urban-rural migration only became a powerful flow in the 1970s. This was at least a decade after car ownership had ceased to be restricted to the middle class; the timing fits better with the closing of the urban-rural gap in service provision (including electrification). It is difficult to imagine that counter-urbanisation could ever have become important in the absence of electricity. While there is still debate over the prominence of the 'service class' in counter-urbanisation, there is little doubt that most in-migrants to the countryside were comparatively wealthy and highly educated.[28] These people were used to 'mod cons' although often they cherished the 'traditional' qualities of the countryside, too. In many respects electricity enabled them, and their counterparts who came to visit rather than live in the countryside, to have it both ways. Although transporting electricity from place to place could be highly visually intrusive, once the wires reached the cottage walls they were relatively discreet. The result was that incomers could lead modern electric lives inside traditional cottage shells, the characteristic if perhaps disingenuous contemporary compromise whereby the content of rural life is radically modernised while its outward appearance remains as unchanged as possible.

The cultural effects of rural electrification were more contentious. This was largely because the modernity that electricity enabled and signified was itself fraught with contestation. For many, although at first perhaps rather few who actually lived there, the countryside was cherished as a bulwark against or refuge from modernity. The visual intrusion of wires, poles and pylons into the rural landscape was often hotly resented. Yet as David Matless has shown, the issue was more complex than this. While there certainly were some, such as the folk-dancing fascist Rolf Gardiner, who deplored almost every rural manifestation of modernity, for most preservationists, including the influential Council for the Preservation of Rural England (CPRE), the aim was more to achieve a harmonious reconciliation between modernity and tradition.[29] Pylons are an interesting case in point. The Design and Industry Association, an organisation with close links to the CPRE, published a didactic book of photographs titled *The Face of the Land*. This included two photographs of electricity wires. One, a clutter of short wooden poles, haphazardly scattered over the landscape, was roundly denounced as 'disquieting'. The other photograph showed much taller steel pylons, doubtless visible from a much greater distance. Yet these were praised as dignified 'standards', a word that, in a rural context, usually refers to mature, free-standing trees. Evidently, the clean lines and visual elegance of the steel pylons and high-tension wires were regarded as an acceptable form of modernity in a rural context, but the untidy and aesthetically illegible tangle of wires and poles in the other photograph was not.[30]

Most inhabitants of the countryside, however, probably felt less ambivalence towards electrical infrastructure. To farmers, the way leaves that electricity distributors were obliged to obtain were a source of income. Many villagers were eager to embrace modernity with open arms. This is the dominant note that Shirley identifies in the Women's Institute scrapbooks that she considers in chapter seven. The front cover of the scrapbook for Binsted

236   *Paul Brassley et al.*

in north Hampshire consists of embroidered hop sacking, featuring a large pylon surrounding by a sprig of blackcurrant, some hops, apples, potatoes, a tractor tyre and other emblems of rural life. Here, pylons are embraced as a positive part of village identity, something to be celebrated because they enhance rural life by bringing electricity to the village. Landscape values are produced here by the life lived in the village, rather than by a detached aesthetic gaze. Shirley emphasises that the Women's Institute scrapbooks avoid falling into binary constructions of rural identity by emphasising the flow connecting past and present, traditional and modern, urban and rural, of which the power lines themselves are a compelling symbol.

Wires, poles and pylons were not the only potentially controversial electrical additions to the rural landscape. Brassley mentions the unsightliness of a transformer placed in a farm garden (chapter 6). Far more intrusive, although rarer, were the power stations that generated the electricity in the first place. Many of these were on already highly urbanised coalfields, and some were in towns. But for others, rural sites were chosen. As Sheail demonstrates, power stations could affect rural life in diverse ways. Usk power station in South Wales antagonised the local population because its hot water emissions threatened the valuable Usk salmon fishery. Their often overwhelming visual presence provoked much opposition, especially in the case of nuclear power stations like Sizewell and Dungeness, where fears about radiation seemed to magnify the perceived effect on the landscape. In time, however, the need to take 'amenity' into consideration when constructing power stations was recognised, section 37 of the 1957 Electricity Act constituting a benchmark in this respect in Britain (chapter 3). Ironically, such are the malleability and subjectivity of landscape preferences, the demolition of decommissioned power stations has also caused dismay. Didcot power station, partly demolished in 2014, is a case in point. When first mooted, the proposal to build a power station in the Vale of the White Horse was greeted with dismay, but the decision to knock down the cooling towers after decades of service provoked an impassioned local opposition and, when this was disregarded, hundreds of local people camped out overnight to witness the last moments of what had become a local icon.[31]

It remains far from clear to what extent preservationists were able to influence policy and decision-making. In the early post-nationalisation years, planners and preservationists seem to have been in a weak position, confronted by a powerful alliance of policy-makers committed to extending electrification and rural consumers convinced that mains electricity could now be theirs on reasonable terms for the asking. A memorandum submitted by Devon County Council (planning authority for Dartmoor National Park) for a conference with the National Parks Commission in July 1955 noted that:

> What has troubled Planning Authorities, and this is certainly true for the Dartmoor National Park, is that if they continue to insist on

Conclusion 237

underground transmission they are accused both by local residents and the District Councils of the area, of depriving inhabitants of the benefits of electricity, or alternatively that the supply will cost consumers twice as much as it would if the transmission was overground.

Reflecting this weak position, and perhaps also divided loyalties on the part of the council as planning authority, Devon County Council had only requested undergrounding of power lines in three of eighty-five applications received since the designation of Dartmoor National Park in 1951.[32]

As late as 1969 a parliamentary secretary in the Ministry for Agriculture won a three-year dispute against 'pylons being erected across his 500-acre farm' in Essex, after the Minister for Power intervened and established that the pylons would be diverted to run instead along the edge of Nazeing Common, referred to by the *Times* as 'a beauty spot in the heart of the countryside'.[33] In this particular instance there were three possible routes, and three corresponding sets of interest groups.[34] The politics of this were complex, and reveal the ways in which farming, history/heritage, emerging understandings of visitor access to the countryside, and settlement all vied for special consideration and entitlement post-war, while in the end it appears that the CPRE and others who would maintain the remaining commons simply did not have the level of influence required to resist change (although how far the balance of forces shifted towards so-called Nimbyism from the 1970s onwards is a question that requires further research).[35] What the Nazeing Common case also clearly demonstrates is the way in which rural electrification might be seen simultaneously as a 'bad thing' and as a 'good thing', and was never a foregone conclusion; one person's electrical utopia was another's dystopia.[36]

Wider implications

Historians of science and technology have often pointed out that technical change is rarely a matter of a new technology replacing an old one overnight, or at least within a very short period of time.[37] Nor is it always a matter of a new technology being imported from outside and uncritically adopted. It is more common for the users to be involved in the process and to shape, convert, or remodel a new technology according to their needs and resources.[38] There are also many examples of existing technologies maintaining or adapting themselves in the face of competition from the new.[39] All these features can be found in the history of rural electrification, and are to some extent being repeated in the current development of rural broadband. As Martyn Warren demonstrates (chapter 11), the provision and uptake of rural broadband in the early twenty-first century offers striking similarities to the electrification of rural Britain more than half a century earlier. In each case, urban areas received the service in question much earlier than rural. The reason the countryside lagged behind the towns with respect to the provision of broadband, as of electricity, was the high cost of supply to the countryside. A monopolistic provider, or providers in the case of electrification, impeded efforts to extend the service in question more fully. Ultimately, in both cases, the government was reluctantly forced to intervene, although it did so in stages. In the case of electricity, the first decisive step was the creation of the Central Electricity Board in 1926 but it was only following nationalisation in 1947 that effectively comprehensive provision was achieved in rural areas. Broadband availability in rural area is, at the time of writing, still far less widespread than in the towns and cities, so it may be that further government intervention will yet be necessary.

Both electricity and broadband are examples of what Jonathan Coopersmith, analysing the early history of electrification in Russia, refers to as 'networked' technologies, where the costs of supply per user are correlated with the density of users. Coopersmith argues that the individual components of networked technologies do not work unless the whole system works. There is no point in having a generating station unless there are also transmission cables, control and distribution systems, and some way of measuring the amount of electricity used by a consumer and collecting payment for it. The implication of this is that there will be significant economies of scale – a thousand consumers can be supplied for much less than ten times the cost of supplying a hundred consumers, and the more each consumer uses the lower the fixed cost per unit consumed. These networks were and are therefore often natural monopolies.

Other examples of networked technologies in a rural context include mains water, sewerage and gas, and the telephone. To a certain extent, each of these appear to have followed a similar trajectory to electricity and broadband with respect to their provision, adoption and use in the countryside, although there are some interesting differences.[40]

Mains water was most similar to electricity in the timing and rate of uptake and in wider discourse surrounding it. In both cases, connection rates were extremely high by the late twentieth century. In 1990, for example, only 0.84% of the population of England was not connected to mains water, although the figure was higher in rural areas. But connection rates for mains electricity were even higher – data supplied by the Electricity Boards to ARUP Economic Consultants implied that only 0.01% of properties lacked mains electricity. Comprehensive data for rural areas is not available, but a case study of South Devon, an area with a very low population density, estimated that 7.1% of dwellings were without mains water supplies by 1986, compared to 0.4% not connected to mains electricity.[41] The difference is probably best explained by the availability and relative cost of adequate alternative supplies. Clean water had been a high priority for consumers and policy-makers for much longer than electricity, and even after the Second World War continued to be regarded as the most fundamental of all household services. However, in many parts of the country, especially the more remote upland areas, clean water could be obtained relatively cheaply

Conclusion 239

and easily from local boreholes. Nor, despite the problem of leaks, did water require the expensive apparatus of transformers and high-voltage cables necessary to transmit electricity cost-effectively across even a few hundred metres. Conversely, the cost of mains supply of water and electricity to remote rural areas (i.e. over long distances) appears to have been broadly similar. The principal engineer of the North-Eastern Electricity Board, for example, regarded £10,000 as a not untypical connection cost for a remote rural dwelling, not dissimilar to Anglian Water's estimate of up to £12,000 for mains water in comparable situations.[42]

The reason that both mains water and electricity achieved near-universal coverage by the end of the twentieth century is that both had come to be seen as something to which all citizens in a modern democracy were entitled. The influential Scott Report of 1942, sometimes regarded as a blueprint for post-war rural legislation and planning, emphasised that electricity was 'an essential service which in due course should be available in the home of practically every citizen in town and country alike, at no higher price to the consumer in the country than in the town'. The Report used similar language in speaking of electricity: 'We consider the provision of a piped water supply an essential service in every village.'[43] This discourses of citizenship and universal provision was reflected in persistent efforts by government to extend provision. As early as 1934, for example, the Rural Water Supply Act made £1 million available for the extension of piped water supplies in rural Britain, although 3,432 of 11,186 parishes in England and Wales were still without piped water in 1939 according to the Scott Report.[44] In the case of electricity, as we have seen, the 1947 Electricity Act did a great deal to extend supplies in rural areas, backed by the legal requirement (originating in the Electric Lighting (Clauses) Act of 1899) to provide supply to any owner or occupier of premises within 50 yards of the distributor main.[45] Gas and sewerage, however, proved to be rather different. In 1939 no more than 25,000 to 30,000 agricultural holdings out of a total of 365, 972 in Britain as a whole were thought to be served with gas, while at least 5,186 of 11,186 parishes had no sewerage systems. The Scott Report, while noting this situation, carefully avoided making any pronouncements about rights to mains supply, in sharp contrast to the emphatic position the Report took on electricity and water. However, it was not only because gas and sewerage were regarded as less necessary than electricity and water. Mains gas and sewers were also very expensive. As a study on rural deprivation noted in 1979, 'the costs of [rural sewerage schemes] have been high and many parishes have still not been connected to mains sewerage.' The same study observed that 'the capital costs of connection to a gas main are very high except where properties are immediately adjacent to a gas main. As a result of this mains gas supplies are largely restricted to towns and large villages. . . .' According to this study, 3.1 million people lacked mains gas in the non-metropolitan counties of England and Wales, 600,000 lacked mains sewerage, but only 7,000 lacked mains water and a negligible number lacked mains electricity.[46]

240   *Paul Brassley et al.*

Telephones in some ways offer a closer comparison to water, electricity and broadband than to gas and sewerage. Telephones offered new opportunities for social connection, but were expensive in exactly the same way as electricity to start with, which held back rural connection in an identical way (as the consumer paid for the cost of the line being installed as well as the final connection), and had older, established competitors. Letters, markets and auction marts, shops, wells and pumps, village hall occasions and institutional meetings, and public houses all offered a chance to communicate. Like the landline, mobile/smartphones and tablets, where there is access, are currently in the process of supplementing and underpinning, sometimes replacing, older sources of information in farming, both formal and informal. Weather apps with location services and Twitter feeds such as @FarmersWeather can supplement the weather forecasts offered by broadcasters and newspapers, which themselves replaced domestic barometers; farmers can and do connect with each other instantly on social media, not just at sales or annual meetings and farming forums; the agricultural press and the agricultural services industry publish on and promote themselves through the same platforms, as much as in print. However, despite increasingly stringent obligations to improve coverage, 2G, 3G and now 4G, mobile broadband coverage remains a problem, and Ofcom has begun arguing a case for operators to share their infrastructure to improve access.[47] The broadband issues are therefore comparable to the case of electricity, but they are also comparable to the slow introduction of the landline telephone.

In each instance, it is not as if there is no alternative. There is still the radio, the paper, the letter, the conversation at the auction mart, but the new technology offers something more immediate and perhaps something that addresses a more profound and underlying consequence attaching to the changes that were predicted and have now taken place in the countryside in the twentieth century: rural depopulation. Rather than the feared loss of skill, however, we look back to see that services have centralised, increased mechanisation and labour efficiency in both intensive systems and on extensive arable farms; family farms and hill farms supplemented on-farm with off-farm income and part-time work. Together these changes have led to villages and farms becoming much more isolated places to live and work.

Changes such as reduced numbers of labourers on farms, the cultural and social marginalisation of farming as cultural divisions between country and city have become more rigid and a sense of entitlement from non-farming communities to access a pristine and idealised countryside have risen, the closure of village services such as shops and other centres of activity, the loss of rural transport, have meant that that isolation became, and remains, increasingly problematic in rural areas from the post-war period. To address the particularly high risks associated with these issues and financial stress, the Samaritans (helpline 0845 6967607) rolled out a County Rural Initiative from 1992 and still operate dedicated support on this. Similar initiatives by other agencies have gone on to recommend and offer help and support on similar lines, such as including telephone numbers of advice lines about managing financial pressures, support for small rural businesses and small family farms, accessing help for those with disabilities, the elderly, carers and parents of young children, as well as mental health and wellbeing.[48]

Modernity is not alien to the countryside, imposed on it as if it were external to it. It has been demanded by rural populations. In the form of production, it has even been driven and supplied by rural populations. But, it has been made to seem rigidly alien to it as policy-makers have consistently failed to see the need to provide adequate support to underpin the transformations needed to keep rural areas abreast of the changes so much more easily introduced in cities. Alongside depopulation, the hardening of the perceptual division between country and city (which has little to do with their actual interdependence) has in some ways left rural populations profoundly disempowered. The acceptability, indeed, normalisation of a technological lag between country and city in Britain has had a very real cost.

Studying the history of rural electrification raises several issues of much wider relevance. In the first place, it forces us to ask what the countryside is *for*. Is it, as some preservationists assumed, primarily there to be looked at and enjoyed for its aesthetic rewards? Or is it, as the members of Binsted Women's Institute appear to have believed, there to be lived in? Should the rural landscape be regarded as complete, in the sense that any changes or further additions to it are likely to be deleterious, or is the making of the landscape a legitimately ongoing process, in which case questions like those asked by the Design and Industries Association about the extent to which certain forms of electrical infrastructure may complement the existing landscape are of critical significance? How far does the value of the countryside depend on its separateness and difference from the urban, as campaigners like Ian Nairn appear to have believed, or, as Shirley argues, would we do better to regard the pylons and transmission lines as an instance and symbol of the profound connectedness and mutual interdependence of town and country (chapter 8)? What does the history of electrification tell us about the relationship between the rural and the modern, and how far it is possible to accommodate the modern within the rural without emptying the rural of its distinctive character?

Further questions prompted by studying the history of rural electrification relate to the uneven spatiality of modernity. Do many of the most characteristic and transformative innovations of modernity, such as electricity and the internet, discriminate systematically against certain kinds of space (for example where there is a comparatively low density of population, as in the countryside)? In such circumstances, how far should local interests be overridden for the sake of 'national advantage', and which groups are best placed to assert or impose their own conception of this? Perhaps the most fundamental question posed by the history of rural electrification, however, is about how far, and under what circumstances and conditions, the democratic state is obliged to provide a basic level of services for all its citizens.

242 *Paul Brassley et al.*

Certainly in the case of electricity, this obligation was eventually recognised, although it has not yet been fully acknowledged in the analogous context of rural broadband. In both cases, however, an initial ideological presumption in favour of provision by private enterprise gave way, in due course and in the face of a demonstrable failure to achieve universality at an affordable price, to a pragmatic recognition of the need for public oversight, regulation and intervention. This was, in the case of electrification at least, ultimately able to overcome what was always the fundamental obstacle – the large outlay of capital required to provide fixed physical connections to areas of highly dispersed settlement.

Notes

1 Moore-Colyer, 'Lighting the landscape: Rural electrification in Wales', *Welsh History Review*, vol. 23 (4), 2007, p. 82.
2 W. C. Dampier Whetham, 'Electric power in agriculture', *JRASE*, vol. 85, 1924, p. 265. In its 21 November 2014 issue *Farmers Weekly* published a survey of various methods (ground and rooftop-mounted photovoltaic, wind, anaerobic digestion, water turbine and biomass boiler) by which farmers could generate electricity for on-farm use and export to the grid. It concluded (p. 18) that there could be between 10 and 20 GW of 'unfulfilled renewable energy generation potential' on UK farms, compared with the 2013 UK renewable generation capacity of 19.7 GW, within a total capacity of 94.1 GW.
3 This follows from Ohm's law, which states that the current (i) through a conductor is proportional to the potential difference (V) between its ends, or V/i = resistance. The voltage drop in a given length of 6.6 kV cable is five times that in a 33kV cable, and the power loss more than twenty times as much. A.E.E. McKenzie, *A second course of electricity*, Cambridge: Cambridge University Press, 1959, pp. 121 and 131.
4 Hannah, *Electricity before nationalisation: A study of the development of the electricity supply industry in Britain to 1948*. London: Macmillan, 1979, pp. 189–190.
5 H. Hedel, 'Early rural electrification in Denmark – A reaction from people outside the town establishment', in D. C. Christensen (ed.), *European Historiography of Technology: Proceedings from the TISC Conference in Roskilde*, Odense: Odense University Press, 1993, p. 92; Hinchliffe, 'Technology, power and space', passim.
6 F. W. Purse, 'Chairman's address to the transmission section', *JIEE*, vol. 86, 1940.
7 E. C. Dickinson and H. W. Grimmitt, 'The design of a distribution system in a rural area', *JIEE*, vol. 70, 1931; Purse, Chairman's address; C. T. Mellins, 'General factors affecting the unification of electricity supply tariffs', *JIEE*, vol. 90 part 1, 1943, p. 322.
8 E. W. Golding, *The electrification of agriculture and the rural districts*. London: English Universities Press, 1937, p. 5; Bill Luckin, *Questions of power: Electricity and environment in interwar Britain*. Manchester: Manchester University Press, 1990, pp. 83–85. On modernising to preserve, see P. Brassley, J. Burchardt, and L. Thompson (eds), *The English countryside between the wars: Regeneration or decline?*. Woodbridge: Boydell and Brewer, 2006, p. 241.
9 Ministry of Transport, *Report of the Committee on Electricity Distribution, May, 1936* (the McGowan Committee). London: HMSO, 1937, p. 86.

Conclusion 243

10 A further film was also produced after the war: See British Pathe, *Rural Electrification, AKA A Way to Plenty* (1948). http://www.britishpathe.com/video/rural-electrification-drive-aka-way-to-plenty/query/electrification.

11 C. Chant (ed.), *Science, technology and everyday life 1870–1950*. London: Routledge/Open University, 1989, p. 108; Hannah, *Electricity before nationalisation*, pp. 189–191.

12 *Report of the Committee on Land Utilisation in Rural Areas*. HM Stationery Office, 1942 (sections 65 and 165).

13 H. Hedel, 'Early rural electrification in Denmark – A reaction from people outside the town establishment', in D.C. Christensen (ed.), *European historiography of technology: Proceedings from the TISC conference in Roskilde*. Odense: Odense University Press, 1993, p. 92.

14 On agriculture cooperation in Europe see F.J. Beltrán Tapia, 'Commons, social capital, and the emergence of agricultural cooperatives in early twentieth century Spain', *European Review of Economic History*, vol. 16, 2012, pp. 511–528; E. Fernández, 'Trust, religion, and cooperation in western agriculture, 1880–1930', *Economic History Review*, vol. 67, 2014, pp. 678–698; S. Garrido, 'Why did most cooperatives fail? Spanish agricultural cooperation in the early twentieth century', *Rural History*, vol. 18, 2007, pp. 183–200; I. Henriksen, M. Hviid, and P. Sharp, 'Law and peace: Contracts and the success of the Danish dairy cooperatives', *Journal of Economic History*, vol. 72, 2012, pp. 197–224; K.H. O'Rourke, 'Culture, conflict and cooperation: Irish dairying before the Great War', *Economic Journal*, vol. 117, 2007, pp. 1357–1379; J. Simpson, 'Cooperation and cooperatives in southern European wine production: The nature of successful institutional innovation, 1880–1950', *Advances in Agricultural Economic History*, vol. 1, 2000, pp. 95–126.

15 K. Sayer, 'Battery birds, 'stimulighting' and 'twilighting': The ecology of standardised poultry technology', *History of Technology*, Special issue, 'By whose standards? Standardization, stability and uniformity in the history of information and electrical technologies', vol. 28, 2008, pp. 149–168.

16 C. Culpin, *Profitable farm mechanization*. London: Crosby Lockwood, 1968, pp. 186–195 and 201–215.

17 E.J.T. Collins, 'The farm horse economy of England and Wales in the early tractor age 1900–40', in F.M.L. Thompson (ed.), *Horses in European economic history: A preliminary canter*. Reading: British Agricultural History Society, 1983, pp. 73–97.

18 P. Brassley, 'The wheelwright, the carpenter, two ladies from Oxford, and the construction of socio-economic change in the countryside between the wars', in P. Brassley, J. Burchardt and L. Thompson (eds), *The English countryside between the wars: Regeneration or decline?* Woodbridge: Boydell, 2006, p. 222.

19 A. Monkhouse, 'Electricity in agriculture and horticulture', in E. Molloy (ed.), *Electrical engineer reference book: A comprehensive work of reference, providing a summary of latest practice in all branches of electrical engineering*. London: George Newnes, 1st edn, 1945.

20 For example, C. Culpin, *Profitable farm mechanization*. London: Crosby Lockwood, 1968, p. 72.

21 P. Wakefield, 'Electricity for farm improvement'. Paper read at the Electricity Council, EDA Division, Rural Electrification Conference, held at the University of Nottingham School of Agriculture. London: The Electricity Council, 1967.

22 Alison Light, *Forever England: Femininity, literature and conservatism between the war*. London: Routledge, 1991.

23 J.W. Robertson Scott, *England's green and pleasant land*. London: Penguin Books, 1925; Stella Gibbons, *Cold comfort farm*. London: Longmans, 1932.

244 Paul Brassley et al.

24 Norman McCord, *The Anti-corn law league, 1838–1846.* London: George Allen & Unwin, 1958, pp. 144–145.

25 On the Countryside Alliance, see Alison Anderson, 'Spinning the rural agenda: The countryside alliance, foxhunting and social policy', *Social Policy & Administration*, vol. 40 (6), 2006, pp. 722–738.

26 James Littlejohn, *Westrigg: The sociology of a Cheviot parish.* London: Routledge & Kegan Paul, 1958, pp. 144–145.

27 Ruth Gasson, *Mobility of farm workers: A study of the effects of towns and industrial employment on the supply of farm labour.* University of Cambridge: Department of Land Economy, Occasional papers, 1974.

28 Keith Hoggart, 'The middle classes in rural England 1971–1991', *Journal of Rural Studies*, vol. 13 (3), 1997, pp. 253–273.

29 David Matless, *Landscape and Englishness.* London: Reaktion Books, 1998, pp. 50–54.

30 The full caption reads: 'The vexed question of electricity pylons can only be touched on. No one can deny a real beauty in the standards of the upper picture [tall modernist national grid pylons], but the lower is disquieting [untidy mess of poles].' *The Face of the Land. The Year Book of The Design and Industries Association 1929–1930*, ed. H.H.P. and N.L.C. [sic] with an Introduction by Clough Williams-Ellis (George Allen & Unwin, London n.d. [c.1930]), p. 36. On the following page: 'When we come to scenery such as that of the South Downs or Lakes, we are entitled to ask whether it is not grotesque folly to mar such national heritages for the sake of uniformity or for less money than buys an old masterpiece.' See also CPRE photographs of pylons, wires and street furniture etc., at MERL coded SR 3 CPRE PH2/30 and SR 3 CPRE PH 2/40. Other captions suggest hostility to some forms of design for lighting/electricity supply, e.g. '*Sevenoaks*: Townside Road exit obtrusive concrete lampstands against Kurle Park' and 'Huge inappropriate lamp standards at rural roundabout – A592 junction with the A66 at Stainton' (SR 3 CPRE PH 2/40).

31 'Didcot power station towers demolished'. http://www.bbc.co.uk/news/uk-england-oxfordshire-28487288. Accessed 11 January 2015.

32 'Item No. 5. Devon County Council. Notes on Electricity Problems in National Parks', Agenda and papers for National Parks Commission, Conference with Park Planning Authorities, 26 July 1955, North Yorkshire Record Office, NYCC/P/YD, file of papers belonging to the Clerk of the Peace.

33 'Beauty spot chosen as Pylon site', *Times*, 15 May 1969, p. 3.

34 (1) The farmer/Parliamentary Secretary Mr Mackie, who believed the pylons would 'ruin his farm, which stands on the site of King Harold's hunting lodge'; (2) Essex Country Council, the CPRE, & the trustees of Nazeing Common, who 'said that the pylons would desecrate the common which attracts hundreds of visitors'; and (3) two councils, the Church of England, & Mr Stanley Newens, the Labour MP for Epping, who fought the pylons passing near to the hamlet of Bumbles Green. Ibid.

35 The area was fortunate in that it had a relatively early gas, electricity and water supply. Gas was supplied to Nazeing from Hoddesdon by 1926. When the Hoddesdon works closed in 1932 the supply was continued from Ponders End (Mdx.). Electricity was first provided in 1926–1927 by the North Metropolitan Supply Company; the supply was extended to Bumble's Green in 1933 and Hoe Lane in 1935. The Eastern Electricity Board now supplies the whole parish, except for a few isolated premises. Water was being piped to part of Nazeing by the Herts. and Essex Water Company from about 1900; the parish is now supplied by the Lee Valley Water Company, and few houses are without a main supply. Main drainage was first provided in 1937, and a further scheme of 1953 extended the sewers to other parts of the parish. ' "Nazeing", *A history of the*

county of Essex', vol. 5, 1966, pp. 140–150. http://www.british-history.ac.uk/report.aspx?compid=42717. Accessed 8 June 2012.

36 See Gooday, *Domesticating electricity: Technology, uncertainty and gender, 1880–1914*. London: Pickering & Chatto, 2008, p. 4.

37 P. Geroski, 'Models of technology diffusion', *Research Policy*, vol. 29, 2000, pp. 603–625.

38 N. Oudshoorn and T. Pinch (eds), *How users matter: The co-construction of users and technologies*. Cambridge, MA: MIT Press, 2003.

39 D. Edgerton, *The shock of the old: Technology and global history since 1900*. London: Profile Books, 2006.

40 The historiography of these utilities also unfortunately resembles that of electrification, in that the rural dimension has been largely ignored. Trevor Williams's standard work, *A history of the British gas industry*. Oxford: Oxford University Press, 1981, for example, barely mentions the countryside at all. A promising reference to the National Farmers Union in the index leads only to a short paragraph discussing wayleaves for mains pipelines. Water and sanitation have attracted more attention from historians but again with an almost wholly urban focus. Harriet Ritvo's *The dawn of green: Manchester, Thirlmere and modern environmentalism* (Chicago: University of Chicago Press, 2009) is a partial exception but is concerned with the effect of urban supply on rural landscapes rather than with rural supply per se.

41 ARUP Economic Consultants, *The Provision of Basic Utilities in Rural Areas. A Report to the Rural Development Commission* [no place of publication or publisher given], 1990, pp. 23, 26, 35, 37.

42 ARUP Economic Consultants, *The Provision of Basic Utilities in Rural Areas*, pp. 23, 31.

43 Ministry of Works and Planning, *Report of the Committee on Land Utilisation in Rural Areas*. Cmnd 6378. London: HMSO, 1942, pp. 50, 52.

44 One-seventh of the rural population were thought to be without piped water. Ministry of Works and Planning, *Report of the Committee on Land Utilisation in Rural Areas*, p. 19.

45 ARUP Economic Consultants, *The Provision of Basic Utilities in Rural Areas*, p. 8.

46 Association of County Councils, *Rural deprivation*. London: Association of County Councils, 1979, pp. 37, 52.

47 Ofcom, 'Five point plan to improving mobile coverage'. http://maps.ofcom.org.uk/mobile-services/. Accessed 9 January 2015; Ofcom UK Mobile Services Map 2013, Level of outdoor mobile coverage by administrative authority. http://maps.ofcom.org.uk/mobile-services/. Accessed 9 January 2015.

48 The deaths associated with these issues (twice as high among men as for other professions) remain indicative of the very real nature of these problems. 'The Future of Local Suicide Prevention Plans in England, A Report by the All Party Parliamentary Group on Suicide and Self-Harm Prevention' (published January 2013). http://www.samaritans.org/sites/default/files/kcfinder/files/press/APPG%20-%20The%20Future%20of%20Local%20Suicide%20Prevention%20Plans%20in%20England.pdf. Accessed 9 January 2015, pp. 1, 34; J. Mcclean, 'Stressed, misunderstood, and lonely: The farmer's lot is not a happy one'. *Independent*, 10 February 1996, http://www.independent.co.uk/news/uk/stressed-misunderstood-and-lonely-the-farmers-lot-is-not-a-happy-one-1318209.html. Accessed 9 January 2015; Samaritans, 'Rural support helping farmers to deal with financial stress in uncertain times' http://www.rural support.org.uk/rural-support-helping-farmers-to-deal-with-financial-stress-in-uncertain-times/. Accessed 9 January 2015; Jane Boys, 'Tackling stress in rural communities' (January 2007). http://archive.defra.gov.uk/rural/documents/living/tackling-stress0106.pdf. Accessed 9 January 2015. Helpline 0845 6967607.

Index

acid rain 48
Acts of Parliament, and Bills
  Agricultural Wages Act 1948 126–7
  Agriculture Act 1947 126
  Electricity (Supply) Act 1919 22, 53
  Electricity (Supply) Act 1926 3, 25,
    30, 53, 74, 85, 117
  Electricity Act 1947 40, 58, 94, 239
  Electricity Act 1957 47, 236
  Electric Lighting (Clauses) Act 1899
    16, 20, 239
  Electric Lighting Act 1882 3, 15, 52,
    224, 227
  Electric Lighting Act 1909 2
  Grampian Electricity Act 1922 47
  Hill Farming Act 1946 61, 65, 231
  Hydro-Electric Development
    (Scotland) Act 1943 47, 76–7
  Land Tenure Bill 1906 125
  Livestock Rearing Act 1951 61, 65,
    231
  Lochaber Water Power Act 1921 46
  National Parks and Access to the
    Countryside Act 1949 129
  North Wales Hydro-Electric Bill
    1955 47
  Opencast Coal Act 1958 47
  Rural Water Supply Act 1934 239
  Town and Country Planning Act
    1947 58
  Wages Councils Act 1947 127
ADSL 207, 209, 216
advertising 59, 119, 147, 191, 230
Affric Beauly Scheme 1952–63 78–9
Aga stoves 126–7, 230
agricultural colleges 192
Agricultural Organisation Society 227
agricultural policy 65
Agricultural Wages Board 126–7

air pollution 42
aluminium 72
Aluminium Corporation 53
amenity 65, 73, 130, 141, 236
amenity clause 46–8
area electricity boards 4, 40, 58, 61, 75,
  94, 129
Asquith, Herbert, Prime Minister 22
Association of Municipal
  Corporations 19
Attlee, Clement, Prime Minister 39
Austria 6, 11

Baldwin, Stanley, Prime Minister
  23, 25
bandwidth 211
Ben Cruachan Electrification
  Scheme 1965 78
Benn, Anthony Wedgwood,
  MP 48
Binsted (Hampshire) 9, 136–45,
  235–6, 241
Birds Eye (frozen food company) 146
Blomfield, Reginald 144
Bowen, Roderic, MP 57
British Aluminium Company 72–3
British Broadcasting Corporation
  (BBC) 213
British Electrical Development
  Association *see* Electrical
  Development Association
British Electricity Authority (BEA) 40,
  41, 43, 75
British Telecom (BT) 209, 211,
  214, 216
broadband 9, 81, 205–17, 233, 237,
  240
  adoption 214–15
  availability/supply 209

Broadband4Britain 210
coverage targets 213
demand 210
download speeds 215
government policy 209–10, 212
local loop unbundling 211
broadband/electrification comparisons
205–6, 216–17
BT Openworld 210

Cambridge Electric Supply
Company 222
Canada 4, 9, 85, 178–99, 222,
224, 229
candles 30, 51
Capenhurst research centre 100
capital grants 61, 65, 100, 106
car ownership 234–5
Central Electricity Authority 41,
44, 94
Central Electricity Board (CEB) 3, 24,
25, 27, 38, 53, 55, 74, 77, 117,
144, 223, 225, 238
Central Electricity Generating
Board (CEGB) 4, 38, 40–2,
45–8, 141–2
Chiswick Electricity Supply
Company 52
cinema 52
City of London Electric Light
Company 60
cleaning 53
Cleveland and Durham County Power
Company 20
Clyde Valley Electrical Power
Company 73
Coal Conservation Committee 3, 22
Cold Comfort Farm 232
collage 138–9
Commission for Rural Communities
(CRC) 211
compulsory purchase 76
Conservative Party 28, 225
consumer cooperatives 161
cooking 53, 59–60
Cooper Report 76
Council for the Preservation of Rural
England (CPRE) 128, 143–4,
235, 237
counter-urbanisation 234
Country Land and Business Association
(CLA) 210
Countryside Agency 210

Countryside Alliance 233
County Development Plans 58
County War Agricultural Executive
Committees 88
crofting 70, 80
crop growth stimulation 56
Culpin, Claude 99
cultural conservatism 230
current (electric)
alternating current (AC) 6, 16, 52,
161, 169, 229
direct current (DC) 6, 16, 52, 71,
161, 169, 229
Czechoslovakia 6, 11

dairy farming 56, 63, 91, 193, 228
dams 78, 184
Denmark 54, 224
Design and Industry Association
235, 241
Development Commission 56, 229
Digital Britain Implementation
Plan 212
digital divide 209, 211, 217
district heat and power schemes 224
Dominion Bureau of Statistics
(Canada) 194
Dunn, Paul 125–8

egg production 56, 85, 191
electrical appliances and equipment:
domestic 1, 7, 17, 49, 55–6, 59–60,
79, 86, 91, 97, 100, 103–8,
119–30, 146–51, 158–60, 172,
187–8, 191, 194, 198, 225, 230,
234
farm 17, 18, 56–7, 63, 85, 93, 97,
99, 103–8, 129, 158–60, 169–71,
197, 228
Electrical Association for Women
(EAW) 59, 146–7, 225
Electrical Development Association
(EDA) 18, 59, 84, 100, 117,
120–3, 140, 230
electric fences 91
Electrician, The 23
electricity
adoption 119
amenity value 95–6
connection costs 58–9, 62, 94,
95, 98, 105–6, 108, 117, 168–9,
239

248 *Index*

consumption 4, 27, 63, 99, 163, 181, 187, 189, 192
costs 18, 63, 185, 195, 222, 225
cultural impact 7–8, 235
demand 2, 7, 16, 23, 26, 84, 92, 99, 105, 109, 121, 128, 185, 192–8, 227–31
distribution 17, 157, 162, 173
farm consumption 94
local undertakings 15–31
marketing 120–1
price 20, 21, 25, 30, 181, 190–4
private companies 15–31
sales, farms 86, 88, 92
supply 2, 18, 22, 23, 29, 88, 118, 169, 187, 222–7
supply, servicing costs 98
supply, three phase 74, 85, 98, 106, 221
supply, to farms 29, 83–111
supply, to villages 29
tariffs 59
Electricity Commissioners 3, 23, 24, 26, 27, 28, 53, 223, 225
Electricity Consultative Councils 40
Electricity Council 3, 41, 63, 100, 109–11, 225, 231
electric light 18, 31, 54, 86, 91, 125, 158, 163, 187, 195–7, 221, 230, 233
electric model farms 160
electric motors 6, 57, 85, 197, 225
Electric Power Supply Committee 22
electric shocks 105
electrification
  advantages and benefits 64, 73, 81
  costs 55, 65, 93
  coverage 62–3, 84, 86, 88–92, 101–3, 109–11, 160–71, 178–9, 183, 186, 198, 224
  domestic impact 64, 151, 167, 169, 171–3
  economic studies 55, 57
  effect of farm size 64, 91
  effects 80, 100–8, 117–30, 158, 175, 231–7
  employment 78, 108, 157
  expansion in the SWEB area 101–2
  farm connections 86, 88–92, 96, 109–11
  generational change 231
  intra-regional differences 164
  landscape impact 45–8, 76, 97, 107, 136, 140–4, 148, 151

state support 160, 162, 178, 181, 231
at various dates and 101–3
electrification committee 1917 (Sweden) 159
Electro-Agricultural Centre (Stoneleigh) 100
electro farming 54, 85
email 207
European Union (EU) 212–13

Faraday, Michael 3
farm electrification handbooks 100
Farmer and Stockbreeder 119, 124
Farmer's Weekly 119, 124
Farm Management Survey 101–8
farms, connections to mains supply *see* electrification, coverage
farm workers 121–3, 171–2
Ferranti 22
fibre-optic cable 207–9, 213
films 117
  Crofter Boy 79
  Frozen Summer 149
  The Modern Electric Refrigerator 149
  Power comes to Widecombe 96–7, 141–2
  Time to Freeze 149
  The Village That Found Itself 226
Finland 7
fire risk 51
Fort Augustus 71
Foyers 72
France 6, 30, 54, 224
Fraser, Dugald 48–9
frozen food 145–51, 173, 234

gaslight 30; *see also* power sources, gas
G.E.C. (General Electric Company) 18, 126
generators *see* private generators
Germany 4, 6, 20, 21, 23, 30, 224
Godalming 3

heating 13
Holford, Sir William 48
House of Commons Environment, Food and Rural Affairs Committee 213
House of Commons Public Accounts Committee 213
housing conditions 122–3
hydroelectricity 5, 9, 52–4, 57, 69–82, 104, 157–64, 169, 180–4, 223–4
Hydro-Electric Power Corporation of Ontario 197

Index 249

Incorporated Municipal Electrical
    Association 23
Institution of Electrical Engineers
    18, 25
internet use 208
Ireland 8

Japan 85
Johnston, Tom, CH, MP 75–7, 81

Kerry Falls Hydroelectric
    scheme 79
Kinlochleven 72
Kitson, Sir James, MP 19

labour costs 92
Labour Party 28, 226–7
Lancashire Power Company 20
Leeds 2, 16, 25, 232
lighting 51
local authorities 3, 8, 52, 223–4, 226
Lodge, Sir Oliver 56
London 15
Lyme Regis 2
Lyons Maid (frozen food company) 148

MacColl, Edward 73–5, 79
MacDonald, James Ramsay, Prime
    Minister 46
McGowan Committee 3, 27, 28, 225
materials handling 108
Matthews, Richard Borlase 85, 117
Megginson, Irene 123–5
Merseyside and North Wales Electricity
    Board (MANWEB) 58, 61, 63
Merz, Charles 74
meter testing 195
Miliken Brothers 144
milk, hygiene standards 56
milking 103–8
milking machines 6, 17, 56,
    104–8, 227
Milk Marketing Board 56, 86, 228
ministers and ministries (UK)
    agriculture (*see* minister and ministries,
        agriculture, fisheries and food)
    agriculture, fisheries and food 4, 13,
        42–5, 56, 92, 95, 99, 126, 237
    food (*see* minister and ministries,
        agriculture, fisheries and food)
    fuel and power 40, 42–4, 59, 61,
        77, 95
    Housing and Local Government
        42, 44

power 4, 45, 58, 96, 237
    trade (including Board of Trade)
        16–22, 28, 73
    transport 24, 26, 27, 28
modernisation and modernity 2,
    8, 118–19, 128, 136–8, 146,
    172, 178, 192, 198, 229, 232,
    234–5, 241
Moretonhampstead meeting 1953 95–6
Morrison, Herbert, MP 39–40, 45

National Coal Board 41
National Farmers' Union 61, 93, 95, 96
National Farm Survey 30, 31, 54, 57,
    88–91, 100
national grid 3, 9, 24, 26, 30, 38–42,
    53, 57, 73–5, 81, 117–18, 139,
    194, 222–5
national identity 8
nationalisation 4, 9, 22, 25, 28, 30,
    31, 38–42, 75–7, 94, 109, 181,
    226–7, 231, 238
National parks 97, 236
Netherlands 6, 224
network services 184, 205, 216, 238
Nicholson, Max 39
Nimbyism 237
North of Scotland Hydro-electricity
    Board (NoSHEB) 40, 48, 76–81
North Wales Power Company 54
North Western Electricity Board 100
Norway 76
Nottinghamshire Power Company 20

Ofcom 211, 214, 240
oil lamps 30, 51, 57, 103, 233; Aladdin
    59, 101, 128–9; Tilley 101, 125,
    128–9, 229
Ontario Hydro-Electric Power
    Commission 186
Openreach 211

peak load problem 185
Political and Economic Planning
    (PEP) 118
population density 158, 167, 179,
    184–5, 209, 211, 222–3, 238
poultry farming 56, 86, 193, 196, 228
power companies 26, 157, 190
power failure 195–6
power lines *see* transmission lines
power sources 119, 125, 130, 182, 228
    coal 4, 5, 30, 103, 126, 160, 178,
        224

250 *Index*

gas 4, 5, 15, 30, 52, 103, 124, 239
horse gins 56, 83
nuclear 41, 47, 181, 236
oil 4, 5, 18, 30, 83, 85, 87–8, 161, 224
paraffin 51, 103, 160
Pelton wheels 53
petrol 18, 56, 85
steam 18, 56, 83, 161, 232
water 18, 30, 52–3, 178 (*see* hydroelectricity)
wind, wave and solar power 5, 81
wood 30, 103, 173, 178, 197–8, 229
power stations 5, 9, 22, 24, 38, 39, 42–5, 47, 225, 236
preservationism 8, 14, 144
private generators 5, 6, 52–4, 79, 85–94, 104–5, 124, 130, 186, 190, 221, 229
pylons 8, 9, 21, 45–8, 58, 136–45, 222, 235
landscape impact 45–8

radio *see* wireless
Raeburn, Dr John 126
Rayburn stoves 126, 230
refrigerators 146–8
Ruck, Ruth Janette 99
rural broadband *see* broadband
rural depopulation 60, 66, 81, 122, 164, 192, 199, 232, 234, 240–2
Rural Development Contribution (RDC) 98
rural electrification subsidy 96
rural industries 158, 161
rural occupations 180
Rural Reconstruction Association 54
rural service provision 233, 240–2
rural-urban divide 233
Russia 6

salmon fishing 42–5, 236
Samaritans 240
Scotland 16, 38, 69–81, 224
pre 20th century economy 70
Southern uplands 69
Scott Committee 1942 13, 57, 84, 226, 239
Scottish Highlands 9, 46, 69–82
Self, Sir Henry 3, 94
sheep shearing 63, 100
smartphones 214
South Downs 45–8

South of Scotland Electricity Board 41
South Wales Electricity Board 58, 61, 63
South Wales Power Company 54
South West Electricity Board (SWEB) 94–6, 100–2, 141
South West Electricity History Society 113
South West England 83, 100–8
startamatic generators 86
Stationary power on farms 87–8
Steward, Stanley 95
Stockholm Exhibition (1930) 160
stoves 197–8
Strategic Review of Telecommunications 211
Strathpeffer 71
street lighting 52
superfast broadband 208, 214
supergrid 41
Swan, Joseph 3
Sweden 9, 30, 54, 157–75, 221, 223, 233

tablets 214
telephone 127, 206–7, 238, 240; mobile 233, 240; *see also* smartphones
television 96, 100, 105
Tennessee Valley Authority 4
tractors 18, 104
transformers 55, 58, 98, 107, 142, 222
transmission lines 26, 31, 54–5, 58, 84, 93–4, 97–8, 107, 129, 140–4, 162, 184, 222
in West Devon 101–2
tunnelling 78

underground transmission 141–3, 145, 236–7
United States of America 4, 6, 23, 148–9, 181, 234
universal service obligation 205, 212
upland farming 65
urban areas, effect of proximity on electrification 88–91
Usk, river 42–5
Usk Board of Conservators 42
Uskmouth Power Station 38, 42–5, 236
Usk River Board 44

Village Scrapbook Today competition 135

Index 251

Wales 9, 42, 51–68
water heating 86, 103
water mains 15, 80, 238
water pollution 44
way leaves 55, 58, 93, 100, 107,
     222, 235
Weir Committee 1926 23, 24, 25, 74
Welsh Reconstruction Advisory
     Council 57
West Cambrian Power Company 54
Whetham, C. Dampier 85
Widecombe 96
Williamson, James T.W. 73

wireless 51, 53, 59, 123, 127, 172,
     234
wirescape 142
wiring costs 93, 99, 105, 168–9, 193,
     198, 229
Women's Institute (WI) 135–51, 192,
     225, 235
World Power Conference, Washington
     1936 30
World War II 38, 75

Yorkshire Electric Power Company 20
Young Farmers' Clubs 100